L. Randall Wray is a professor of Economics at the University of Missouri-Kansas City, USA, as well as Research Director, the Center for Full Employment and Price Stability, and Senior Scholar at the Levy Economics Institute of Bard College, New York. A student of Hyman P. Minsky while at Washington University in St. Louis, Wray has focused on monetary theory and policy, macroeconomics, financial instability, and employment policy. He has published widely in journals and is the author of *Understanding Modern Money: The Key to Full Employment and Price Stability* (1998) and *Money and Credit in Capitalist Economies* (1990). He is the editor of *Credit and State Theories of Money* (2004) and the co-editor of *Contemporary Post Keynesian Analysis* (2005), *Money, Financial Instability and Stabilization Policy* (2006), and *Keynes for the Twenty-First Century: The Continuing Relevance of The General Theory* (2008). Wray is also the author of numerous scholarly articles in edited books and academic journals, including the *Journal of Economic Issues, Cambridge Journal of Economics, Review of Political Economy, Journal of Post Keynesian Economics, Economic and Labour Relations Review, Economie Appliquée,* and the *Eastern Economic Journal.* Wray received a B.A. from the University of the Pacific and an M.A. and Ph.D. from Washington University in St. Louis. He has served as a visiting professor at the University of Rome, the University of Paris, and UNAM (Mexico City). He was the Bernardin-Haskell Professor, UMKC, Fall 1996, and joined the UMKC faculty as Professor of Economics, August 1999.

Modern Money Theory

A Primer on Macroeconomics for Sovereign Monetary Systems

L. Randall Wray
University of Missouri-Kansas City

First published 2012 by
PALGRAVE MACMILLAN

Palgrave Macmillan in the UK is an imprint of Macmillan Publishers Limited, registered in England, company number 785998, of Houndmills, Basingstoke, Hampshire RG21 6XS.

Palgrave Macmillan in the US is a division of St Martin's Press LLC, 175 Fifth Avenue, New York, NY 10010.

Palgrave Macmillan is the global academic imprint of the above companies and has companies and representatives throughout the world.

Palgrave® and Macmillan® are registered trademarks in the United States, the United Kingdom, Europe and other countries

ISBN: 978–0–230–36888–0 hardback
ISBN: 978–0–230–36889–7 paperback

Contents

List of Illustrations   viii

Preface   ix

Box: Definitions   xv

1 The Basics of Macroeconomic Accounting   1
   1.1 The basics of accounting for stocks and flows   1
   1.2 MMT, sectoral balances, and behavior   6
   1.3 Government budget deficits are largely nondiscretionary: the case of the Great Recession of 2007   15
   1.4 Accounting for real versus financial   21
   1.5 Recent US sectoral balances: Goldilocks and the global crash   27
   1.6 Stocks, flows, and balance sheet: a bathtub analogy   30

2 Spending by Issuer of Domestic Currency   39
   2.1 What is a sovereign currency?   39
   2.2 What backs up currency and why would anyone accept it?   44
   2.3 Taxes drive money   47
   2.4 What if the population refuses to accept the domestic currency?   52
   2.5 Keeping track of stocks and flows: the money of account   58
   2.6 Returning to real versus nominal stocks and flows   62
   2.7 Sustainability conditions   65

3 The Domestic Monetary System: Banking and Central Banking   76
   3.1 IOUs denominated in the national currency: government and private   76
   3.2 Clearing and the pyramid of liabilities   83
   3.3 Central bank operations in crisis: lender of last resort   89

3.4   Balance sheets of banks, monetary creation by banks, and interbank settlement   92
3.5   Exogenous interest rates and quantitative easing   97
3.6   The technical details of central bank and treasury coordination: the case of the Fed   98
3.7   Treasury debt operations   105

4   Fiscal Operations in a Nation That Issues Its Own Currency   110
4.1   Introductory principles   110
4.2   Effects of sovereign government budget deficits on saving, reserves, and interest rates   114
4.3   Government budget deficits and the "two-step" process of saving   120
4.4   What if foreigners hold government bonds?   126
4.5   Currency solvency and the special case of the US Dollar   133
4.6   Sovereign currency and government policy in the open economy   138
4.7   What about a country that adopts a foreign currency?   144

5   Modern Money Theory and Alternative Exchange Rate Regimes   148
5.1   The gold standard and fixed exchange rates   149
5.2   Floating exchange rates   150
5.3   Commodity money coins? metalism versus nominalism, from Mesopotamia to Rome   153
5.4   Commodity money coins? metalism versus nominalism, after Rome   159
5.5   Exchange rate regimes and sovereign defaults   164
5.6   The Euro: the set-up of a nonsovereign currency   169
5.7   The crisis of the Euro   173
5.8   Endgame for the Euro?   181
5.9   Currency regimes and policy space: conclusion   185

6   Monetary and Fiscal Policy for Sovereign Currencies: What Should Government Do?   187
6.1   Just because government can afford to spend does not mean government ought to spend   187
6.2   The "free" market and the public purpose   190
6.3   Functional finance   193

6.4	Functional finance versus the government budget constraint	198
6.5	The debate about debt limits (US case)	203
6.6	A budget stance for economic stability and growth	208
6.7	Functional finance and exchange rate regimes	211
6.8	Functional finance and developing nations	216
6.9	Exports are a cost, imports are a benefit: a functional finance approach	217
7	**Policy for Full Employment and Price Stability**	221
7.1	Functional finance and full employment	221
7.2	The JG/ELR for a developing nation	227
7.3	Program manageability	230
7.4	The JG/ELR and real world experience	233
7.5	Conclusions on full employment policy	236
7.6	MMT for Austrians: can a libertarian support the JG?	238
7.7	Inflation and the consumer price index	241
7.8	Alternative explanations of hyperinflation	246
7.9	Real-world hyperinflations	252
7.10	Conclusions on hyperinflation	256
7.11	Conclusion: MMT and policy	258
8	**What Is Money? Conclusions on the Nature of Money**	261
8.1	Is money a physical thing?	262
8.2	Propositions on the nature of money	264
8.3	Money is debt	269
8.4	Liquidity and default risks on money IOUs	274
8.5	Why are banks special?	279
	Conclusions	282
	Notes	283
	Bibliography	284
	Index	289

Illustrations

Figures

1.1	Federal government tax receipts, consumption expenditures, and transfer payments	16
1.2	Propensity to save out of disposable income	17
1.3	Sector financial balances as a percentage of GDP, 1952q1 to 2010q4	29
3.1	Case 1a: government imposes a tax liability and buys a bomb by crediting an account at a private bank	99
3.2	Final position, Case 1a	100
3.3	Case 1b: government deficit spends, which creates private net wealth	101
3.4	Final position, Case 1b	101
3.5	Case 2: government must sell bond before it can deficit spend	102
3.6	Government buys bomb, writing check on private bank	102
3.7	Final position, Case 2	103
3.8	Case 3: Treasury can write checks only on its central bank account	103
3.9	Treasury moves deposit to central bank account	103
3.10	Treasury buys bombs	104
3.11	Final position, Case 3	104
5.1	Government debt as a percentage of GDP, 1995–2010	174
5.2	General government deficit, 1995–2010	174
5.3	Sectoral balances as a percentage of GDP: Euro area	176
5.4	Sectoral balances as a percentage of GDP: France	177
5.5	Sectoral balances as a percentage of GDP: Spain	177
5.6	Sectoral balances as a percentage of GDP: Italy	178

Tables

3.1	Balance sheet of a typical bank	92
3.2	Bank A balance sheet	92
3.3	Bank B balance sheet	94

Preface

In recent years an approach to macroeconomics has been developed that is called "modern money theory" (MMT). The components of the theory are not new, but the integration toward a coherent analysis is. My first attempt at a synthesis was in my 1998 book, *Understanding Modern Money*. That book traced the history of money as well as the history of thought undergirding the approach. It also presented the theory and examined both fiscal and monetary policy from the "modern money" point of view. Since that time, great strides have been made in applications of the theory to developing an understanding of the operational details involved. To put it simply, we have uncovered how money "works" in the modern economy. The findings have been reported in a large number of academic publications. In addition, the growth of the "blogosphere" has spread the ideas around the world. "Modern money theory" is now widely recognized as a coherent alternative to conventional views. However, academic articles and short blogs do not provide the proper venue for a comprehensive introduction to the approach.

This Primer seeks to fill the gap between formal presentations in the academic journals and the informal blogs. It will begin with the basics to build to a reasonably sophisticated understanding.

In addition, it will explicitly address another gap: the case of developing nations. The MMT approach has often been criticized for focusing too much on the case of the US, with many critics asserting that it has little or no application to the rest of the world's nations that do not issue the international reserve currency. To be sure, that criticism is overdone because modern money theorists have applied the approach to a number of other countries, including Australia, Canada, Mexico, Brazil, and China. Still, much of the literature explicitly addresses the case of developed nations that operate with floating exchange rates. Some supporters have even argued that MMT cannot be applied to fixed exchange rate regimes. And there has been very little application of MMT to developing nations (many of which do adopt exchange rate pegs).

So this Primer also fills that gap – it explicitly addresses alternative exchange rate regimes as well as the situation in developing nations. In that sense it is a generalization of modern money theory.

Unlike my 1998 book, this Primer will not revisit the history of money or the history of thought. The exposition will remain largely theoretical. I will provide a few examples, a little bit of data, and some discussion of actual real world operations. But for the most part the discussion will remain at the theoretical level. The theory, however, is not difficult. It builds from simple macro identities to basic macroeconomics. It is designed to be accessible to those with little background in economics. Further, the Primer mostly avoids criticism of the conventional approach to economics; there are many critiques already, so this Primer aims instead to make a positive contribution. That helps to keep the exposition relatively short. Where appropriate, there will be boxes that provide slightly more technical discussions and case studies. In addition, boxes will provide answers to frequently asked questions. The material in boxes can be skipped by readers in a hurry. Alternatively, the reader can return to the boxes after completing each chapter.

In this Primer we will examine the macroeconomic theory that is the basis for analyzing the economy as it actually exists. We begin with simple macro accounting, starting from the recognition that at the aggregate level spending equals income. We then move to a sectoral balance approach showing that the deficits of one sector must be offset by surpluses of another. We conclude by arguing that it is necessary to ensure stock-flow consistency: deficits accumulate to financial debt; surpluses accumulate to financial assets. We emphasize that all of these results apply to all nations today as they follow from macroeconomic identities.

We next move to a discussion of currency regimes – ranging from fixed exchange rate systems (currency board arrangements and pegs), to managed float regimes, and finally to floating exchange rates. We can think of the possibilities as a continuum, with many developed nations toward the floating rate end of the spectrum and many developing nations toward the fixed exchange rate end.

We will examine how a government that issues its own currency spends. We first provide a general analysis that applies to all currency regimes; we then discuss the limitations placed on domestic policy as we move along the exchange rate regime continuum. It will be argued that the floating exchange rate regime provides more domestic policy space. The argument is related to the famous open economy "trilemma" – a country can choose only two of three policies: maintain an exchange rate peg, maintain an interest rate peg, and allow capital mobility. Here, however, it will be argued that a country that chooses an exchange rate target may not be able to pursue domestic policy devoted to achieving full employment with robust economic growth.

Later – much later – we will show how the "functional finance" approach of Abba Lerner follows directly from MMT. This leads to a discussion of monetary and fiscal policy – not only what policy *can* do but also what policy *should* do. Again, the discussion will be general because the most important goal of this Primer is to set out theory that can serve as the basis of policy formation. This Primer's purpose is not to push any particular policy agenda. It can be used by advocates of "big government" as well as by those who favor "small government." My own biases are well-known, but MMT itself is neutral.

As mentioned above, one major purpose of this Primer is to apply the principles developed by recent research into sectoral balances and the modern money approach to the study of developing nations. The Levy Economics Institute has been at the forefront of such research, following the work of Wynne Godley and Hyman Minsky, but most of that work has focused on the situation of developed nations. Jan Kregel, in his work at UNCTAD, has used this approach in analysis of the economies of developing nations. Others at Levy have used the approach to push for implementation of job creation programs in developed and developing nations. This Primer will extend these analyses, explicitly recognizing the different policy choices available to nations with alternative exchange rate regimes.

Finally, we will explore the nature of money. We will see that logically money cannot be a commodity; rather, it must be an IOU. Even a country that operates with a gold standard is really operating with monetary IOUs, albeit with some of those IOUs convertible on demand to a precious metal. We will show why monetary economies typically operate below capacity, with unemployed resources including labor. We will also examine the nature of creditworthiness; that is, the reason why some monetary liabilities are more acceptable than others. As my professor, the late and great Hyman

Minsky, used to say, "anyone can create money; the problem lies in getting it accepted." Understanding what money is provides the first step to an analysis of what went wrong in the events leading up to the global financial crisis of 2007. It also helps us to understand the problems faced in Euroland, especially from 2010.

This monograph actually began as an effort to provide a basic Primer on macroeconomics that can be used by home country analysts in developing nations, as an alternative to the macroeconomic textbooks that suffer from a variety of flaws. The purpose was not to critique orthodox theory but rather to make a positive contribution that maintains stock-flow consistency while also recognizing differences among alternative exchange rate regimes. Jesus Felipe at the Asian Development Bank urged me to put together a version that could be more widely circulated. At the same time, many bloggers have asked those who have written on MMT to provide a concise explication of the approach. Many professors have also asked for a textbook to use in the classroom.

This Primer is designed to fulfill at least some of those requests, although a textbook for classroom use will have to wait. To keep the project manageable, I will not go deeply into operational details. That would require close analysis of specific procedures adopted in each country. This has already been done in academic papers for a few nations (as mentioned above, for the United States, Australia, Canada, and Brazil, with some treatment of the cases of Mexico and China). As I am aiming for a nonspecialist audience, I am leaving those details out of the main text, although there will be some treatment of them in boxes. What I do provide is a basic introduction to MMT that does not require a great deal of previous study of economics. I will stay free from unnecessary math or jargon. I build from what we might call "first principles" to a theory of the way money really "works." And while it was tempting to address a wide range of policy issues and current events – especially given the global financial mess today – I will try to stay close to this mission.

To test the Primer on a large cross section of potential readers, I began to post sections of it at the New Economic Perspectives blog site run by my colleague Stephanie Kelton. These appeared on a separate page, the Modern Money Primer, each Monday. Comments were collected through Wednesday night, with my response to the comments then published. That allowed me to adjust the text that appears here. In some cases, my responses were incorporated within this Primer; other responses became the basis for some of the boxes. I thank all of the participants for their help; their critical analyses helped to sharpen the exposition.

I thank the MMT group that I have worked with over the past 20 years as we developed the approach together: Warren Mosler, Bill Mitchell, Jan Kregel, Stephanie Kelton, Pavlina Tcherneva, Mat Forstater, Ed Nell, Scott Fullwiler, and Eric Tymoigne, as well as many current and former students among whom I want to recognize Joelle LeClaire, Heather Starzinsky, Daniel Conceicao, Felipe Rezende, Flavia Dantas, Yan Liang, Fadhel Kaboub, Zdravka Todorova, Andy Felkerson, Nicola Matthews, Shakuntala Das, Corinne Pastoret, Mike Murray, Alla Semenova, and Yeva Nersisyan. I want to thank Warren Mosler for his many years of support of our program at the University of Missouri-Kansas City, along with Maurice Samuels, Cliff Viner, and Scott Ramsey.

I also thank the Asian Development Bank – and especially Jesus Felipe – for funding of the initial project, and participants of two ADB workshops held in Kazakhstan for comments that helped to sharpen the focus on developing countries. Others – some of whom were initially critical of certain aspects of the approach (a few probably still are!) – have also contributed to development of the theory: Charles Goodhart, Marc Lavoie, Mario Seccareccia, Michael Hudson, Rob Parenteau, Marshall Auerback, Geoff Ingham, Geoffrey Gardiner, Martin Watts, James Juniper, and Jamie Galbraith. Other international colleagues, including Peter Kreisler, Arturo Huerta, Claudio Sardoni, Bernard Vallegeas, Andrea Terzi, Philip Arestis and John McCombie, and Xinhua Liu let me try out the ideas before audiences abroad. Special thanks to Eric Tymoigne for reading the manuscript and helping with formatting.

Many bloggers have helped to spread the word, including Edward Harrison, Lambert Strether, Dennis Kelleher, Rebecca Wilder, Yves Smith, Joe Firestone, Mike Norman, Cullen Roche, Paolo Barnard, Roger Erickson, and Tom Hickey. I also thank the folks at New Economic Perspectives from Kansas City (and especially Stephanie Kelton, Felipe Rezende, Mitch Green, Bill Black, and Erik Dean), Lynn Parramore (formerly at New Deal 2.0, now at Alternet), Selise and Joe Firestone at FDL, Huffington Post, Nouriel Roubini and Joshua Glazer at Economonitor (which sponsors my Great Leap Forward blog), and

Benzinga – all of whom posted my blogs (and above all, wearing two hats, Bill Mitchell at billyblog! – the "grandfather" of modern money blogs). All those at CFEPs in the United States and Coffee in Australia and Europe, as well as the Levy Economics Institute in New York, have helped to promote the ideas over the past decade. Thanks especially to Dimitri Papadimitriou and Jan Kregel, and also the late Hyman Minsky and Wynne Godley for their support and for making the Levy Institute a welcoming and stimulating environment. A big *thanks* to all.

Enough with the preliminaries. We get started with the theory in Chapter 1.

Box: Definitions

Throughout this Primer we will adopt the following definitions and conventions:

The word "money" will refer to a general, representative unit of account. We will not use the word to apply to any specific "thing" – that is a coin or central bank note.

Money "things" will be identified specifically: a coin, a bank note, a demand deposit. Some of these can be touched (paper notes); others are electronic entries on balance sheets (demand deposits, bank reserves). So "money things" is simply shorthand for "money denominated IOUs."

A specific national money of account will be designated with a capital letter: US Dollar, Japanese Yen, Chinese Yuan, UK Pound, EMU Euro.

The word currency is used to indicate coins, notes, and reserves issued by government (both by the treasury and the central bank). When designating a specific treasury or its bonds, the word will be capitalized: US Treasury; US Treasuries.

Bank reserves are private bank deposits at the central bank, denominated in the money of account. They are used for clearing among banks, to meet cash withdrawals, and for making payments for customers to the government.

Net financial assets are equal to total financial assets less total financial liabilities. This is not the same as net wealth (or net worth) because it ignores real assets.

An IOU (I owe you) is a financial debt, liability, or obligation to pay, denominated in a money of account. It is a financial asset of the holder. There can be physical evidence of the IOU (for example, written on paper, stamped on coin) or it can be recorded electronically (for example, on a bank balance sheet). Of course, an IOU is a liability of the issuer but it is an asset of the holder (who is also called the creditor).

Three Sectors Balance: We can divide the economy into three sectors: domestic government, domestic private (or nongovernment, including households, firms, and not-for-profits), and foreign. At the aggregate we know Spending = Income for the economy as a whole. But any individual sector can spend more than (run a deficit), or less than (run a surplus), its income. From the macro identity, if one sector runs a surplus, at least one other runs a deficit. Let E = spending and Y = income, then we can write: Government $Y - E$ + Private $Y - E$ + Foreign $Y - E = 0$. Or: Government balance + Private balance + Foreign balance $= 0$. In terms of Gross Domestic Product (GDP), which is the sum of consumption (C), investment (I), government (G), and net exports ($X - M$, or exports minus imports), the three sectors balance identity is similar to: Government balance ($T - G$) + Private balance ($S - I$) + Foreign balance ($M - X$), where S = saving, T = taxes. Either way the balance is measured; it sums to zero in the aggregate.

1
The Basics of Macroeconomic Accounting

In this chapter we are going to begin to build the necessary foundation to understand modern money. Please bear with us. It may not be obvious at first why this is important. But you cannot possibly understand the debate about the government's budget (and critique the deficit hysteria that has recently gripped many nations) without understanding basic macro accounting. So be patient and pay attention. No higher math or knowledge of intricate accounting rules will be required. This is simple, basic stuff. It is a branch of logic. But it is extremely simple logic.

1.1 The basics of accounting for stocks and flows

One's financial asset is another's financial liability

It is a fundamental principle of accounting that for every financial asset there is an equal and offsetting financial liability. The checking deposit (also called a demand deposit or a sight deposit) is a household's financial asset, offset by the bank's liability (or IOU). A government or corporate bond is a household asset, but represents a liability of the issuer (either the government or the corporation). The household has some liabilities, too, including student loans, a home mortgage, or a car loan. These are held as assets by the creditor, which could be a bank or any of a number of types of financial institutions such as pension funds, hedge funds, or insurance companies. A household's net financial wealth is equal to the sum of all its financial assets (equal to its financial wealth) less the sum of its

1

financial liabilities (all of the money-denominated IOUs it issued). If that is positive, it has positive net financial wealth.

Inside wealth versus outside wealth

It is often useful to distinguish among different types of sectors in the economy. The most basic distinction is between the public sector (including all levels of government) and the private sector (including households and firms). If we were to take all of the privately issued financial assets and liabilities, it is a matter of logic that the sum of financial assets must equal the sum of financial liabilities. In other words, net private financial wealth would have to be zero if we consider only private sector IOUs. This is sometimes called "inside wealth" because it is "inside" the private sector. In order for the private sector to accumulate net financial wealth, it must be in the form of "outside wealth", that is, financial claims on another sector. Given our basic division between the public sector and the private sector, the outside financial wealth takes the form of government IOUs. The private sector holds government currency (including coins and paper currency) as well as the full range of government bonds (short-term bills, longer maturity bonds) as net financial assets, a portion of its positive net wealth.

A note on nonfinancial wealth (real assets)

One's financial asset is necessarily offset by another's financial liability. In the aggregate, net financial wealth must equal zero. However, real assets represent one's wealth that is not offset by another's liability, hence at the aggregate level net wealth equals the value of real (nonfinancial) assets. To be clear, you might have purchased an automobile by going into debt. Your financial liability (your car loan) is offset by the financial asset held by the auto loan company. Since those net to zero, what remains is the value of the real asset – the car. In most of the discussion that follows we will be concerned with financial assets and liabilities, but will keep in the back of our minds that the value of real assets provides net wealth at both the individual level and at the aggregate level. Once we subtract all financial liabilities from total assets (real and financial) we are left with nonfinancial (real) assets, or aggregate net worth. (See the discussion below in Section 1.4.)

Net private financial wealth equals public debt

Flows (of income or spending) accumulate to stocks. The private sector accumulation of net financial assets over the course of a year is made possible only because its spending is less than its income over that same period. In other words, it has been saving, enabling it to accumulate a stock of wealth in the form of financial assets. In our simple example with only a public sector and a private sector, these financial assets are government liabilities – government currency and government bonds. These government IOUs, in turn, can be accumulated only when the government spends *more* than it receives in the form of tax revenue. This is a government deficit, which is the flow of government spending less the flow of government tax revenue measured in the money of account over a given period (usually a year). This deficit accumulates to a stock of government debt – equal to the private sector's accumulation of financial wealth over the same period.

A complete explanation of the process of government spending and taxing will be provided later. What is necessary to understand at this point is that the net financial assets held by the private sector are exactly equal to the net financial liabilities issued by the government in our two-sector example. If the government always runs a *balanced budget*, with its spending always equal to its tax revenue, the private sector's net financial wealth will be zero. If the government runs continuous budget surpluses (spending is less than tax receipts), the private sector's net financial wealth must be negative. In other words, the private sector will be indebted to the public sector.

We can formulate a resulting "dilemma": in our two-sector model it is impossible for both the public sector and the private sector to run surpluses. And if the public sector were to run surpluses, by identity the private sector would have to run deficits. If the public sector were to run sufficient surpluses over some period to retire all its outstanding debt, by identity the private sector would run equivalent deficits, running down its net financial wealth until it reached zero and then turned negative.

Rest of world debts are domestic financial assets

Another useful division is to form three sectors: a domestic private sector, a domestic public sector, and a "rest of the world" (ROW) sector that consists of foreign governments, firms, and households. In this case, it is possible for the domestic private sector to accumulate net claims on the ROW, even if the domestic public sector runs a *balanced budget,* with its spending over the period exactly equal to its tax revenue. The domestic private sector's accumulation of net financial assets in that case is equal to the ROW's issue of net financial liabilities. Finally, and more realistically, the domestic private sector can accumulate net financial wealth consisting of both domestic government liabilities as well as ROW liabilities. It is possible for the domestic private sector to accumulate government debt (adding to its net financial wealth) while also issuing debt to the ROW (reducing its net financial wealth). In the next section we turn to a detailed discussion of sectoral balances.

Basics of sectoral accounting, relations to stock and flow concepts

Let us continue with our division of the economy into three sectors: a domestic private sector (households and firms); a domestic government sector (including local, state or province, and national governments); and a foreign sector (the rest of the world, including households, firms, and governments). Each of these sectors can be treated as if it had an income flow and a spending flow over the accounting period, which we will take to be a year. There is no reason for any individual sector to balance its income and spending flows each year. If it spends less than its income, this is called a *budget surplus* for the year; if it spends more than its income, this is called a *budget deficit* for the year; a *balanced budget* indicates that income equalled spending over the year.

From the discussion above it will be clear that a budget surplus is the same thing as a saving flow and leads to net accumulation of financial assets (an increase in net financial wealth). By the same token, a budget deficit reduces net financial wealth. The sector that runs a deficit must either run down its financial assets that had been accumulated in previous years (when surpluses were run), or must issue new IOUs to offset its deficits. In common parlance, we say that it "pays for" its deficit spending by exchanging its assets for spendable bank deposits (called "dissaving"), or it issues debt ("borrows") to obtain spendable bank deposits. Once it runs out of accumulated assets, it has no choice but to increase its indebtedness every year that it runs a deficit budget. On the other hand, a sector that runs a budget surplus will be accumulating net financial assets. This surplus will take the form of financial claims on at least one of the other sectors.

Another note on real assets

A question arises: what if one uses savings (a budget surplus) to purchase real assets rather than to accumulate net financial assets? In that case, the financial assets are simply passed along to someone else. For example, if you spend less than your income, you can accumulate deposits in your checking account. If you decide you do not want to hold your savings in the form of a checking deposit, you can write a check to purchase, say, a painting, an antique car, a stamp collection, real estate, a machine, or even a business firm. You convert a financial asset into a real asset. However, the seller has made the opposite transaction and now holds the financial asset. The point is that if the private sector taken as a whole runs a budget surplus, someone will be accumulating net financial assets (claims on another sector), although activities within the private sector can shift those net financial assets from one "pocket" to another.

Conclusion: one sector's deficit equals another's surplus

All of this brings us to the important accounting principle that if we sum the deficits run by one or more sectors, this must equal the surpluses run by the other sector(s). Following the pioneering work by Wynne Godley, we can state this principle in the form of a simple identity:

Domestic Private Balance + Domestic Government Balance + Foreign Balance = 0

For example, let us assume that the foreign sector runs a *balanced budget* (in the identity above, the foreign balance equals zero). Let us further assume that the domestic private sector's income is $100 billion while its spending is equal to $90 billion, for a budget surplus of $10 billion over the year. Then, by identity, the domestic government sector's budget deficit for the year is equal to $10 billion. From the discussion above, we know that the domestic private sector will accumulate $10 billion of net financial wealth during the year, consisting of $10 billion of domestic government sector liabilities.

As another example, assume that the foreign sector spends less than its income, with a budget surplus of $20 billion. At the same time, the domestic government sector also spends less than its income, running a budget surplus of $10 billion. From our accounting identity, we know that over the same period the domestic private sector must have run a budget deficit equal to $30 billion ($20 billion plus $10 billion). At the same time, its net financial wealth will have fallen by $30 billion as it sold assets and issued debt. Meanwhile, the domestic government sector will have increased its net financial wealth by $10 billion (reducing its outstanding debt or increasing its claims on the other sectors), and the foreign sector will have increased its net financial position by $20 billion (also reducing its outstanding debt or increasing its claims on the other sectors).

It is apparent that if one sector is going to run a budget surplus, at least one other sector *must* run a budget deficit. In terms of stock variables, in order for one sector to accumulate net financial wealth, at least one other sector must increase its indebtedness by the same amount. It is impossible for all sectors to accumulate net financial wealth by running budget surpluses. We can formulate another "dilemma": if one of three sectors is to run a surplus, at least one of the others must run a deficit.

No matter how hard we might try, we cannot all run surpluses simultaneously. It is a lot like those children in Lake Wobegon (an imaginary town featured in Garrison Keillor's *Prairie Home Companion* weekly radio show in the United States) who are supposedly all above average. For every kid above average there must be one below average. And for every deficit there must be a surplus.

1.2 MMT, sectoral balances, and behavior

In the previous section we introduced the basics of macro accounting. In this section we will go a bit deeper into the accounting, looking at the relation between flows (deficits) and stocks (debts). To avoid making mistakes we need to make sure that we have "consistency" between our flows and our stocks. We want to make sure that all spending and saving comes from somewhere and goes somewhere.

And we must make sure that one sector's surplus is offset by a deficit in another sector. This is a lot like keeping track of the scores in a baseball game, and in fact most financial "scores" really are electronic entries in the modern world (like those on an electronic scoreboard).

We will also try to say something about causation. It is not sufficient to say that at the aggregate level, the private balance plus the government balance plus the foreign balance equals zero. But, for example, we would like to be able to understand why the US private sector balance was negative during the Clinton Goldilocks years while the government balance was positive – how did we get to that point, and what sorts of processes did it induce?

Obviously that is necessary before we can really analyze the situation and formulate policy. Unlike the macro accounting identity (which must be true), it is not possible to say with certainty what causes a particular sector's balance. It is quite easy to say that if the government runs a surplus and if the foreign balance is positive (foreign sector spends less than its income) then the domestic private sector must by accounting identity be negative (running a deficit). It all must sum to zero.

Explaining why the US private sector had a deficit during the Goldilocks years is harder; it is even more difficult to project if and for how long that deficit might continue. Projections are darned hard to get right – if they were easy, we would all make lots of money placing bets on outcomes. Another way of stating this is to say that a good understanding of MMT does not give one a monopoly on explanations of causation. We must not be overly confident. As the late and great Wynne Godley used to put it, he did not make forecasts; rather, he made contingent projections.

For example, carrying on with the work of Wynne Godley, the Levy Economics Institute (www.levy.org) makes such projections. Typically it begins with CBO (US Congressional Budget Office) projections of the path of government deficits and of economic growth over the next few years. CBO projections are largely determined by current law (i.e., laws governing spending and taxing, as well as mandates over deficit reduction). However, the CBO's projections are not always stock-flow consistent and do not adopt the three-sector balances approach. In other words, they are in that sense incoherent. But given projections over the government balance and GDP growth as well as empirical estimates of various economic parameters (propensity to consume and import, for example), one can produce a stock-flow-consistent model that produces the implied sectoral balances as well as path of debt. The Levy Institute often finds that economic growth rates (for example) plus government deficit projections used in CBO forecasts imply highly implausible balances in the other two sectors (domestic private and foreign) as well as private debt ratios. To do that kind of analysis you must go beyond the simple accounting identities, but you should ensure your analysis doesn't violate the identities.

Deficits→savings and debts→wealth

We have established in our previous section that the deficits of one sector must equal the surpluses of (at least) one of the other sectors. We have also established that the debts of one sector must equal the financial wealth of (at least) one of the other sectors. So far this all follows from the principles of macro accounting. However, the economist wishes to say more than this, for, like all scientists, economists are interested in causation. Economics is a social science, that is, the science of extraordinarily complex social systems in which causation is never simple because economic phenomena are subject to interdependence, hysteresis, cumulative causation, "free will" influenced by expectations, and so on. Still, we can say something about causal relationships among the flows and stocks that we discussed previously. Some readers will note that the causal connections adopted here follow from Keynesian theory.

a) *Individual spending is mostly determined by income.* Our starting point will be the private sector decision to spend. For the individual, it seems plausible to argue that income largely determines spending because one with no income is certainly going to be severely constrained when deciding to purchase goods and services. However, on reflection it is apparent that even at the individual level, the link between income and spending is loose: one can spend less than one's income, accumulating net financial assets, or one can spend more than one's income by issuing financial liabilities and thereby becoming indebted. Still, at the level of the individual household or firm, the direction of causation largely runs from income to spending even if the correspondence between the two flows is not perfect. There is little reason to believe that one's own spending significantly determines one's own income.

b) *Deficits create financial wealth.* We can also say something about the direction of causation regarding accumulation of financial wealth at the level of the individual. If a household or firm decides to spend more than its income (running a budget deficit), it can issue liabilities to finance purchases. These liabilities will be accumulated as financial wealth by another household, firm, or government that is saving. Of course for this net financial wealth accumulation to take place we must have one household or firm willing to deficit spend, and another household, firm, or government willing to accumulate wealth in the form of the liabilities of that deficit spender. We can say that "it takes two to tango". However, it is the decision to deficit spend that is the initiating cause of the creation of net financial wealth. No matter how much others might want to accumulate financial wealth, they will not be able to do so unless someone is willing to deficit spend.

Still, it is true that the household or firm will not be able to deficit spend unless it can sell accumulated assets or find someone willing to hold its liabilities. We can suppose there is a propensity (or desire) to accumulate net financial wealth by at least some individual households, firms, governments, or foreigners. This does not mean that every individual firm or household will be able to issue debt so that it can deficit spend, but it does ensure that many firms and households will find willing holders of their debt. And in the case of a sovereign government, there is a special power – the ability to tax – that virtually guarantees that households and firms will want to accumulate the government's debt. (This is a topic we pursue later.)

We conclude that while causation is complex, and while "it takes two to tango", causation tends to run from individual deficit spending to accumulation of financial wealth, and from debt to financial wealth. Since accumulation of a stock of financial wealth results from a budget surplus, that is, from a flow of saving, we can also conclude that causation tends to run from deficit spending to saving.

c) *Aggregate spending creates aggregate income.* At the aggregate level, taking the economy as a whole, causation is more clear cut. A society cannot decide to have more income, but it can decide to spend more. Further, all spending must be received by someone, somewhere, as income. Finally, as discussed earlier, spending is not necessarily constrained by income because it is possible for households, firms, or government to spend more than income. Indeed, as we discussed, any of the three main sectors can run a deficit with at least one of the others running a surplus. However, it is not possible for spending at the aggregate level to be different from aggregate income since the sum of the sectoral balances must be zero. For all of these reasons, we must reverse causation between spending and income when we turn to the aggregate; while at the individual level, income causes spending, at the aggregate level, spending causes income.

d) *Deficits in one sector create the surpluses of another.* Earlier we showed that the deficits of one sector are by identity equal to the sum of the surplus balances of the other sector(s). If we divide the economy into three sectors (domestic private sector, domestic government sector, and foreign sector), then if one sector runs a deficit at least one other must run a surplus. Just as in the case of our analysis of individual balances, it "takes two to tango" in the sense that one sector cannot run a deficit if no other sector will run a surplus. Equivalently, we can say that one sector cannot issue debt if no other sector is willing to accumulate the debt instruments.

Of course, much of the debt issued within a sector will be held by others in the same sector. For example, if we look at the finances of the private domestic sector we will find that most business debt is held by domestic firms and households. In the terminology we introduced earlier, this is "inside debt" of those firms and households that run budget deficits held as "inside wealth" by those households and firms that run budget surpluses. However, if the domestic private sector taken as a whole spends more than its income, it must issue "outside debt" held as "outside wealth" by at least one of the other two sectors (domestic government sector and foreign sector). Because the initiating cause of a budget deficit is a desire to spend more than income, the causation mostly goes from deficits to surpluses and from debt to net financial wealth. While we recognize that no sector can run a deficit unless another wants to run a surplus, this is not usually a problem because there is a propensity to net save financial assets. That is to say, there is a desire to accumulate financial wealth – which by definition is somebody's liability.

Conclusion

Before moving on it is necessary to emphasize that everything in this section applies to the macro accounting of any country. While examples used the Dollar, all of the results apply no matter what currency is used. Our fundamental macro balance equation,

Domestic Private Balance + Domestic Government Balance + Foreign Balance = 0

will strictly apply to the accounting of balances of any currency. Within a country there can also be flows (accumulating to stocks) in a foreign currency, and there will be a macro balance equation in that currency also.

Note that nothing changes if we expand our model to include a number of different countries, each issuing its own currency. There will be a macro balance equation for each of these countries and for each of the currencies. Individual firms or households (or, for that matter, governments) can accumulate net financial assets denominated in several different currencies; vice versa, individual firms or households (or governments) can issue net debt denominated in several different currencies. It can even become more complicated, with an individual running a deficit in one currency and a surplus in another (issuing debt in one currency and accumulating wealth in another). Still, for every country and for every currency there will be a macro balance equation.

Technical note:

The main differences between the personal saving rate and the household net saving as a percent of GDP are the following (thanks to Scott Fullwiler):

1. Household net saving is as a percent of GDP, whereas personal saving rate is as a percent of disposable income;
2. Household net saving subtracts all household spending, including consumption and residential investment, whereas personal saving only subtracts consumption spending.

A few additional smaller differences for the really wonky:

1. Household net saving adds an allowance for household capital consumption (i.e. depreciation), personal saving doesn't;
2. Household net saving imputes insurance and pension reserves to households from government sector, personal saving doesn't; and
3. Household net saving includes wage accruals less disbursements from businesses to households, personal saving doesn't.

Box: Frequently asked questions

Q: The Primer claimed: "No matter how much others might want to accumulate financial wealth, they will not be able to do so unless someone is willing to deficit spend." But what about undesired inventory accumulation?

A: If a firm is producing "widgets" it does so to "realize" them in the form of money things – it wants to sell them to get a credit to its bank account. If it cannot sell them, they are added to inventory and count in the GDP accounts (technically NIPA) as investment. There will be an offsetting flow which is saving. Within the private sector, the increase to investment equals the increase to saving – this activity has no impact on the overall private sector's balance (which includes households and firms). But let us imagine that foreigners order those widgets; in that case, the firm gets to sell them (receiving a credit to its bank account), but there will be no increase to domestic investment. Instead, exports have increased – there is a positive entry to the current account balance. Ignoring all other entries, the US domestic private sector gets a surplus on its balance (saving) while the foreign sector "deficit spends".

This will not answer all possible questions that follow from this. After we look at the "circuit approach" later in the Primer we will see how the firm financed its production of widgets and what the implication is for the firm if it fails to "realize" them in the form of sales for money things. You can think of the "saving" of the household sector as the counterpart to the undesired inventory accumulation by the widget manufacturer. The manufacture of the widget produces household income that can be consumed or saved; of course the firms hope workers never save – because that means lost potential sales. If households do save, widgets go to inventory as investment. The firm can then be in trouble – not able to cover its costs. But foreigners or the government can step in to fill the demand gap, buying goods that otherwise would accumulate as unsold inventory.

Q: Is spending really determined by income? What about borrowing to spend?

A: Of course, it is true that wealthier people can fairly easily spend even if their flow of income is zero – they can sell off assets or borrow against them. But for many households it is "mostly" true that income determines spending. And it is common sense to most people. The bigger theoretical point, however, is that at the aggregate level we need to think about reversing the causation. My household's income is mostly determined by my employer's decision to spend on my wages and salaries. So household consumption really depends to a great extent on its income (consumption is called "induced spending") but its income in turn comes from somewhere – largely spending by firms and governments on wages, profits, and interest. And that spending by firms is undertaken on the expectation of sales (expenditures by households, foreigners, governments, or other firms). We then also have government and investment and export spending that are at least to some extent "autonomous" from income (they don't depend so much on today's income). These are important issues both for explanation and for projections of economic performance. There is also a logical angle: a society can decide to spend more but it cannot decide to have more income (unless it spends more). Spending is thus logically prior.

Q: Is spending really related to stocks (not flows)? For example, when somebody hands you a five-dollar bill, you spend out of your stock of cash. You can only spend out of wealth, not out of income.

A: When my boss pays me my $5 wages, that is indeed an income flow, for example, $5 per hour, per week, per month, or per year. Flows occur over time (even if the time is short). I can accumulate my income (wages) flow in the form of green paper dollar notes – the flows accumulate to a stock of dollar bills. (Stocks are measured at a point in time. Now, for example.) If instead I spend the wages as I receive them, that is a consumption flow financed out of wages flow. But if I save all my wages as accumulated stacks of dollar bills for a period of a year, and at the end of the year I choose to run down my wealth by splurging on a new BMW, I am then dissaving (reducing stock of wealth) to finance consumption.

Note that if I accumulated BMWs as my wealth (rather than dollar notes) then I would first have to sell the BMWs before I could finance consumption. That is of course the advantage of accumulating "cash" – I don't have to sell it before spending. You could say that it is rather arbitrary whether to count hoarding of five-dollar notes as a saving flow into my stock of wealth, that I then run down to finance consumption, versus spending the five-dollar income flow to finance consumption. That is to say, as we collapse the time period toward an "instant" then the distinction between flows and stocks disappears. An instantaneous flow reduces to a stock as time approaches zero. And that of course is correct, too.

Income can be received as a flow of claims (rather than currency or other means of payment). I work all month long, accumulating wage claims on my employer. (These claims are legally enforceable in court.) Then I finally get my paycheck and deposit it in my bank account. Now I spend down my deposit until my next paycheck. If we want to be technically wonky we would say I was receiving an income flow every day of the month that finances a consumption flow every day of the month. But the "payment" of the wage actually takes place on a single day as a credit to my bank account (increasing my stock of wealth). (Technically, the claim on my employer is converted to a bank deposit – usually a debit to my employer's bank account and a credit to mine.) I could not really spend my wages (claims on my employer) until I got my paycheck – except by borrowing against the claims.

Q: Isn't it savers who force deficit spending and not the other way? If households won't spend, GDP declines, lowering tax revenue and thus causing a budget deficit.

A: Good point. It takes two to tango, of course. But carrying on from above, at the aggregate level (at least), it makes more sense to say that spending "causes" income which in turn "causes" saving. Here is why. If I am creditworthy I can always decide to spend more (the bank takes my IOU, gives me its IOU, and I deficit spend). I cannot (easily) decide to have more income. I need income to save more. Still, it takes two to tango. So, yes, if I have income I can decide to consume less and save more. That will have an implication on someone else's income flow (since I am not buying her widgets). And that means undesired deficit spending (and perhaps inventory accumulation – as above).

1.3 Government budget deficits are largely nondiscretionary: the case of the Great Recession of 2007

In previous sections we have examined the three balances identity and established that the sum of deficits and surpluses across the three sectors (domestic private, government, and foreign) must be zero. We have also attempted to say something about causation because it is not enough to simply lay out identities. We have argued that while household income largely determines spending at the individual level, at the level of the economy as a whole it is best to reverse that causation: spending determines income.

Individual households can certainly decide to spend less in order to save more. But if all households were to try to spend less, this would reduce aggregate consumption and national income. Firms would reduce output, thus would lay off workers, cut the wage bill, and thereby lower household income. This is J. M. Keynes's well-known "paradox of thrift" – trying to save more by cutting aggregate consumption will not increase saving. We'll have more to say about that later.

However, there is an issue of immediate interest given the deficit hysteria that has gripped the United States (as well as many other countries). In the aftermath of the global financial crisis (GFC), social spending by government (for example, on unemployment compensation) has risen while tax revenues have collapsed. The deficit has grown rapidly leading to widespread fears of eventual insolvency or bankruptcy. Those, too, are issues for later. The implication of growing deficits has been attempts to cut spending (and perhaps to increase taxes) to reduce deficits. The national conversation (in the United States, the United Kingdom, and Europe, for example) presumes that government budget deficits are discretionary. If only the government were to try hard enough, it could slash its deficit.

However, anyone who proposes to cut government deficits must be prepared to project impacts on the other balances (private and foreign) because by identity the budget deficit cannot be reduced unless the private sector surplus or the foreign surplus (flip side to the domestic current account deficit) is reduced. In this section, let us look at the rise of government budget deficits since the GFC hit. We will ask whether the deficit has been, and might be, under discretionary control; if not, then that raises questions about the attempts by deficit hysterians to reduce deficits.

In the aftermath of the Great Recession of 2008, many government budgets moved sharply to large deficits. (See the Figure below.) While observers attributed this to various fiscal stimulus packages (including bailouts of the auto industry and Wall Street in the United States, and bank bailouts in Ireland), the largest portion of the increase in the deficit in most countries came from automatic stabilizers and not from discretionary spending.

This is easily observable in the graph below for the situation in the United States which shows the rate of growth of tax revenues (mostly automatic), government consumption expenditures (somewhat discretionary), and transfer payments (again mostly automatic) relative to the same quarter of the previous year:

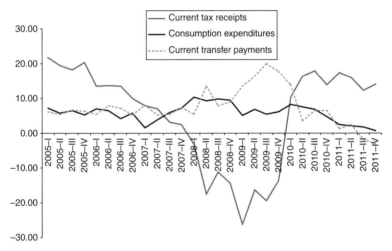

Figure 1.1 Federal government tax receipts, consumption expenditures and transfer payments (growth rate relative to the same quarter of the previous year)
Source: Bureau of Economic Analysis and author's calculations.

In 2005 tax revenues were humming, with a growth rate hitting 15 percent per year – far above GDP growth – hence reducing non-government sector after-tax income – and faster than government spending, which grew just above 5 percent. Such fiscal tightening (called fiscal drag) often is followed by a downturn, and the downturn that accompanied the GFC was no exception. When it came, the budget deficits increased, mostly automatically. While government consumption expenditures remained relatively stable over the downturn (after a short spike in 2007–2008), the rate of growth of tax revenues dropped sharply from a 5 percent growth rate to a 10 percent negative growth rate over just three quarters (from Q4 of 2007 to Q2 of 2008), reaching another low of negative 15 percent in Q1 of 2009. Tax receipts quite simply fell off a cliff.

Transfer payments grew at an average rate of 10 percent since 2007, with the higher rate in part due to the rotten economy. Decreasing taxes coupled with increased transfer payments automatically pushed the budget into a larger deficit, notwithstanding the flat consumption expenditures. The automatic stabilizer – and not the bailouts or stimulus – is the main reason why the economy did not go into a freefall as it had in the Great Depression of the 1930s. As the economy slowed, the budget automatically went into a deficit, putting a floor on aggregate demand. With counter-cyclical spending and pro-cyclical taxes, the government's budget acts as a powerful automatic stabilizer: deficits increase sharply in a downturn.

After the global crash, the US household sector retrenched (as it always does in recession), and saving remains high. Slow growth has been the major cause of the rapidly growing budget deficit, and the slow growth, in turn, is due to a high propensity to save by the retrenching household sector. See the next graph:

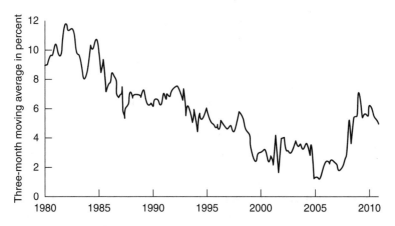

Figure 1.2   Propensity to save out of disposable income
Source: BEA.

What we see is a rather remarkable reduction of household saving on trend since the mid-1980s. The cause is beyond the scope of this section. But the flipside to that has been the rise of household debt. That trend turned around sharply after the GFC, with households saving like it was 1992 all over again. Given loss of jobs, and stagnant incomes (at best) for most Americans, the likelihood that the household propensity to spend will reverse course soon seems unlikely. (Note that saving as a percent of disposable income is not exactly the same as the household balance that goes into our three-sector balance equation. That is why although this is a small positive saving number, in the sectoral balances equation households actually spent more than their income. See the note at the end of Section 1.2 above for the wonky stuff.)

To reduce the US government sector deficit from 9 percent or so of GDP (that it reached after the crisis) toward balance requires some combination of a private sector movement toward deficit and a current account movement toward surplus amounting to a total of 9 percent points of GDP. That is huge. The problem is that actually trying to balance the budget through spending cuts or tax increases could reduce economic growth (it might actually cause a sharp downturn, but we do not need to make that case). Lower economic growth could conceivably reduce the US current account deficit – by making Americans too poor to buy imports, by lowering US wages and prices to make our exports more competitive, and by reducing the value of the dollar. Note that all of those are painful adjustments for Americans. And it might not work, because it requires the United States to slow without that affecting the global economy; if global growth also slows, US exports may not increase.

Let us summarize the main points. First, the three balances must balance to zero. This implies it is impossible to change one of the balances without having a change in at least one other. Second, at the aggregate level, spending (mostly) determines income. A sector can spend more than its income, but that means another spends less. While we can take government spending as more-or-less discretionary, government tax revenue (government's equivalent to its income) depends largely on economic performance. As the chart above showed, tax receipt growth is highly variable, moving procyclically (growing rapidly in boom and collapsing in slump).

Government can always decide to spend more (although it is politically constrained), and it can always decide to raise tax rates (again, given political constraints), but it cannot decide what its tax revenue will be because we apply a tax rate to variables like income and wealth that are outside government control. And that means the budgetary outcome – whether surplus, balanced, or deficit – is not really discretionary.

Turning to the foreign sector, exports are largely outside control of a nation (we say they are "exogenous" or "autonomous to domestic income"). They depend on lots of factors, including growth in the rest of the world, exchange rates, trade policy, and relative prices and wages (efforts to increase exports will likely lead to responses abroad). It is true that domestic economic outcomes can influence exports – but impacts of policy on exports are loose (as discussed, slower growth by a large importer like the United States can slow global growth).

On the other hand, imports depend largely on domestic income (plus exchange rates, relative wages and prices, and trade policy; again, if the United States tried to reduce imports this would almost certainly lead to responses by trading partners that are pursuing trade-led growth). Imports are largely pro-cyclical, too. Again, the current account outcome – whether deficit, surplus, or balanced – is also largely nondiscretionary.

What *is* discretionary? Domestic spending – by households, firms, and government – is largely discretionary. And spending largely determines our income. Sectoral balances, however, should be taken as mostly nondiscretionary because they depend in very complex ways on the discretionary variables plus the nondiscretionary variables and on the constraints imposed by the macro identity. It makes most sense to promote spending that will utilize domestic resources close to capacity, and then let sectoral balances fall where they may. As we will argue later, the best domestic policy is to pursue full employment and price stability – not to target arbitrary government deficit or debt limits, which are mostly nondiscretionary anyway.

Box: The paradox of thrift and other fallacies of composition

One of the most important concepts in macroeconomics is the notion of the fallacy of composition: what might be true for individuals is probably not true for society as a whole.

The most common example is the paradox of thrift: while an individual can save more by reducing spending (on consumption), society can save more only by spending more (for example, on investment). This example can drive home the fallacy of composition.

Students and others who haven't been exposed to macroeconomics naturally extrapolate from their own individual situation to society and the economy as a whole. This often leads to the problem of the fallacy of composition. Of course, that isn't just restricted to economics. While a few people could quickly exit the doors of a crowded movie theater, all of us could not.

Any individual can increase her saving by reducing her spending – on consumption goods. So long as her decision does not affect her income – and there is no reason to assume that it would – she ends up with less consumption and more saving. The example I always use involves Mary, who usually eats a hamburger at her local fast-food chain every day. She decides to forgo one hamburger per week, to accumulate savings. Of course, so long as she sticks to her plan, she will add to her savings (and financial wealth) every week.

The question is this: what if everyone did the same thing as Mary – would the reduction of the consumption of hamburgers raise aggregate (national) saving (and financial wealth)?

The answer is that it will not. Why not? Because the fast-food chains will not sell as many hamburgers, they will begin to lay off workers, and reduce orders for bread, meat, catsup, pickles, and so on.

All those workers who lose their jobs will have lower incomes, and will have to reduce their own saving. You can use the notion of the multiplier to show that this process comes to a stop when the lower saving by all those who lost their jobs equals the higher saving of all those who cut their hamburger consumption. At the aggregate level, there is no accumulation of savings (financial wealth).

Of course that is a simple and even silly example. But the underlying explanation is that when we look at the individual's increase of saving, we can safely ignore any macro effects because they are so minimal that they have only an infinitely small impact on the economy as a whole.

But if everyone tries to increase saving, we cannot ignore the effects of lower spending on the economy as a whole. That is the point that has to be driven home.

1.4 Accounting for real versus financial (or nominal)

So far in this chapter we have focused on accounting for financial flows and stocks. That is appropriate for a Primer that is devoted to "modern money". It is often said that "money makes the world go 'round", and certainly in a capitalist economy the purpose of much of the production is for profit, that is, to realize monetary sales receipts that are greater than monetary costs. True enough, and certainly that is a huge part of our modern economy.

And yet there is also "real stuff" that is being produced, and life itself would be impossible without producing goods and services to be consumed. That is to say the economist also needs to be concerned with the "provisioning process" itself. The final point to make here is that much of the provisioning process takes place outside markets and does not directly involve money.

How can we account for the real stuff? That is the topic of this section.

The state's monetary unit is a handy measuring device that we use to measure credits, debts, and something fairly esoteric we might call "value". By now the reader is probably fairly clear on the credits and debits part of this. I owe taxes to the government and these are measured in so many Dollars. It is my debt and the government's asset and we can record it on electronic balance sheets. I have deposits in my bank measured in Dollars that are the bank's IOU and my credit (again, they exist only as electronic charges on a computer tape).

"Value" is more difficult. We need a measuring unit that is appropriate to measuring heterogeneous things. We cannot use color, weight, length, density, and so on. For reasons I will not go into right now, we usually use the state's money of account. Otherwise, we can only measure value in terms of the thing itself. For example, it is fairly easy to measure the value of sugar in terms of sugar: sugar weight will work, and if the crystals are uniform we could actually count them out. Usually however we measure sugar by volume, at least for kitchen purposes. But we cannot just say "cup", we must say "cup of sugar" and then define what we mean by sugar.

Now, I could borrow a cup of sugar from you and write "IOU a cup of sugar". However, we might as well agree to write the IOU in Dollars since we live in a heavily monetized society that uses the state's money or nominal measure – the Dollar – as the unit of account. Let us say the going price of sugar at the store is about a Dollar for a cup of sugar, so I write the IOU as "IOU a Dollar". I might repay you in a Dollar (state's IOU), a cup of sugar, or something else that we agree to *value* at a Dollar.

When I go to tally up all of my wealth I will include all the Dollar IOUs I hold against banks, the government, other financial institutions, friends and family and so on. That is my gross *financial* wealth. (It could include even some of those "real cup of sugar IOUs" if there is a reasonable expectation that I could collect Dollars from those owing me sugar.) Against that I count up all of my own IOUs – to banks, government, family and friends. (And again, if I issued cup of sugar IOUs in which payment could be enforced in Dollars I should include them. If my cup of sugar credits and debts will never be converted to Dollars then I should treat these as real assets and liabilities – and I can subtract the liabilities from the assets to obtain net cup of sugar real wealth. More below on real wealth.) When I subtract these financial IOUs from my gross financial wealth I am left with my *net* financial wealth.

Now clearly I am not done. I've got a house and a car (and maybe some sugar in the kitchen cabinet). Assume I've got some debt against them, as I took out a loan (issued my own IOU to the bank or auto finance company, etc.) to finance purchases. That is part of my financial IOUs included in the calculation above. But I've been paying for years and so the outstanding IOU is much less than the value of my car and home. I count the monetary *value* of the car and home and add that to my financial assets to get *gross* assets.

Exactly how I value the house and car is tricky and subject to accounting rules. But that is not important to understand the principle here. We take the total value of gross assets (financial plus real) and subtract the outstanding liabilities (usually financial, but there could be some real sugar IOUs) to get net wealth. That of course will be comprised of *real* assets plus net financial wealth. So total net wealth will be greater than net financial wealth because I've got real assets (car, house, and sugar).

(I could have negative net financial wealth that is – hopefully – more than offset by positive real assets. Otherwise I am "underwater". As a result of the global financial crisis, many Americans are "underwater" in home mortgages: the outstanding mortgage debt is greater than the monetary value of their home. We cannot say for sure that they are underwater in terms of their total wealth – we'd need to count up the value of all their other assets and liabilities – but it is likely that many are.)

Most of the time in this Primer we are focused on the monetary part of the economy – indeed on what Keynes called "monetary production" and Marx called M-C-M', in which production begins with money (M), to produce a commodity for sale (C) for "more money" (M', profits). We focus on that because that is basically what capitalism is all about and we are mostly concerned with how "modern money" works in a capitalist economy; this is a *modern* money primer, after all. (Note, however, that "taxes drive money" – see Section 2.3 – also applies to earlier societies that used money even though they were not capitalist.)

Still, even in capitalism it is obvious that not all production involves money in the beginning and not all is undertaken on the prospect of making profit. In about two hours I am going to fix dinner and wash dishes. I am not going to get paid, much less earn any profits. Now at least some of this "production" process does begin with money: I bought most of the ingredients for the cooking, and purchased both water and soap for washing. But part of the ingredients (especially my labor) will not be purchased.

Is this kind of production important? Undoubtedly – even in a highly developed capitalist economy like that of the United States it is hard to see how any of the monetary production could take place without all of the unpaid labor involved in "reproducing" the "labor power" (these are Marx's terms; you can replace them with "supporting the family that supplies workers"). Domestic services, childrearing, recreation and relaxation, and so on are critical and mostly do not involve monetary transactions. We can – and sometimes do – put monetary values on them anyway. Not only is there a "flow" dimension (recall the discussion from the previous sections) in the form of daily dishwashing, but there is also a "stock" dimension – accumulation of the knowledge and skills our youngsters will need later (often called "human capital" by economists). That (growing) stock should be added to our "real assets" and hence to our total net wealth. Obviously these things are very difficult to measure in Dollar terms. And often they are even harder to realize in money form; you no doubt have human "capital" skills you cannot sell.

Box: Accounting through balance sheets

A balance sheet is an accounting document that records what an economic unit owns and owes.

Assets	Liabilities and Net Worth
Financial Assets (FA) Real Assets (RA)	Financial Liabilities (FL) Net Worth (NW)

A balance sheet must balance, that is, the following equality must hold:

$$FA + RA = FL + NW$$

Net worth (NW) can be considered to be the residual variable that makes the adjustment to preserve the equality, that is, net worth is the difference between assets and liabilities.

Financial assets are financial claims on other economic units and real assets are physical things (cars, buildings, machines, pens, desks, inventories, etc.). Financial liabilities are claims of others on the economic unit.

Given that a balance sheet must always balance, any change in one component of the balance sheet must lead to an offsetting change in at least one other component.

Household buys a car

For example, if a household buys a car for $100 by writing a check on its bank account, the outstanding bank account balance is reduced by $100 ($\Delta$FA: –$100) and the household gains a car worth the same amount (ΔRA: +100):

Household Balance Sheet

Change in Assets	Change in Liabilities and NW
ΔFA (bank account): –$100 ΔRA (car): +$100	0

As you can see the sum of all assets has not changed, and neither did the liability (and NW) side. Households may also pay for a portion of the value of the car (say $30) by taking out a car loan (increase in financial liabilities):

Household Balance Sheet

Change in Assets	Change in Liabilities and NW
ΔFA (bank account) = −$70 ΔRA (car) = +$100	ΔFL (car loan) = +$30

Both sides of the balance sheet have increased by $30, thus preserving the equality.

Impact on the rest of the private domestic sector in a closed economy

We only looked at the household balance sheet in isolation, but when a household buys a new car, the car manufacturer (a nonfinancial business) receives the funds and loses the car. If households borrowed, banks now have a claim of $30 on the household and the household used its bank deposit ($70) plus the borrowed funds ($30) to pay the car dealer. Here are the other two balance sheets:

Nonfinancial business balance sheet

Change in Assets	Change in Liabilities and NW
ΔFA (bank account)= +$70 + $30 ΔRA (car) = −$100	

Bank balance sheet

Change in Assets	Change in Liabilities and NW
ΔFA (car loan) = +$30	ΔFL (bank account) = +$30

Note that all these accounting entries show up in the balance sheet of an economic unit and in the balance sheet of at least one other economic unit: the household borrowed $30 so a bank lent $30, the household purchased a car for $100 so a car dealer sold a car for $100, and so on.

Households, banks, and nonfinancial businesses broadly represent what we call the private sector. If you try to compute the overall impact of the purchase of the car on the private sector by summing all balance sheet changes above you get:

Consolidated private sector balance sheet

Change in Assets	Change in Liabilities and NW
ΔFA (bank account)= –\$70 + \$100 ΔRA (car) = +\$100 – \$100 ΔFA (car loan) = +\$30	ΔFL (bank account) = +\$30 ΔFL (car loan) = +\$30

So the overall impact is

Consolidated private sector balance sheet

Change in Assets	Change in Liabilities and NW
ΔFA (bank account) = +\$30 ΔFA (car loan) = +\$30	ΔFL (bank account) = +\$30 ΔFL (car loan) = +\$30

Thus overall the private sector owes to itself \$60, which if we consolidate even more means that nothing changed in the private sector: "I owe you, you owe me, let's cancel each other's debt." Private sector "inside" financial wealth nets to zero. Only the real asset – the car – remains.

Introducing the government

What if instead of the household buying the car, the government bought it? Let us assume for simplicity the government finances its purchase by issuing cash to the car manufacturer

Government balance sheet

Change in Assets	Change in Liabilities and NW
ΔRA (car)= +\$100	ΔFL (cash) = +\$100

In the private sector, the manufacturer receives cash (ΔFA: +100) and sells a car in exchange (ΔRA: –100)

Nonfinancial businesses balance sheet

Change in Assets	Change in Liabilities and NW
ΔFA (cash) = +\$100 ΔRA (car) = –\$100	

In this case the private sector has accumulated a financial claim against the government, that is, this financial claim does not cancel out within the private sector. If one consolidates both the Government and Private Sector to get a view of the domestic economy, the balance sheet looks like this:

Domestic economy consolidated balance sheet

Change in Assets	Change in Liabilities and NW
ΔFA (cash) = +\$100 ΔRA (car) = −\$100 + \$100	ΔFL (cash) = +\$100

Again the result is that the economy owes itself and so overall the financial balance nets to zero. Importantly, however, the private sector's financial balance is positive (it holds cash) and the government's is negative (cash is its liability). We call this positive financial balance of the private sector "outside wealth" because it is a claim on an entity outside the private sector.

Likewise, if we added a foreign sector, our domestic private sector could have a net financial claim on foreigners – again counted as positive outside wealth. And even the domestic government could hold "outside wealth" in the form of a claim on foreigners. So the domestic economy would have a net financial asset, the claim on foreigners.

1.5 Recent US sectoral balances: Goldilocks and the global crash

In this section we apply what we've learned to a real world example. Let us look at the US "Goldilocks economy" of the mid-1990s to find the seeds of the GFC, using our sectoral balance approach. As a reminder, President Bill Clinton headed government when the United States emerged from a long period of substandard economic growth. Suddenly the United States began to grow at a robust pace, lowering unemployment to levels not seen since the 1960s. Amazingly, however, inflation remained low. This is why it was labeled the Goldilocks economy – neither too hot nor too cold, indeed, just right. And yet it crashed at the end of the 1990s. And after a recovery that reproduced some of the same features of the Goldilocks economy in the 2000s under President Bush (this time called the Great Moderation), it crashed again into what is called the "Great Recession" in the United States and the "Global Financial Crisis" (GFC) elsewhere. Let's see how the sectoral balance approach makes it possible to discern what went wrong.

To be clear, what follows uses our sectoral balances identity plus some real world data to provide an interpretation of the causes of the crash. As always, interpretations are subject to disagreement. The identity as well as the data are not. But an identity plus data cannot decisively "prove" what caused the crash.

Beginning in 1998 some of us who had adopted the MMT approach began to warn that the Goldilocks economy had produced unsustainable sectoral balances in the United States. We had recognized that the economy of the time was in a bubble, driven by what I perceived to be unsustainable deficit spending by the private sector – which had been spending more than its income since 1996. As we now know, we called it too soon; the private sector continued to spend more than its income until 2006. The economy then crashed, a casualty of the excesses. What I had not understood in 2002 was just how far the financial sector would go in building up private sector debt. It kept the debt bubble going through all sorts of lender fraud until it finally collapsed in 2008 – a decade after we had first warned of the problem. (See L. Randall Wray, "The Perfect Fiscal Storm", 2002, available at http://www.epicoalition.org/docs/perfect_fiscal_storm. htm.)

So let's see what lessons we can learn from "Goldilocks" that help us to understand the GFC. At the end of the 1990s Goldilocks did fall into a recession, ending Clinton's budget surpluses, but the deficit under President Bush then grew to 5 percent of GDP, helping the economy to recover. With recovery, the private sector moved right back to huge deficits fueling a real estate boom as well as a consumption boom (financed by home equity loans). See the chart below (thanks to Scott Fullwiler). Note that we have divided each sectoral balance by GDP (since we are dividing each balance by the same number – GDP – this does not change the relationships; it only "scales" the balances). This is a convenient scaling that we will use often in the Primer. Since most macroeconomic data tend to grow over time, dividing by GDP makes it easier to plot (and rather than dealing with trillions of dollars – so many zeroes! – we express everything as a percent of total spending). Take a look at the next chart.

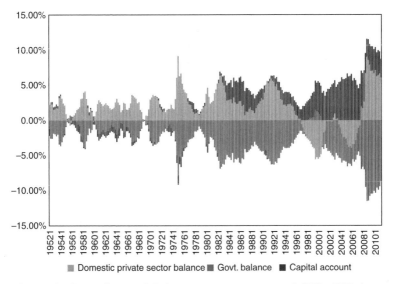

■ Domestic private sector balance ■ Govt. balance ■ Capital account

Figure 1.3 Sector financial balances as a percentage of GDP, 1952q1 to 2010q4

It shows the "mirror image": a government deficit from 1980 through to the Goldilocks years is the mirror image of the domestic private sector's surplus plus our current account deficit (shown as a positive number because it reflects a positive capital account balance: the rest of the world runs a positive financial balance against the USA). (Note: the chart confirms what we learned from the previous sections: the sum of deficits and surpluses across the three sectors must equal zero – that is why there's a mirror image from zero.) During the Clinton years, as the government budget moved to surplus (shown as above the line), it was the private sector's deficit that was the mirror image to the budget surplus plus the current account deficit.

This mirror image is what almost no one except those following MMT, as well as the Levy Economic Institute's researchers who used Wynne Godley's sectoral balance approach, understand, which is why most did not see the private deficit/government surplus relationship. After the financial collapse, the domestic private sector moved sharply to a large surplus (which is what it normally does in recession), the current account deficit fell (as consumers bought fewer imports), and the budget deficit grew mostly because tax revenue collapsed as domestic sales and employment fell.

Unfortunately, just as policymakers learned the wrong lessons from the Clinton Goldilocks budget surpluses – thinking that the federal budget surpluses were desirable while they actually were just the flipside to the private sector's deficit spending – they are now learning the wrong lessons from the global crash after 2008. They've managed to convince themselves that it is all caused by government sector profligacy. This in turn has led to calls for spending cuts (and, more rarely, tax increases) to reduce budget deficits in many countries around the world (notably, in the United States and United Kingdom and in Europe – which is a topic we will take up later).

The reality is different: Wall Street's excesses led to too much private sector debt that crashed the economy and reduced government tax revenues. This caused a tremendous increase of federal government deficits. (As a sovereign currency issuer, the federal government faces no solvency constraints [readers will have to take that claim at face value for now; it is the topic for Chapter 2].) However, the downturn hurt state and local government revenue. Hence those governments responded by cutting spending, laying off workers, and searching for revenue.

Federal, state, and local government deficits probably will not fall until robust recovery returns, ending the perfect fiscal storm that destroyed tax revenues. Robust recovery will reduce the overall government sector's budget deficit as the private sector reduces its budget surplus. It is probable that the US current account deficit will grow a bit when America recovers. If you want to take a guess at what our "mirror image" in the graph above will look like after economic recovery, perhaps we will return close to the USA's long-run average: a private sector surplus of 2 percent of GDP, a current account deficit of 3 percent of GDP, and a government deficit of 5 percent of GDP. In our simple equation it will look like this:

Private Balance (+2) + Government Balance (–5) +
Foreign Balance (+3) = 0

And so we are back to the concept of zero!

1.6   Stocks, flows, and balance sheet: a bathtub analogy

Each item in the balance sheet of a firm, household, or government records the outstanding amount of an asset or a liability. The outstanding amount is a stock, that is, the measure of an item at a point in time. Stocks are affected by flows because inflows accumulate to a stock, while outflows reduce a stock.

Maybe a better way to look at it is in terms of a bathtub. Below is a bathtub half full of water. The water in the tub is called the stock of water. Currently, there is no water flowing in the tub from the faucet, and there is a stopper on the drain so no water is flowing out of the tub. Thus the stock of water remains the same. This initial level of water will be used as point of reference below.

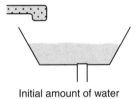

Initial amount of water

This would be similar to having money in a checking account (a stock of deposits) and neither receiving any deposits (no inflow), nor spending any deposits (no outflow). It also would be similar to having an outstanding amount of debts and not taking on more debt nor repaying any debts.

What would happen if suddenly we turn on the faucet? Water would flow into the tub and the stock of water would rise.

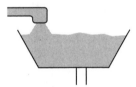

Outstanding amount of water rises

This would be similar to receiving a monetary income and saving all of it, so the amount of deposits in a checking account would rise. This would also be similar to buying a new car and keeping the old one: the stock of cars owned would rise. Of course if we now turn off the faucet and remove the stopper on the drain, the water in the tub would flow out of the tub and the stock of water would decline until nothing is left in the tub. The equivalent of this in terms of a checking account would be that someone does not receive income but still spends. This is called dissaving and would lead to a decline in the outstanding funds in the checking account until all the deposits were gone. Similarly, if someone repays her debts and does not borrow more, her outstanding amount of debts declines.

Finally, if both the faucet and drain are open, the outstanding amount of water will rise if the inflow of water from the faucet is greater than the outflow of water through the drain. In terms of a checking account that would mean that the income inflow is greater than the outflow due to spending, which means the individual is saving. The income saved adds to the outstanding stock of funds in the checking account. If the individual spends more than income, dissaving depletes the checking account. In terms of the tub, if more water flows out the drain than flows from the faucet, the tub empties.

More water flowing in than out   More water flowing out than in

One of the central goals of national accounting (Flow of Funds Accounts and National Income and Product Accounts) is to account for all the flows and all the stocks for all assets and liabilities of the private sector, the government, and the rest of the world. The common measure used to measure stocks and flows is the monetary unit of account (Dollar, Euro, etc.). It is not always easy to measure everything in monetary terms because the monetary value of some stocks and flows is hard to know. One reason is that some things are not purchased directly or at all (What is the monetary value of public lighting? What about a public park? What is the value of the vegetables grown in your garden?). Another reason is that some inflows and outflows escape measurements (there are leakages in the water pipes and water evaporates from the tub) because there is no recording for them. Some people lose some of their cash; someone's old car may get stolen and a claim is not reported. More broadly, there are a lot of underground economic activities that are not recorded anywhere. Thus in practice some statistical discrepancies will emerge in accounting from difficulty of measurement or unavailability of data.

One of the central goals of national accounting is to see how economic sectors relate to each other. For example, when the government spends on goods and services (G), this leads to an inflow of income to the private sector. On the other hand, taxes (T) are a drain on the private sector. In the graph below, G is greater than T, so the bathtub savings of the private sector rises.

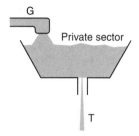

Government deficit and private sector

In this case the government is deficit spending and the private sector is saving, so the water in the tub increases. This gives us the first part of the well-known National Income and Product Accounts accounting identity:

$$S \equiv (G - T)$$

The size of the private sector saving (S) is equal by definition to the size of the fiscal deficit (G – T). They can never be different from one another (hence the three bars equals sign, which stands for "true by identity").

Technically this is true for a two-sector economy, with a government sector and a household sector. Once we add business firms to the household sector, that is like adding another faucet, for investment spending by firms. That augments our identity to: $S \equiv (G - T) + I$.

If we added a foreign sector, we would need another faucet (exports) and drain (imports), and then our full identity would be: $S \equiv (G - T) + I + NX$ (I is private domestic investment, and NX is net exports)

Box: Objections to accounting identities

Many people are skeptical when they first encounter accounting identities. In this Box we will deal with three objections:

1. Is an accounting identity something like simple arithmetic, that is, 2 + 3 = 5? Isn't that really just rigging the results?

2. Couldn't we just as well choose different identities? Why are these the important ones?
3. Why is an "imbalance" (i.e. a sectoral surplus or deficit) called a "sectoral balance"?

With regard to the first question, yes we did in some sense "rig" the results. We first rule out black helicopters that drop bags of cash into backyards in the dark of night. We also rule out expenditures by some that go "nowhere" – that is, expenditures that are not received by anyone. Finally, we rule out expenditures that are not in some manner "paid for".

Suppose our whole economy consists of you and me (I'll be Robinson Crusoe, you get to be Friday). If I spend, you receive income. If you spend, I get income. I can consume or save, and you can consume or save. We denominate our spending and income and saving or surpluses and deficits in "dollars" and record transactions by scratch marks on the big rock by the pond. We've discovered double entry bookkeeping and use it because it is a handy way of keeping track. (We trust each other, but we've got bad memories. I accept your IOUs denominated in dollars, and you accept mine but we want a record of them.) That is the set-up of our mental experiment – the rabbits and the hat. Nothing up our sleeves.

Say that you hire me to collect coconuts from your trees, and I hire you to catch fish in my pond. You own the coconuts, I own the fish due to our property rights in our respective resources. As workers we have a right to our wages but not to the coconuts or fish we collect. We each work five hours at a dollar an hour. We record these on our balance sheets on the big rock: on your balance sheet, your financial asset is my IOU; my financial asset is your IOU. At the end of the first day we each had income of $5 (recorded as assets) and we each issued an IOU to pay wages of $5 (recorded as liabilities).

On my balance sheet I hold your $5 IOU as my asset, and I have issued my IOU to you in the amount of $5, which I record on my liability side. And vice versa. It looks like this:

Me: Asset = Your $5 IOU; Liability = My $5 IOU
You: Asset = My $5 IOU; Liability = Your $5 IOU

Now I want to buy coconuts from you and you want to buy fish from me. I "pay for" the coconuts by delivering your IOUs. You "pay for" fish by delivering to me my IOUs. Let us say I purchase $5 worth of coconuts (I return all $5 of your IOUs – crossing off the entry on the big rock) and you purchase $4 worth of fish (returning to me $4 of my IOUs and retaining $1 of my IOU) because you are more frugal. It looks like this:

Me: Asset = $5 coconuts; Liability = My $1 IOU; my assets exceed my liabilities by $4, which is my net worth until I eat the coconuts.

You: Asset = $4 fish + My $1 IOU; Liability = 0; so your net worth is $5 until you eat the fish.

Once we eat, all that is left is the "financial" part of these balance sheets, and my $1 IOU is my liability and it equals your financial asset of a $1 claim on me.

My deficit spending has been $1 and your surplus (or saving) has been $1. They are equal (not magically – we put the rabbits in the hat), and indeed your saving accumulation takes the form of a money claim on me (my debt).

When we net out all the money claims, what we are left with is the real stuff (coconuts and fish) until we eat it.

To be sure, we have left out of this analysis much of what is interesting about the economy – no banks, no government, no green paper currency, and so on. All we did was to play a little game of IOU and U-O-Me. But we did demonstrate the simple sectoral balance conclusion: the financial deficit of one sector (me) equals the surplus of the other (you). And that once we net out the financials, we are left with the real stuff (fish and coconuts). No magic involved.

We can all of us accumulate in real (nonfinancial) terms. For example, we can all grow our own crops in our backyards, accumulating corn that is not offset by a financial liability. For most of the time humans have been around we managed without money. Still, we fed, clothed, cared for, and fought with, our fellow humans. For the most part, MMT is concerned with "money", that is, the financial accounting part, and it is here where every deficit is offset by an equal surplus (somewhere) and every debt is held by someone as financial wealth – so the net is zero. In terms of our Lake Wobegone analogy, we can all accumulate in real terms (we all have IQs above zero) but our finances net to zero (our IQs average to – well – average).

Turning to the second objection, some prefer alternative identities. For example, rather than using the domestic private, government, and foreign sector division we can choose to divide up into alternative sectors. We could divide into sectors according to hair color: blonde + black + red + blue + brown + silver, etc.... For the purposes of this Primer, however, our division is more useful. It is not unusual to separate the foreign sector from the domestic sector on the basis that it (mostly) uses a different currency (actually, multiple currencies – just about one different currency for each nation), so we are going across exchange rates. It is also not unusual to separate government from private, and that is particularly useful in discussion of "sovereign currency", which after all is the main purpose of this Primer. For convenience we add state and local government to the national government even though only the nation's government is the issuer of the sovereign currency. What is, admittedly, unusual is to add the households and firms together (as well as not-for-profits). This is in part due to data limitations – some data are collected this way. But we do this mostly to distinguish the currency "user" (households and firms) from the "issuer" (sovereign government).

We should say a word about a more common approach adopted in almost all economics textbooks. And that is to begin with the Gross Domestic Product (GDP) identity (GDP = consumption + investment + government purchases + net exports; which equals gross national income). Without getting overly technical, the GDP comes out of the NIPA accounts (national income and product accounts) that have some well-known disadvantages for those of us who worry about stock-flow consistency (the topic of future sections). NIPA actually imputes some values and things don't quite add up (a rather large and nasty "statistical discrepancy" is used to fudge to get to the identity). Just as one example: most Americans own their own homes, but certainly we all "consume" what is called "housing services" – the sheer enjoyment we get out of having some shelter over our heads in a rainstorm. So statisticians "impute" a price we would pay (make up some economic value for that enjoyment), adding it to GDP. What we do not like about that is that no one really has to "pay for" the consumption of "housing services" for owner-occupied housing (say you paid off your mortgage five years ago, but the statistician records $12,000 worth of enjoyment you consumed this year without paying for it this year).

Another area that is problematic comes in the treatment of saving. Typically this can be done in one of two ways: either saving is simply a residual (your income less your consumption) or it is the accumulation to your wealth. In many calculations, when there is a real estate price boom, the value of the housing stock increases, which means our wealth increases. But that must mean our saving increased. However, there was no income source that allowed us to save in financial terms. In economics terms it is an "unrealized" capital gain. To be realized there must be an actual sale.

Since this Primer is very concerned about "accounting for" all spending, all income, all consumption, and all saving, we do not want to include such imputations that do not have a financial flow counterpart. So we prefer to work from the flow of funds accounts, which are stock-flow consistent (or, at least, closer to consistency). Now, in truth, NIPA data are more readily available for many countries than are flow of funds data, and so sometimes we are forced to use the GDP equation rather than our sectoral balances equation. That is probably good enough for the game of horseshoes (where being "close" to the target can be sufficient), and even for most economics questions.

Here is a comparison:

**Domestic Private balance +
Government balance + Foreign balance = 0**

**(Saving – Investment) +
(Taxes – Government Purchases) + (Imports – Exports) = 0**

You can see that these are reasonably close approximations. Roughly, if private saving exceeds investment, then the private sector will be running a surplus; if taxes are less than government purchases, the government is running a deficit; and if imports exceed exports the foreign sector is running a surplus. We can get even more wonky and put in government transfer payments (things like unemployment compensation that add to private sector income) and international factor payments (flows of profits earned by American firms from abroad – that reduce our foreign imbalance). But we won't do that here. We will usually work from the sectoral balances (thus, flow of funds) rather than from the GDP identity (NIPA) but readers can do the mental gymnastics if they want to do the conversion.

Finally, why would we call an "imbalance" a "balance": that is, if the private sector runs a deficit, why would we refer to that as the private sector's "balance"? Well, you have a checking account "balance" at your bank that is probably positive. If you write a check for more than your "balance", and if you have automatic overdraft coverage, then you will now have a negative "balance" in your account! So you would still call that a "checking account balance" even though it is "imbalanced". The "balance" can be either positive, zero, or negative for any sector.

2
Spending by Issuer of Domestic Currency

In previous sections we have examined in some detail the three balances approach developed largely by Wynne Godley. In some sense all of that is preliminary to examining the *nature* of modern money. Further, a key distinguishing characteristic of MMT is its view on *how government really spends*. Beginning with this chapter we will develop our theory of sovereign currency.

We will examine spending by government that issues its own domestic currency. We first present general principles that are applicable to any issuer of domestic currency. These principles apply to both developed and developing nations, and regardless of exchange rate regime. We later move on to analysis of special considerations that apply to developing nations. Finally we will discuss implications of the analysis for different currency regimes.

In the next section we examine the concept of a *sovereign currency*.

2.1 What is a sovereign currency?

Domestic Currency

We first introduce the concept of the money of account: the Australian Dollar, the US Dollar, the Japanese Yen, the British Pound, and the European Euro are all examples of a money of account. The first four of these monies of account are each associated with a single nation. By contrast, the Euro is a money of account adopted by a number of countries that have joined the European Monetary Union (EMU). Throughout history, the usual situation has been "one nation, one currency", although there have been a number of exceptions to this rule, including the modern Euro. Most of the discussion that follows will be focused on the more common case in which a nation adopts its own money of account, and in which the government issues a currency denominated in that unit of account. When we address the exceptional cases, such as the European Monetary Union, we will carefully identify the differences that arise when a currency is divorced from the nation.

Note that most developing nations adopt their own domestic currency. Some of these peg their currencies, hence surrender a degree of domestic policy space, as will be discussed below. However, since they do issue their own currencies, the analysis here of the money of account does apply to them.

Note also we recognize that individual households and firms (and even governments) can use foreign currencies even within their domestic economy. For example, within Kazakhstan (and many other developing nations) some transactions can occur in US Dollars, while others take the form of Tenge. And individuals can accumulate net wealth denominated in Dollars or in Tenge. However, the accounting principles that apply to a money of account will still apply (separately) to each of these currencies.

One nation, one currency

The overwhelmingly dominant practice is for a nation to adopt its own unique money of account: the US Dollar (US$) in America; the Australian Dollar (A$) in Australia; the Kazakhstan Tenge. The government of the nation issues a currency (usually consisting of metal coins and paper notes of various denominations) denominated in its money of account. Spending by the government as well as tax liabilities, fees, and fines owed to the government are denominated in the same money of account. The court system assesses damages in civil cases using the state money of account. For example, wages are counted in the nation's money of account and in the event that an employer fails to pay wages due, the courts will enforce the labor contract and assess monetary damages on the employer to be paid to the employee.

A government might also use a foreign currency for some of its purchases, and might accept a foreign currency in payment. It might also borrow – issuing IOUs – in a foreign currency. Usually this is done when the government is making purchases of imports or when it is trying to accumulate foreign currency reserves (for example when it pegs its currency). While important, this does not change the accounting of the domestic currency. That is, if the Kazakhstan government spends more Tenge than it collects in Tenge taxes, it runs a budget deficit in Tenge that exactly equals the nongovernment sector's accumulation of Tenge claims on government through its budget surplus (assuming a balanced foreign sector, it will be the domestic private sector that accumulates the Tenge claims).

We will argue that the government has much more leeway (called "domestic policy space") when it spends and taxes in its own currency than when it spends or taxes in a foreign currency. For the Kazakhstan government to run a budget deficit in US Dollars, it would have to get hold of the extra Dollars by borrowing them. This is more difficult than simply spending by issuing Tenge to a domestic private sector that wants to accumulate some net saving in Tenge.

It is also important to note that in many nations there are private contracts that are written in foreign monies of account. For example, in some Latin American countries as well as some other developing nations around the world it is common to write some kinds of contracts in terms of the US Dollar. It is also common in many nations to use US currency in payment in private transactions. According to some estimates, the total value of US currency circulating outside America exceeds the value of US currency used at home. Thus one or more foreign monies of account as well as foreign currencies might be used in addition to the domestic money of account and the domestic currency denominated in that unit.

Sometimes this is explicitly recognized, and permitted by, the authorities, while other times it is part of the underground economy that tries to avoid detection by using foreign currency. It might be surprising to learn that in the United States foreign currencies circulated alongside the US dollar well into the nineteenth century; indeed, the US Treasury even accepted payment of taxes in foreign currency until the middle of the nineteenth century.

However, such practices are now extremely rare in the developed nations that issue their own currencies (with the exception of the Euro nations, each of which uses the Euro that is effectively a "foreign" currency from the perspective of the individual nation). Still it is not uncommon in developing nations for foreign currencies to circulate alongside domestic currency, and sometimes their governments willingly accept foreign currencies. In some cases sellers even prefer foreign currencies over domestic currencies.

This has implications for policy, as discussed later.

Sovereignty and the currency

The national currency is often referred to as a "sovereign currency", that is, the currency issued by the sovereign government. The sovereign government retains for itself a variety of powers that are not given to private individuals or institutions. Here we are only concerned with those powers associated with money.

The sovereign government alone has the power to determine which money of account it will recognize for official accounts (as discussed, it might choose to accept a foreign currency for some payments, but that is the sovereign's prerogative). Further, modern sovereign governments alone are invested with the power to issue the currency denominated in its money of account.

If any entity other than the government tried to issue domestic currency (unless explicitly permitted to do so by government) it would be prosecuted as a counterfeiter, with severe penalties.

Further, the sovereign government imposes tax liabilities (as well as fines and fees) in its money of account, and decides how these liabilities can be paid – that is, it decides what it will accept in payment so that taxpayers can fulfill their obligations.

Finally, the sovereign government also decides how it will make its own payments: what it will deliver to purchase goods or services, or to meet its own obligations (such as payments it must make to retirees). Most modern sovereign governments make payments in their own currency and require tax payments in the same currency.

In the next section we will continue this discussion, investigating "what backs up" modern money.

Box: Frequently asked questions

Let us examine two commonly posed questions.

Q: What is the relation between the sovereign currency and the medium of exchange?

A: We first introduced the money of account in Chapter 1: the Dollar in the United States and the Pound in the United Kingdom. This is a unit of account, a measuring unit like the "inch", "foot", and "yard". It does not exist even as an electronic entry; no bloodhound could sniff it out. It is purely abstract and representational.

Next we introduced the concept of "money things", denominated in the money of account, some of which can be touched. (Similarly, our unit used to measure length cannot be sniffed by a dog, but it does measure physical things that can be sniffed: the inchworm is an inch in length, my foot is a foot – more or less – and the football field is 100 times the distance from Henry the First's nose to thumb. Probably more, actually, as we know those kings exaggerated the size of their anatomical features, like rap stars today.) These things can include coins, paper notes, and electronic entries. We'll say a lot more about the nature of those *things* that get measured by the money of account.

In this section we introduced the sovereign currency – the national money of account adopted by a sovereign government. While a money of account could – in theory – be created and adopted by private entities, the sovereign currency is adopted by the sovereign government and is usually the primary money of account if not the only money of account used within a sovereign nation.

The word "currency" is frequently used to designate not only the money of account adopted by sovereign government, but also to designate a money thing issued by the sovereign government and denominated in the money of account. In the United States it is the coin issued by the Treasury and the note issued by the Fed. In other words, we use the term "Dollar" to indicate both the sovereign currency (money of account) and the money thing (paper note or coin) issued by the US government.

We have not yet got to the "medium of exchange". Most textbooks begin with the medium of exchange (Crusoe and Friday look about for handy seashells to function as convenient media of exchange). I reject that story and purposely wait to introduce the concept. But to jump ahead a bit, **yes** the "money thing" currency issued by government generally functions as a medium of exchange. Other privately issued money things also frequently function as media of exchange. That is a *function* of money things, and really does not help us to understand much about the *nature* of money.

When you walk into a relatively new diner or any other "mom and pop" firm in the United States, there often is a frame hanging on the wall, with a Dollar bill and some sort of statement like "the first dollar we ever earned". Here, money *functions* as a memento – reflecting the pride of the owner of the establishment. Two decades ago, there were lots of stories of Wall Street traders using hundred Dollar bills *functioning* as cocaine delivery devices. I don't think it is useful to put undue emphasis on the various functions of money. Let us at least first try to understand its *nature*.

Q: What is bank money? Is that different from government money? Is it risky? Has government simply allowed banks to "print up" government money?

A: Again, we will get into this in detail in coming sections. However, to break the suspense, banks (and other institutions as well as individuals) can issue IOUs denominated in the money of account. We do not call these "currency". They are not issued by sovereign government. They are "money things". Yes, some are more "special" than others: the IOU of the Bank of America (a private bank – not Uncle Sam's bank) is more "special" than the IOU that you issue. Yes, it can function as a medium of exchange. The reasons for the "specialness" will be examined later. But an obvious one is that to some degree Uncle Sam stands behind BofA – for example, he guarantees demand deposits (your checking account).

So, yes I do understand the worry that Uncle Sam has essentially licensed BofA to "counterfeit" Dollars; if the bank goes bust, Uncle Sam will pay out nice new Dollar bills to depositors. This raises many issues of concern, and some of those are directly relevant to the global financial crisis we are going through, in which Uncle Sam has effectively done just that. But for right now, that really would take us too far afield.

2.2   What backs up currency and why would anyone accept it?

When I first started teaching, most students thought the US Dollar had gold backing, that it was valuable because Fort Knox was filled with gold, and if they drove to the Fort with a stash of cash, they could load up their cars with gold. (They were shocked to find out there had not been any gold backing since they were babies.) Today, very few students entertain such beliefs; they have all learned that our currency is "fiat" – it has "nothing" backing it up, or so many claim!

Let us take a peek behind the currency. Is there anything *there*?

Do reserves of metal or foreign exchange back the currency?

There has long been confusion surrounding sovereign currency. For example, many policymakers and economists have had trouble understanding why the private sector would accept currency issued by government as it makes purchases.

Consistent with the views my students used to hold, many have argued that it is necessary to "back up" a currency with a precious metal in order to ensure acceptance in payment. Historically, governments have sometimes maintained a reserve of gold or silver (or both) against domestic currency. It was thought that if the population could always return currency to the government to obtain precious metal, then currency would be accepted because it would be thought to be "as good as gold". Sometimes the currency itself would contain precious metal, as in the case of gold coins. In the United States, the Treasury did maintain gold reserves in an amount equal to 25 percent of the value of the issued currency through the 1960s. (Interestingly, American citizens were not allowed to trade currency for gold; only foreign holders of US currency could do so.)

However, the United States and most nations have long since abandoned this practice. And even with no gold backing, US currency is still in high demand all over the world, so the view that currency needs precious metal backing is erroneous. We have moved on to what is called "fiat currency": one that is not backed by reserves of precious metals. While some countries do explicitly back their currencies with reserves of a foreign currency (adopting, for example, a currency board arrangement in which the domestic currency is converted on demand at a specified exchange rate for US Dollars or some other currency), most governments of developed countries issue a currency that is not "backed by" foreign currencies.

In any case, we need to explain why a currency like the US Dollar, UK Pound, or Japanese Yen can circulate without such "backing".

Legal tender laws

One explanation that has been offered to explain acceptability of government "fiat" currency (that has no explicit promise to convert to gold or foreign currency) is legal tender laws. Many sovereign governments have enacted legislation requiring their currencies to be accepted in domestic payments. Indeed, paper currency issued in the

United States proclaims "This note is legal tender for all debts, public and private"; Canadian notes say "This note is legal tender"; and Australian paper currency reads "This Australian note is legal tender throughout Australia and its territories". By contrast, the paper currency of the United Kingdom simply says "I promise to pay the bearer on demand the sum of five pounds" (in the case of the five-Pound note). If you were to present a five-Pound note to the Queen, she promises to give you another five-Pound note!

Further, throughout history there are examples of governments that passed legal tender laws, but still could not create a demand for their currencies which were not accepted in private payments, and sometimes even rejected in payment to government. (In some cases, the penalty for refusing to accept a king's coin included the burning of a red-hot coin into the forehead of the recalcitrant, indicating that without such extraordinary compulsion, the population refused to accept the sovereign's currency.) Hence, there are currencies that readily circulate without any legal tender laws as well as currencies that were shunned even with legal tender laws. Further, as we know, the US Dollar circulates in a large number of countries in which it is not legal tender (and even in countries where its use is discouraged and perhaps even outlawed by the authorities). We conclude that legal tender laws, alone, cannot explain why currency is accepted.

If "modern money" is mostly not backed by foreign currency, and if it is accepted even without legal tender laws mandating its use, why is it accepted? It seems to be quite a puzzle. The typical answer provided in textbooks is that you will accept your national currency because you know others will accept it. In other words, it is accepted because it is accepted. The typical explanation thus relies on an "infinite regress": John accepts it because he thinks Mary will accept it, and she accepts it because she thinks Walmart will probably take it.

What a thin reed on which to hang monetary theory!

Personally, I'd be embarrassed to write that in my own textbook, or to try to convince a skeptical student that the only thing backing money is the "greater fool" or "hot potato" theory of money: I accept a Dollar bill because I think I can pass it along to some dupe or dope.

That is certainly true of counterfeit currency: I would take it only on the expectation that I could surreptitiously pass it along. But I'm certainly not going to try to convince readers of this Primer of such a silly theory. In the next section we will provide a more convincing argument. See if you can anticipate the answer.

Are you satisfied with the "gold standard", "fiat money", "legal tender", "hot potato", and "dupe a dope" theories of money? Is gold money? Can it be money? If gold no longer backs money, why does the Fed hold gold? Could a currency be backed by nothing more than "trust" – the expectation that someone, somewhere, will take it?

Have fun pondering.

Box: Frequently asked questions

Q: Why is gold so important if it is not what backs our currency?

A: Well, it is bright, it is shiny, and it is the "noble element" that never changes: doesn't rust, easy to clean up, can be smashed into impossibly thin sheets, and looks good in ears and teeth and on fingers. It also benefits from an almost mystical quality with several thousand years at the top of the totem pole of desirable prestige goods. Oh, and yes, many countries pegged their currencies to gold in not-so-recent years. Finally, its value is maintained by fairly robust manufacturing demand as well as propensity of governments to lock most of it up behind bars (in places like Fort Knox). Speculators bet that governments will not release the imprisoned gold, which would instantly wipe all of them out. To hedge their bets, they help to put goldbugs (like Alan Greenspan) in government. So far as I can tell, there are no rival explanations for the fascination with gold.

Q: Isn't fiat money accepted because it "stores value"?

A: What value is stored in a piece of paper that merely says "I promise to pay you five of my IOUs"? Zero. This appears to be another infinite regress argument: yes, if there is a demand for fiat currency that is expected to continue into the future, then it will be a store of value. But we need to explain why anyone would want it in the first place. That is why we focus on the tax liability.

2.3 Taxes drive money

In the last section we raised the following question: where currency cannot be exchanged for precious metal, and if legal tender laws are neither necessary nor sufficient to ensure acceptance of a currency, and if the government's "promise to pay" really amounts to nothing more than exchanging one five-dollar note for another five-dollar note, then why would anyone accept a government's currency? In this section we explore the MMT answer.

Sovereignty and taxes

One of the most important powers claimed by sovereign government is the authority to levy and collect taxes (and other payments made to government, including fees and fines). Tax obligations are levied in the national money of account: Dollars in the United States, Canada, and Australia; Yen in Japan; Yuan in China; and Pesos in Mexico. Further, the sovereign government also determines what can be delivered to satisfy the tax obligation. In most developed nations, it is the government's own currency that is accepted in payment of taxes.

We will examine in coming sections exactly how payments are made to government. While it appears that taxpayers mostly use checks drawn on private banks to make tax payments, actually when government receives these checks it debits the *reserves* of the private banks. Effectively, private banks *intermediate* between taxpayers and government, making payment in currency (technically, reserves that are the IOUs of the nation's central bank) on behalf of the taxpayers. Once the banks have made these payments, the taxpayer has fulfilled her obligation, so the tax liability is eliminated.

We are now able to answer the question posed earlier: why would anyone accept government's "fiat" currency? Because the government's currency is the main (and usually the only) thing accepted by government in payment of taxes and other money due to government. To avoid the penalties imposed for nonpayment of taxes (including prison), the taxpayer needs to obtain the government's currency.

It is true, of course, that government currency can be used for other purposes: coins can be used to make purchases from vending machines; private debts can be settled by offering government paper currency; and government money can be hoarded in piggy banks for future spending. However, these other uses of currency are all *subsidiary*, deriving from government's willingness to accept its currency in tax payments.

Ultimately, it is because anyone with tax obligations can use currency to eliminate these liabilities that government currency is in demand, and thus can be used in purchases or in payment of private obligations. The government cannot readily force others to use its currency in private payments, or to hoard it in piggybanks, but government can force use of currency to meet the tax obligations that it imposes.

For this reason, neither reserves of precious metals (or foreign currencies) nor legal tender laws are necessary to ensure acceptance of the government's currency. All that is required is imposition of a tax liability to be paid in the government's currency. It is the tax liability (or other obligatory payments) that stands behind the curtain.

What does government promise? What does a government IOU owe you?

The "promise to pay" that is engraved on UK Pound notes is superfluous and really quite misleading. The notes should actually read "I promise to accept this note in payment of taxes". We know that the UK Treasury will not really pay anything (other than another note) when the five-Pound paper currency is presented. However, it will *and must* accept the note in payment of taxes. If it refuses to accept its own IOU in payment, it is defaulting on that IOU.

What was it that President George W. Bush said? "There's an old saying in Tennessee – I know it's in Texas, probably in Tennessee – that says, fool me once, shame on – shame on you. Fool me – you can't get fooled again."

Forgive him as he probably listened to Roger Daltry and The Who a bit too much back in his college days. What he meant is that the sovereign can fool me once – shame on government – but it cannot fool me again. (That, folks, is what led to the creation of the Bank of England! The King of England defaulted on his IOUs, so he was not considered creditworthy. The Bank of England was created to intermediate between an untrustworthy King and his subjects – it would take his IOUs, and issue its own IOUs to finance his spending. But that is a story for another day.)

This is really how government currency is *redeemed* – not for gold, but in payments made to the government. We will go through the accounting of tax payments later. It is sufficient for our purposes now to understand that the tax obligations to government are met by presenting the government's own IOUs to the tax collector.

Conclusion

We can conclude that *taxes drive money*. The government first creates a money of account (the Dollar in Australia, the Tenge in Kazakhstan, and the Peso in the Philippines), and then imposes tax obligations in that national money of account. In all modern nations this is sufficient to ensure that many (indeed, most) debts, assets, and prices will also be denominated in the national money of account.

(Note the asymmetry that is open to a sovereign: it *imposes* a liability on you so that you will *accept* its IOU. It is a nice trick, and you can do it too, if you are king of your own little castle. You can tax the kids in your own family currency ("Johnsons"), and pay them for chores done around the house so that they can earn the currency required to pay the tax. If you punish them for nonpayment of taxes, they'll work hard to get the family "Johnsons"!)

The government is then able to issue a currency that is also denominated in the same money of account, so long as it accepts that currency in tax payment. It is not necessary to "back" the currency with precious metal, nor is it necessary to enforce legal tender laws that require acceptance of the national currency. For example, rather than engraving the statement "This note is legal tender for all debts, public and private", all the sovereign government needs to do is to promise "This note will be accepted in tax payment" in order to ensure general acceptability domestically and even abroad.

Box: Here are two questions to ponder:

1. Does this work only for taxes? Could other obligatory payments work?
2. What if you do not, personally, owe taxes? Why would you accept the government's currency?

In this section we were concerned with why government "fiat" currency is accepted. The short answer was that "taxes drive money": since you have a tax liability that must be cleared by delivering the government's own currency back to government, you want to obtain government currency. So in that sense it is the tax liability that drives the desire to obtain government currency.

But does it have to be a tax? Clearly the answer is "no": if government imposes a fine on you equal to five Dollars, you need five Dollars in the form government is willing to accept to pay your fine – sovereign currency. Until the twentieth century, taxes were relatively less important; what mattered more were fines and tithes and fees.

To go further, let us say government monopolizes the water supply (or energy supply, or access to the gods for salvation, etc.); it can then name what you need to deliver to obtain water (or energy, religious dispensation, etc.). In that case, if it says you must obtain a government IOU, then you need government IOUs – currency – to obtain water in order to avoid death by dehydration. In early nineteenth-century England, a lot of the activities necessary to keep your family alive were illegal by dictate of the Crown. You had to pay a fine after you killed game to feed your family, or collected firewood to keep them warm. You needed the crown's currency to pay the fine – hence "fines drove money". Fees and tithes can also drive money. You get the picture: all you need to drive a currency is an involuntary obligation to deliver the currency – and that can be a tax, fee, fine, or even religious tithe. Or even a payment to obtain water or any other necessity.

Of course it is not enough to merely impose the obligation (tithe, fee, fine, tax); the obligation must also be enforced. A tax liability that is never enforced will not drive a currency. A tax that is only loosely enforced can create some demand for the currency, but it will be somewhat less than the tax liability for the simple reason that many will expect they can evade the tax.

We can next move on to the second question: why would those who do not have tax liabilities also be willing to accept currency?

If some segment of society owes the tax (or fee or fine) denominated in the currency, others will accept it. Note this is not an infinite regress argument. It is the tax standing behind the currency, but it is not necessary for every individual to owe the tax. For example, let us say that Microsoft head Bill Gates owes $1.5 trillion in taxes. I'd be happy to accept Dollars since I know Gates will accept them when I purchase Microsoft software. And that also explains why foreigners want dollars – not because they personally owe Dollar taxes, but because a sufficient number of people like Bill Gates do.

From inception we know that if the total tax liability in dollars is, say, $100 billion, the taxpayers will want a minimum of $100 billion. (How much more? $120 billion? $180 billion? We cannot say for sure, but we will investigate it later.) Government can spend into the economy at least that amount – and probably more.

This explains why people want the currency, but it does not really tell us how much it is worth. How much will the dollar be worth? Well, that depends on what must be done to obtain it. We will have much more to say about that later. But what if the tax liability is too low? Let us say the tax liability is $100 billion but government tries to spend $1,000 billion. This is ten times what the taxpayers need to cover their liabilities. It is possible – even probable – that government will not be able to find takers for the $1,000 billion it wants to spend. It can bid the price it is willing to pay (for labor, finished output, or resource inputs) up, but still find no takers. We could register "inflation" and still find government cannot spend as much as it wants.

A better solution – obviously – is to raise the tax liability toward $1,000 billion, rather than to increase the price government is willing to pay. Again, that is something we will come back to, but it also sheds some light on what determines the value of the currency. As we'll see, we need to separate the willingness to accept currency from the value of the currency. Raising the tax liability will increase the desire to obtain currency although that does not tell us exactly how much the value of currency (in terms of price of labor or other resources or produced output) will rise.

2.4   What if the population refuses to accept the domestic currency?

In the last sections we asked, and answered, the question: why would anyone accept a "fiat currency" that has no intrinsic value without precious metal backing? We have argued that legal tender laws, alone, are not sufficient because it is generally too difficult for government to enforce them (except perhaps in its own payments). Further, we know that "fiat currencies" are often accepted even where their use is not required for all payments "public and private" (i.e. where there are no legal tender laws).

We concluded that "taxes drive money": if a sovereign has the power to impose and enforce a tax liability, it can ensure a demand for its currency. This is a transaction for which government can easily ensure its "fiat currency" is used: in payments made to itself.

We also concluded that other kinds of obligations will work: if you need the currency to pay fees, fines, or tithes, you will demand at least enough currency to make those payments. And, finally, we argued that an authority that monopolizes a needed resource (land, energy) can "name the price", that is, dictate what must be delivered to obtain it. So that, too, could drive a currency – and, again, it is because the authority can choose the form in which the payment is made.

The best kind of payment to be used to drive a currency is an obligatory one – one that must be made in order to stay out of prison, or to avoid death by thirst. An obligatory payment that must be made in the sovereign's own currency will guarantee a demand for that currency. And we argued that even if one does not personally owe taxes (or fees, etc.) to the sovereign, one might still accept the currency knowing that others *do* have tax liabilities and thus will accept the currency. But how much currency will be accepted? Can the sovereign issue *more than* the tax liability? How much more?

Imposing and enforcing a tax liability ensures that at least those subject to taxes will want the domestic currency, in an amount at least equal to the tax liability that will be enforced. In the developed nations, the population is willing to accept more domestic currency than what is needed for tax payments – typically government does not find sellers unwilling to sell for its currency. The normal case – let us say, in the United States or the United Kingdom or Japan – is that anything for sale domestically is for sale in the domestic currency. These sovereign governments never find that they cannot buy something by issuing their own currency.

To be clear: if there is something for sale with a US Dollar price, it can be bought by delivering US currency. (We will just note a caveat here, to be explained more fully later: sometimes, especially for payments made by mail, paper currency and coins are not accepted. But when a payment is made by check or electronically, there is a transfer of bank reserves – a kissing cousin to sovereign currency. Later we'll see what bank reserves really are.)

However, the situation can be very different in developing nations in which foreign currencies might be preferred for "private" transactions (payments that do not involve the sovereign). To be sure, the population will want sufficient domestic currency to meet its tax liability, but the tax liability can be limited by tax avoidance and evasion. This will limit the government's ability to purchase output by making payments in its own currency. With a foreign currency used in private payments, and with widespread tax avoidance and evasion, the population might not want much of the government's own currency.

We can get a rough idea of the limit imposed on a government whose population prefers foreign currency. Let us say that the government imposes a tax liability equal to one-third of measured GDP. However, because the informal sector escapes accounting (it is typically hard to capture the nominal value of exchange in the informal sector for the purposes of including it in GDP), let us assume that GDP only represents half of the true level of output.

Further assume that government is only able to collect half of imposed taxes due to evasion. This means that collected taxes equal only one-sixth of measured GDP and only one-twelfth of true output and income. (Hello, Greece! Just kidding, but that is one of the claims frequently made – that tax evasion and avoidance as well as informal sector transactions led to very low tax collections in Greece, which in turn generated a big government deficit.)

At a minimum, in such a situation government will be able to move one-twelfth of national output to the public sector through its spending of the domestic currency (since those who really do have to pay taxes need the domestic currency to meet their obligations). In practice, the government will probably be able to capture more than one-twelfth of national output because some "private" entities (domestic and perhaps foreign) will want to accumulate domestic currency as well as other claims on government (such as government bonds). Recall from previous discussion that government deficits allow accumulation of net financial wealth in the form of government IOUs. Hence it is likely that government will be able to purchase somewhat more than a twelfth of GDP, while collecting taxes equal to a twelfth of national income, and with some households or firms (or foreigners) accumulating the rest of the currency spent as net financial wealth.

(These calculations are necessarily approximate because we are ignoring possible effects of taxing and spending on the behavior of the population. For example, imposing a tax can drive more production into the "grey market", leaving measured GDP and taxable income even lower. That is the thinking behind the "Laffer Curve": higher tax rates lower GDP and thus lower tax revenue.)

To capture a larger percent of national output, government needs to pursue policies that will a) reduce tax evasion and b) formalize more of the informal sector. Both of those actions would increase taxes on the population and would allow government to obtain more output since the demand for the government's currency would be higher.

If taxes are at just one-twelfth of national output, it might not be effective for government to simply increase its spending to try to move more resources to the public sector – this could just result in inflation, as sellers would accept more domestic currency only at higher prices (as they already have all the currency they need to meet the tax obligation they think will be enforced). And beyond some point government might not find any sellers for additional currency. While it would be incorrect – for reasons explored later – to argue that taxes "pay for" government spending, it is true that inability to impose and enforce tax liabilities will limit the amount of resources government can command.

The problem is not really one of government "affordability" but rather of limited government ability to mobilize resources because it cannot impose and enforce taxes at a sufficient level to achieve the desired result. Government can always "afford" to spend more (in the sense that it can issue more currency), but if it cannot enforce and collect taxes it will not find sufficient willingness to accept its domestic currency in sales to government.

Put simply, the population will find it does not need additional domestic currency if it has already met the tax liability the government is able to enforce (plus some accumulation of currency for contingency purposes). In that case, raising taxes would increase demand for government's currency (to pay the taxes), which would create more sellers to government for its currency. Until government can impose and collect more taxes, its real spending will be constrained by the population's willingness to sell for domestic currency. And that, in turn, can be caused by a preference for use of foreign currency for domestic purposes other than paying taxes. While this is not a big problem in developed countries, it can be a serious constraint in developing nations.

In this section we have presumed government spends and taxes using currency (notes and coins). In practice, governments use checks and, increasingly, electronic entries on bank accounts. Indeed, government uses private banks to accomplish many or most transactions related to spending and taxing. In coming sections we will provide a more "realistic" account of taxing and spending using bank accounts rather than actual currency. This does not change anything of substance – but it does require some understanding of banking, central banking, and treasury operations, discussed in the following pages.

Box: Frequently asked questions

Q: How are unsold goods accounted for? And does that affect the sectoral balances?

A: Recall that we have discussed (briefly in a Box in Chapter 1) unsold inventories. Suppose it is the end of the year 1974 and we are Ford Motor Company and we produce 1,000 Ford Pintos (remember those – the ones with exploding gas tanks?) that we cannot sell. Unsold inventory gets counted as investment. Ford carries the inventory at its market price; let us say Ford uses the average price of Pintos that it actually did sell in 1974. Assume it cannot sell them in 1975, either (due to deep recession, bad publicity about the gas tanks, and so on). How to value them? All things equal, Ford would prefer not to book a loss of value; it carries them at original value, otherwise the value of its inventory declines, impacting 1975 profits and net worth. Suppose in 2011 it is still carrying those Pintos in inventory. You see the problem. We have to assign a dollar value to them.

Now let's address the problem of dual currencies. Suppose Ford produces cars in America but sells them in America and Japan. Assume it imports all the electronic components from Japan. It can keep two sets of books – one for Dollars and one for Yen. It has income and outgo in each currency. Clearly it could run a deficit in one and a surplus in the other (or surpluses in both, or deficits in both, etc. you get the picture). All other firms, households, and levels of government can do the same in Dollars and Yen. Adding up all the sectors, we get to our three balances in each of the currencies. But Ford's shareholders do not want to know that it has a surplus in Dollars of 1 billion and a deficit in Yen of 100 billion – it wants the overall balance for Ford's income. Just as we have to convert Pintos to Dollars, we have to convert those Yen to Dollars. We need an exchange rate. But Yen and Dollars float, changing every day in relative value. It is going to make a huge difference what exchange rate we use.

The cleanest way is to keep the accounts separate and there will be sectoral balances in each currency that do balance. But a government as well as a firm needs a budget in one currency (generally it is going to be the domestic currency) and so if income and outgo occur in more than one, exchange rates must be used to get everything into that currency of denomination. This is true even if the government/firm/household actually has bank accounts denominated in the foreign currency. This complicates matters because now the sectoral balances will not balance (exactly) unless everyone uses the same exchange rate all the time – which would happen if we pegged.

More broadly, you should not think that aggregate economic data like GDP or the CPI (consumer price index), or the sectoral balances are measured precisely. These are estimates, using data that is constructed. What *is* important is consistency. This always shocks students the first time they hear it. But the CPI (consumer price index) does not come from heaven. It is constructed, it is revised, and it is subject to great debate among wonky people with thick glasses. And believe it or not, it does matter exactly how these data are constructed. But do not get misled by that. Certainly at the level of logic, the three balances do balance. If we could measure things exactly, they would balance in practice. Knowing that they should balance, the statistician who puts them together ensures they do balance – by construction. This is not easy; a "statistical discrepancy" is added to ensure they do, and if you need a big one of those, that is not good. And, yes, dealing with valuing those inventories is a big headache; I can remember when Wynne Godley used to fret over that, and I didn't understand why. Now I do.

Q: You said sovereign government can buy anything for sale in its own currency, but why can't it just go to foreign exchange markets, get foreign currency, then buy everything for sale in all currencies?

A: Because it takes at least two to tango. Domestically, government ensures sellers by imposing a tax in its own currency. It cannot typically tax foreigners in their own countries – that impinges on sovereignty and the foreign government would not allow enforcement of the tax. (Imagine what would happen if Greece tried to close its budget deficit by imposing a tax on Germans!) So, for example, the government in Kazakhstan cannot force Italians to pay taxes in Tenge. To buy stuff from Italians, the Kazak government *might* be forced to use Euros. (Note the caveat: Italians might take Tenge, in which case there is no affordability problem.) So let us say Italians don't want the Tenge. Yes, the Kazak government can go to forex markets and trade Tenge for Euros. Here's the problem: it is now subject to forex market demand for Tenge. It can never run out of Tenge, but the exchange rate can move against the Tenge. At the extreme, it could find no takers even at an infinite exchange rate against the Euro. (Zimbabwe! Weimar!) I am not saying this is probable. I am just saying we need to be careful in our claims. Domestically, government can buy anything for sale if it is for sale in terms of its own currency. And it can create that demand by imposing taxes. Externally, all bets are off. If stuff is for sale only in foreign currency, the government of Kazakhstan might not be able to buy it with its Tenge.

2.5   Keeping track of stocks and flows: the money of account

In this section we will return to our distinction between stocks and flows, and think of the financial system as a giant scoreboard that keeps track in the money of account.

Stocks and flows are denominated in the national money of account

In previous sections we examined the definitions of stocks and flows, as well as the relations between the two. (It might be helpful if you quickly review the previous discussion on stocks and flows, and the relation between the two: flows accumulate to stocks.) Financial stocks and financial flows are denominated in the national money of account. In this section we will go through the details of keeping track of stocks and flows in the money of account. That will also lead us into a discussion of the relation between "money" and "spending": how do we "pay for" things?

As discussed previously, the money of account is almost always the domestic currency – the money of account chosen by the government. In some cases, however, the accounts can be kept in a foreign currency. For the purposes of this section we will ignore that complication; all the record keeping discussed here will be presumed to take place in a single national unit of account. Let us begin with the case of an employee earning wages.

While working, the employee earns a flow of wages denominated in a money of account accumulating a monetary claim on the employer. On payday, the employer eliminates the obligation by providing a paycheck that is a liability of the employer's bank. Again, that is denominated in the national money of account. If desired, the worker can cash the check at her bank, receiving the government's currency – again an IOU, but this time a debt of the government. Alternatively, the check can be deposited in the worker's bank, leaving the worker with an IOU of her bank, denominated in the money of account.

Wage income that is not used for consumption purchases represents a flow of saving, accumulated as a stock of wealth. The saving can be held as a bank deposit, that is, as financial wealth (the bank's liability). When it comes time to pay taxes, the worker writes a check to the treasury, which then debits the reserves of the worker's bank (and the bank debits the worker's deposit). Reserves are just a special form of government currency used by banks to make payments to one another and to the government. Like all currency, reserves are the government's IOU.

So when taxes are paid, the taxpayer's tax liability to the government is eliminated. At the same time, the government's IOU that takes the form of bank reserves is also eliminated. The tax payment reduces the worker's financial wealth because her bank deposit is debited by the amount of the tax payment.

We can conceive of a flow of taxes imposed on workers, for example, as an obligation to pay 10 percent of hourly wages to government. A liability to government accumulates over the weeks as wages are earned, which is a claim on the worker's wealth. The tax liability, measured in the money of account, is eliminated when taxes are paid by reducing the worker's financial wealth (debiting deposits also measured in the money of account) and the bank's reserves are simultaneously debited by government.

At the same time, the government's asset (the tax liability owed by the worker) is eliminated when taxes are paid, and the government's liability (the reserves held by private banks) is also eliminated.

Sometimes it is useful to compare these flows to water flowing in a river that gets accumulated as a stock behind a dam. (Recall our bathtub example from Chapter 1.) However, it is important to understand that these monetary stocks and flows are conceptually nothing more than accounting entries, measured in the money of account. Unlike water flowing in a stream, or held in a reservoir behind a dam, the money that is flowing or accumulating does not need to have any physical presence beyond ink on paper or electrical charges on a computer hard drive. (See the bathtub approach to stocks and flows in Chapter 1.)

Indeed, in the modern economy, wages can be directly credited to a bank account, and taxes can be paid without use of checks by debiting accounts directly. We can easily imagine doing away with coins and paper notes as well as checkbooks, with all payments made through electronic entries on computer hard drives. All financial wealth could similarly be accounted for without use of paper. Indeed, most payments and most financial wealth are already nothing more than electronic entries, denominated in a national money of account. A payment leads to an electronic debit of the account of the payer, and a credit to the account of the payee – all recorded using electrical charges.

The financial system as electronic scoreboard

The modern financial system is an elaborate one of recordkeeping, a sort of financial scoring of the game of life in a capitalist economy.

For those who are familiar with the sport of American football, financial scoring can be compared with the sport's scoreboard. When a team scores a touchdown, the official scorer awards points, and electronic pulses are sent to the appropriate combination of LEDs so that the scoreboard will show the number six. As the game progresses, point totals are adjusted for each team.

The points have no real physical presence, they simply reflect a record of the performance of each team according to the rules of the game. They are not "backed" by physical things, although they are valuable because the team that accumulates the most points is deemed the "winner" – perhaps rewarded with fame and fortune.

Further, sometimes points are taken away after review by officials determines that rules were broken and that penalties should be assessed. The points that are taken away don't really go anywhere, they simply disappear as the scorekeeper deducts them from the score.

Similarly, in the game of life, earned income leads to "points" credited to the "score" that is kept by financial institutions. Unlike the game of football, in the game of life every "point" that is awarded to one player is deducted from the "score" of another – either reducing the payer's assets or increasing her liabilities. Accountants in the game of life are very careful to ensure that financial accounts always balance. The payment of wages leads to a debit of the employer's "score" at the bank, and a credit to the employee's "score", but at the same time the wage payment eliminates the employer's implicit obligation to pay accrued wages as well as the employee's legal claim to wages.

So while the game of life is a bit more complicated than the football game, the idea that record keeping in terms of money is a lot like record keeping in terms of points can help us to remember that money is not a "thing" but rather is a unit of account in which we keep track of all the debits and credits, or "points". And these "scores" are almost always kept in the sovereign's money of account.

Box: Frequently asked questions

Q: Is all money debt?

A: Yes, all money "things" are debt. Again, that is a topic for detailed treatment later.

Q: Can banks refuse instructions to make transfers out of one person's account and into another – say from the employer's account to the worker's?

A: Yes, the bank might refuse in two cases: apparent fraud or insufficient funds. We certainly applaud any bank that refuses to shift funds out of our account if it suspects fraud! We are not quite so happy when it refuses to clear a check in the case of an overdraft of our account because we get charged fees.

Q: What is the difference between money of account and the medium of exchange?

A: Think of it this way: money of account is the measure (foot, yard, inch); medium of exchange is the thing being measured (shoe, arm, earlobe). Domestic currency is the government's IOU and demand deposits are bank IOUs, but both of these are measured in the money of account (Dollar, Yen, Euro). They are issued by quite different entities. An IOU is a debt, so government IOUs are debts, just as demand deposits are debts of the bank. We denominate these debts in the money of account, and both of these types of debts can be used as media of exchange.

2.6   Returning to real versus nominal stocks and flows

A few hundred years ago, many people built their own homes, after carving a clearing in the wilderness, killing off the lions, tigers, and bears that Dorothy (of *Wizard of Oz* fame) feared, and running off the indigenous population (a particularly shameful episode in the history of many conquests from which modern nations arose). They tilled the soil and planted seeds. Perhaps they sold a bit of their farm's production, and bought a few goods and paid some taxes. But for the most part they lived their lives without much use for money. They had few financial debts and few financial assets. But clearly they had real assets, and those assets were productive (even if the output was mostly consumed). We can put a monetary value on all that if we want. From the perspective of those "settlers" (a really poor choice of words, but commonly used to ignore what was being done to indigenous humans, animals, and the environment more generally) it would be a rather silly exercise to do such an accounting, of course.

At least until they decided to sell the farm and retire on a beach in Florida.

Today if you build a work shed that enhances the value of your property, you can add that to your total net wealth (less any borrowing or running down of saving to purchase materials of course). When you sell the property you realize that value in monetary form (including the extra value due to the work shed you built).

The question is: where did that money come from? Well, the purchaser of your property issued an IOU to a mortgage lender; the loan had to be a wee bit bigger to cover the extra property value due to the workshed you built. You realize the "real asset", the work shed, in monetary form when you sell the property.

Let us say, however, that the purchaser paid "cash" (wrote a check on a demand deposit). We can quickly get into an infinite regress because now we must find out how the purchaser got the credit to her demand deposit. Perhaps she just sold a house on the Left Coast (California) to a purchaser who took out a mortgage loan. So her demand deposit can be traced back to a bank loan, because the way banks make loans is by accepting an IOU (held as the bank asset) and creating a demand deposit (the bank's IOU, held by the depositor). So we again find that a loan created the "money" that the purchaser of your house had in her checking account.

You can go through an infinite number of scenarios and you will see that it all goes back to a loan. The demand deposit is a bank IOU, created when the bank accepted an IOU. Think about it this way: all bank deposits came from bank keystrokes created when banks accepted IOUs of borrowers. So all purchases with demand deposits have a loan somewhere in the background.

There is one important exception. Let us say that the purchaser was retired and living on Social Security. She saved her benefit payments for years to buy your house (and work shed). Each month the Treasury keystroked her benefit payment into existence. The Social Security payment shows up as a bank IOU to her (demand deposit) and at the same time the bank gets a credit to its reserve account at the Fed. (As we'll see later, the bank will probably buy treasuries rather than hold reserves, but that just substitutes what is effectively a "saving deposit at the Fed" for a "demand deposit at the Fed" since government bonds are really equivalent to central bank reserves that pay higher interest and have longer maturity.)

When government spends, it creates "net financial assets" for the nongovernment sector in the form of reserves or treasuries or cash. When the government makes the Social Security payment there are four keystroke entries:

Retiree: + demand deposit owned
Bank: + reserves owned + demand deposit owed
Government: + reserves owed

Note that by double entry bookkeeping, every item is entered twice – once as "owned" and once as "owed". The bank's position nets to zero: it owns reserves exactly equal to the demand deposit it owes. The government's IOU goes up and that is exactly equal to the retiree's increase to her demand deposit. That increase of the demand deposit is the addition to nongovernment net financial assets.

(For the really wonky, there are two other entries in the background. Creation of the Social Security program with rules for qualifying participants leads to an entry on the government's liability side of its balance sheet equal to benefits owed, and to an entry on the nongovernment's asset side of its balance sheet equal to benefits owned; both of these are in the future, of course. When government makes the benefit payment, its "benefits owed to qualifying population" are debited, and the nongovernment's "benefits owed and to be paid by government" are debited. A stroke of the Congressional pen put government into debt for the amount of benefits owed, and created wealth for the private sector in the amount of benefits they will receive. A keystroke then turns that into "reality" by monetizing the benefits as government monetary IOUs in the form of bank reserves are created, and recipients get credits to demand deposits. We will look at some sample balance sheets later.)

What I am getting at is that the private sector does not need to "go into debt" to get "money" so long as the government supplies it. But this is not a commodity money, as we discuss later: it is still an IOU, in the form of central bank reserves. So if we take the (closed) economy as a whole, net financial assets do still sum to zero: the government's IOU equals the retiree's demand deposit. But for the nongovernment sector, it is net financial wealth.

What about real wealth? Again, the government owns lots of real assets: bridges, roads, parks, public buildings, bombs, aircraft carriers, and so on. Those add to the total national net wealth.

Finally, we need to look at real and financial claims against foreigners, and foreign real and financial claims against domestics. Obviously both real and financial (as well as their sum) can be positive or negative. These will largely be denominated in different currencies, so exchange rates will need to be brought into the calculations.

Some readers might wonder why a self-sufficient farmer could not grow his own food and make most of the things he needs, but spend some spare time prospecting to dig gold he uses in markets for luxury items. Couldn't he become quite wealthy while never really participating in the market economy, accumulating a huge hoard of gold?

Well, that is really just our workshed example, except that his gold wealth is bright and shiny but much less useful. Rather than clearing a forest and building a house plus nice woodshed, I dig holes in the ground to find gold. I can value it at market price (just like my woodshed). Now I want to sell it because I want a credit to my banking account. How does someone buy the gold from me? In exactly the same manner as the home mortgage example discussed above: the buyer goes to a bank, proffers an IOU, gets a credit to a demand deposit, writes a check, and transfers the demand deposit to gold seller.

Or, say that the buyer already has a sufficient credit to his demand deposit. Well, that is another infinite regress; it came from a loan.

The exception, again, is the government. If I sell gold to the government, it credits my demand deposit and credits my bank's reserves. A gold purchase by government is exactly the same as a Social Security payment, except that the government now has to go to all the bother of locking up the gold and keeping the bandits away so that the gold does not get freed and put to superior use as dental crowns in mouths. (That makes a lot of sense, doesn't it? We need to start a campaign: free the gold!)

In conclusion, I hope this distinction between real and financial is now clear. And let me add that I absolutely agree that a lot of the most interesting activity in any society takes place outside (or mostly outside) the monetary sphere. And it is important activity; the monetary sphere would not last long without these nonmonetary activities. My own view is that this continual "monetization" of ever more activities is highly problematic and probably threatens survival of our species as well as that of many of the other species on earth. I also resist assigning monetary values to things like caring for your own children – something economists are wont to do.

But, after all, this is a Primer on modern money and so that is where we turn most of our focus, while ignoring much of the really interesting stuff that is studied by anthropologists, political scientists, psychologists, and art historians.

2.7 Sustainability conditions

This section gets a little technical, although I've tried to use simple examples to provide intuition. A mathematical appendix is attached, but it is not at all necessary to understand it in order to follow the main points. Here we deal with what techno-wonky types worry about: is there a maximum government deficit ratio that is sustainable? And, is there a maximum current account balance (foreign sector deficit) that is sustainable? Of course, regular folks do worry about them too. After the government debt crisis among the so-called "PIIGS" (Portugal, Ireland, Italy, Greece, and Spain), many people wonder just how big government deficits can become without setting off a crisis. And many worry about the sustainability of the US trade deficit. So we will tackle the sustainability conditions in this section. Let us deal with these in order.

"Sustainability conditions" for government deficits

It has become trendy among economist wonks to look at government budget stances to determine whether they can continue forever. Many objections could be raised to such purely mental exercises. An obvious one is that no government has ever lasted forever, and so any such exercise is a waste of time. Economist Herb Stein quipped that unsustainable processes will not be sustained. Something will change. That gets us somewhat closer to the problem with such approaches. And, finally, if we are dealing with sovereign budget deficits we must first understand WHAT is not sustainable, and what is. That requires that we need to do sensible exercises. The one that the deficit hysterians propose is not sensible.

Let us first look at a somewhat simpler unsustainable process. Suppose that some guy – we'll use the name Morgan – decides to replicate the "Supersize me" experiment (based on the 2004 documentary by Morgan Spurlock). His caloric intake is 5,000 calories a day, and he burns 2,000 daily. The excess 3,000 calories lets him gain one pound of body weight each day. If he weighed 200 pounds on January 1, by the end of the year he weighs 565 pounds. After 100 years he's up to 36,700 pounds – a bit on the pudgy side. But we don't stop there. After 100,000 years he weighs 36,700,000 pounds, and after a few million years, he's heavy enough to affect the earth's rotation on its axis and its revolutions about the sun. But, according to our policy wonks, that still is not a long enough period – we've got to carry this out to infinity, at which point Morgan is infinite-sized, like the universe, and if he is growing faster than the expansion of the universe, the entire rest of the universe will eventually be infinitesimally smaller than Morgan. So, yes, this is unsustainable. Aren't we all clever?

But would the process actually work that way? Of course not. First, Morgan is not going to live an infinite number of years; second, he's either going to blow up (literally) or go on a diet; and, third, and most important, his body is going to adjust. As his body mass increases, he will burn more than 2,000 calories a day – perhaps he'll get up to a 5,000 calorie a day burn rate – and his body will use the food in a less efficient manner. So he will stop gaining weight long before he becomes the universe's black hole. Herb Stein was right.

Our little mental exercise was fundamentally flawed. It assumed a fixed caloric input (inflow) and a fixed caloric burn rate (consumption flow) with the difference between the two accumulating as a stock (weight gain) at a fixed rate (essentially, "savings" in the form of fat). No adjustments to behavior or metabolism are allowed. And then the whole absurd setup is carried to the ultimate absurdity by the use of infinite horizon projections. Anything carried to a logical absurdity is unsustainable. As you will see, this is the rigged game used by deficit warriors to "prove" the US Federal budget deficit is unsustainable.

The trick used by deficit warriors is similar but with the inputs and outputs reversed. Rather than caloric inputs, we have GDP growth as the input; rather than burning calories, we pay interest; and rather than weight gain as the output we have budget deficits accumulating to government debt outstanding. To rig the little model to ensure it is not sustainable, we have the interest rate higher than the growth rate – just as we had Morgan's caloric input at 5,000 calories and his burn rate at only 2,000 – and this will ensure that the debt ratio grows (just as we ensured that Morgan's waistline grew without limit). Let us see how this works.

We will start with a simple example. Let us have two sectors, government and private. Our government runs surpluses, spending less than its income (tax revenue); the private sector by identity runs a deficit (spends more than its income). We know this means the private sector is running up debt, held by the government as its asset (surpluses are realized in the form of private sector IOUs). The private sector must service the debt by paying interest; that of course adds to its deficit (interest is additional spending it must make out of its income). In comparison to our Supersizing Morgan, the sustainability conditions will be determined by the interest rate paid, the growth rate of income (or GDP), and the deficit of the private sector.

James Galbraith laid out the typical model used to evaluate sustainability of deficit spending. The key formula is:

$$\Delta d = -s + d * [(r - g)/(1 + g)]$$

Here, d is the starting ratio of debt to GDP, s is the "primary surplus" or budget surplus after deducting net interest payments (as shares of GDP), r is the real interest rate, * means multiply, and g is the real rate of GDP growth (for his paper, go here: http://www.levyinstitute.org/publications/?docid=1379).

This is wonky but the key idea is that (given a relation between the primary surplus and starting debt – both as ratios to GDP) so long as the interest rate (r) is above the growth rate (g), the debt ratio is going to grow. (Galbraith has put these key terms in "real" – that is, inflation adjusted – terms but that really does not matter; we can keep it all in nominal terms since "deflation" by the inflation rate merely reduces all terms by the inflation rate.) Note that the starting debt ratio (d) as well as the primary surplus (what the private sector's budget would be if it did not have to pay interest) also play a role. (Galbraith proves that the starting debt ratio does not matter much – just as Morgan's initial weight will not matter since in any case he will grow to an infinite size.)

But we do not need to get too hung up in math to see that if the interest rate is above the growth rate, we get a rising debt ratio. If we carry this through eternity, that ratio gets big. Really big. OK, that sounds bad. And it is. Remember, that is a big part of the reason that the GFC (global financial crisis) hit: an over-indebted private sector. The GFC is the equivalent to an explosion of Morgan that would prevent him from growing to an infinite size. (A debt diet would have been far preferable, but Fed chairmen Greenspan and Bernanke opposed "interfering" with Wall Street lender fraud as they allowed the US financial system to "supersize" until the bubble burst.)

Now change all this around. Let us say that the government runs a continuous budget deficit while the private sector runs a surplus. Assume that the government's deficit is a constant percent of GDP (for example, the deficit remains 6 percent of GDP forever). We can obtain the same equation. To be clear, a persistent deficit does not imply a growing debt ratio – that would depend on the relation between r (the interest rate) and g (the growth rate) – but if the deficit grows fast enough to maintain a constant deficit-to-GDP ratio then the debt ratio will explode. Surely that is unsustainable if carried to the infinite hereafter. (See the Appendix below for more complex math.)

But wait a minute. Is such a mental exercise sensible? We already saw that our supersizing Morgan is going to adjust: he will diet, explode, increase his metabolism, or reduce the efficiency of his absorption of calories. If he does not explode, he will reach some "equilibrium" in which his intake of calories will equal his burn rate so that his waistline will stop growing.

What about our supersizing government? Here are some possible consequences of a persistent deficit that grows fast enough to imply rising interest payments and debt ratios:

a) Inflation: this tends to increase tax revenues so that they grow faster than government spending, thus lowering deficits. (Many, including Galbraith, would point to the tendency to generate "negative" real interest rates.) In other words the growth rate will rise above the interest rate, and reverse the dynamics so that the deficit ratio declines and the debt ratio stops growing. (That is equivalent to an increase of Morgan's caloric burn rate, so he stops growing.)

b) Austerity: government can try to adjust its fiscal stance (increasing taxes and reducing spending to lower its deficit). That is equivalent to a diet by Morgan. Of course, it takes "two to tango" – raising tax rates might not change the government's balance, as it could lower growth rates, and thereby actually increase the rate of growth of the debt ratio.

c) The private sector will adjust its flows (spending and saving) in response to the government's stance. If government continually spends more than its income, it will be adding net wealth to the private sector, and its interest payments will add to private sector income. It is not plausible to believe that as the government's debt ratio goes toward infinity (which means that the private sector's net wealth ratio goes to infinity) there is no induced spending in the private sector. That is usually called the "wealth effect". In other words, government debt is private wealth and as private wealth grows without limit this will eventually cause spending to rise relative to private sector income, reducing government deficits as tax revenues rise. In addition, private sector income includes government interest payments, so rising government interest payments on its debt could induce consumption. When all is said and done, the private sector will not be happy consuming less than its income flow – given its rising wealth – and will adjust its saving behavior. If the private sector tries to reduce its surpluses, this can be done only by reducing the government sector's deficits. It takes two to tango and the likely result is that tax revenues and consumption will rise, the government's deficit will fall, and the private sector's surplus will fall.

d) Government deficit spending and interest payments could increase the growth rate; it can be pushed above the interest rate. This changes the dynamics and can stop the growth of the debt ratio.

The interest rate is a policy variable (as will be discussed below). Ignoring the dynamics discussed in the previous points, to avoid an exploding debt ratio all the government needs to do is to lower the interest rate it pays below the economic growth rate. End of story; sustainability achieved.

Finally, and this is the most contentious point. Suppose none of the dynamics just discussed come into play, so the government's debt ratio rises on trend. Will a sovereign government be forced to miss an interest payment, no matter how big that becomes? The answer is a simple "no". It will take more explication of MMT to explain why. But let us put this in the simple terms that Chairman Bernanke actually used to explain all the Fed spending to bail out Wall Street: government spends using keystrokes, or electronic entries, on balance sheets. There is no technical or operational limit to its ability to do that. So long as there are keyboard keys to stroke, government can stroke them to produce interest payments credited to balance sheets.

And that finally gets us to the difference between perpetual private sector deficit spending versus perpetual government sector deficits: the first really is unsustainable while the second is not. Now, we need to be clear. We have argued that persistent government budget deficits that increase government debt ratios and thus private wealth ratios will lead to behavioral changes. They could lead to inflation.

They could lead to policy changes. Hence they are not likely to last "forever". So when we say they are "sustainable" we merely mean in the sense that sovereign government can continue to make all payments as they come due – including interest payments – no matter how big those payments become. Government might choose not to make those payments. And the mere act of making those payments will likely cause changes in growth rates and budget deficits and growth of debt ratios.

"Sustainability" of current account ratios

What about the sustainability of current account deficits? To be more specific the current account includes the balance of trade (and, more broadly, the balance between exports and imports) plus some other items including "factor payments" (interest and profits paid and received). The United States obviously runs a trade deficit (and exports are less than imports), but the factor payments are in America's favor (she receives more in profits and interest from abroad than she pays to foreign creditors and owners). In any event, her negative current account balance is offset by a positive capital account balance. To put it simply, there is a "flow" of Dollars abroad due to the current account deficit that is matched by the "flow" of Dollars back to the United States due to her capital account surplus. This is often (misleadingly) presented as US "borrowing" of Dollars to "pay for" her trade deficit. We could just as well put it this way: the United States imports more than it exports because the rest of the world wants to accumulate savings in Dollar-denominated assets. I do not want to go into that in detail since it is the subject of later sections.

But here's the question: is a continuous current account deficit possible? A simple answer is yes, so long as "two want to tango": if the rest of the world wants Dollar assets and Americans want the rest of the world's exports (imported into the United States), this will continue.

Hold it, say the worriers. As the rest of the world accumulates Dollar claims on the United States, they also receive interest payments. That is a factor payment that increases our current account deficit. You can see the relation to the point above about government deficits and interest payments. The world will be flooded with Dollars twice over: once from our excessive propensity to import and once from our interest payments on debt.

There is another interesting point: even though the United States is the "biggest debtor on earth", those factor payments flow in her favor. She pays extremely low interest rates and profit rates to foreigners, and earns much higher interest rates and profits on her holdings of foreign investments and debt. Why is that? Because the United States is the safest investment on earth. Anytime there is a financial crisis anywhere in the world, where do international investors run? To the US Dollar.

Ironically, that happens even when the crisis begins in the United States! Why? The United States has a sovereign government with a sovereign currency. Its interest rate is set by the Fed, which can always set the rate below the US growth rate (and, indeed, as Galbraith points out, the US inflation-adjusted interest rate is often below the "real" growth rate). In spite of the deficit hysteria whipped up in the United States and abroad, no investor in her right mind believes there is any default risk on US Treasury debt. So when global fears rise, investors run to the Dollar. This could change, but probably not in your lifetime.

In short, we make no projection about continued US current account deficits but we believe they will continue far longer than anyone imagines. They are sustainable. They will be sustained until the rest of the world decides not to accumulate more Dollars and Americans decide they really do not want the cheap commodities and environment-destroying oil produced by the rest of the world. When that will happen, we cannot know. It is nothing to lose sleep over. Yes, we can calculate "sustainability conditions" but it would just be a mental exercise. We've already done enough of that; it is titillating but ultimately unsatisfying.

Technical appendix: Dynamics of the debt-to-GDP ratio

The level of government debt outstanding (D) follows the following path through time:

$$D_t = D_{t-1} + Def_t$$

That is, every year the outstanding debt increases by the size of the deficit. The fiscal deficit is the difference between government spending (G), and taxes (T), plus interest payments on outstanding debt (iD), where i is the interest rate.

$$Def_t = G_t - T_t + iD_{t-1}$$

Let us look at what happens to the debt-to-GDP ratio under different deficit configurations that produce ever-larger debt ratios.

Case 1: Balanced Primary Budget: The Government Spends as Much on Goods and Services as the Amount It Taxes

Let us assume that the primary balance is zero ($G = T$) so:

$$D_t = D_{t-1} + iD_{t-1}$$

or:

$$D_t = D_{t-1}(1+i)$$

Assume the gross domestic product (Y) grows at a rate g and so follows the following path:

$$Y_t = Y_{t-1}(1+g)$$

Thus the debt-to-GDP ratio is:

$$\frac{D_t}{Y_t} = \frac{D_{t-1}(1+i)}{Y_{t-1}(1+g)}$$

Solving recursively and using d as the debt-to-GDP ratio we get:

$$d_t = d_0 \left(\frac{1+i}{1+g}\right)^n$$

It is pretty clear that if $i > g$ the ratio tends toward infinity when n tends toward infinity, and toward zero if $i < g$. If $g = i$ then $d_t = d_0$ for all t (the ratio is constant).

Case 2a: Permanent Primary Deficit: The Government Spends More on Goods and Services than the Amount of Taxes It Receives

Let's use S to indicate the primary balance with $S > 0$ denoting a primary deficit ($G - T > 0$), then in this case:

$$D_t = D_{t-1} + i D_{t-1} + S_t$$

Therefore:

$$\frac{D_t}{Y_t} = \frac{D_{t-1}(1+i) + S_t}{Y_{t-1}(1+g)}$$

Again solving recursively and noting s_0 is the ratio S_0/Y_0, we have:

$$d_t = \left(d_0 + \frac{s_0}{i}\right)\left(\frac{1+i}{1+g}\right)^n - \frac{s_0}{i}\frac{1}{(1+g)^n}$$

We reach the same results as Case 1. If $i < g$ then d_t tends toward zero and if $i > g$ the debt-to-GDP ratio tends toward infinity. When $i = g$ now $d_t = d_0 + s_0/i$. Thus a government may spend more on goods and services than the amount of taxes it receives but still may have a declining or constant debt-to-GDP ratio as long as the cost of the debt service (interest rate) is lower than or equal to the growth rate of economic activity.

Case 2b: Constant primary-deficit-to-GDP ratio

In Case 2a the level of primary deficit was constant but it declined relative to GDP. Now let us assume that the level of the primary deficit increases at the same rate as GDP, which implies that their ratio is constant. Start again with

$$D_t = D_{t-1}(1+i) + S_t$$

Now divide by Y_t and assume that s is constant for all time periods:

$$d_t = d_{t-1}\frac{(1+i)}{(1+g)} + \bar{s}$$

Following the same recursive method we get:

$$d_t = d_0\left(\frac{1+i}{1+g}\right)^n + \bar{s}\left(\frac{1+g}{g-i}\right)\left(1 - \left(\frac{1+i}{1+g}\right)^n\right)$$

Again, if $g > i$ then the debt-to-GDP ratio converges toward $\bar{s}\left(\frac{1+g}{g-i}\right)$ but if $i \geq g$, the debt-to-GDP ratio rises continuously.

Case 3: Constant deficit-to-GDP ratio

Finally, assume the deficit-to-GDP ratio is constant forever. In this case, we have:

$$\frac{Def}{Y} = \frac{G - T + iD}{Y} = x$$

Thus:

$$d_t = d_{t-1} + x$$

Through recursive calculation we get:

$$d_t = d_0 + nx$$

As n tends toward infinity, d_t also does. Thus, a constant deficit-to-GDP ratio means the debt has to explode even if GDP grows as fast as the deficit.

3
The Domestic Monetary System: Banking and Central Banking

3.1 IOUs denominated in the national currency: government and private

All "modern money" systems (which apply to those of the "past 4000 years at least" as Keynes put it) are state money systems in which the sovereign chooses a money of account and then imposes tax liabilities in that unit. It can then issue currency used to pay taxes. In this chapter we return to our analysis of the operation of today's monetary system, examining the denomination of IOUs in the state money of account.

IOUs denominated in national currency: government.

In earlier sections we have noted that assets and liabilities are denominated in a money of account, which is chosen by a national government and given force through the mechanism of taxation. On a floating exchange rate, the government's own IOUs – currency – are nonconvertible in the sense that the government makes no promise to convert them to precious metal, to foreign currency, or to anything else. Instead, it promises only to accept its own IOUs in payments made to itself (mostly tax payments, but also payments of fees and fines). This is the necessary and fundamental promise made: the issuer of an IOU must accept that IOU in payment. So long as government agrees to accept its own IOUs in tax payments, the government's IOUs will be in demand (*at least* for tax payments, and probably for other uses as well).

On the other hand, when government promises to convert on demand (to foreign currency or precious metal), holders of the government's liabilities have the option of demanding conversion. This might in some cases actually increase the acceptability of the government's currency. At the same time, it commits government to conversion on demand, which as discussed earlier requires that it have accumulated reserves of the foreign currency or precious metal to which it promises to convert. Ironically, while it might be able to find more willingness to accept its currency since it is convertible, it also knows that increasing currency issue raises the possibility it will not be able to meet demand for conversion. For this reason, government knows it should limit its issue of a convertible currency. Should holders begin to doubt government will be able to convert on demand, the game is over unless government has sufficient access to foreign currency or precious metal reserves (either to its hoards, or to loans of reserves). It can be forced to default on its promise to convert if it does not. Any hint that default is imminent will ensure a run on the currency. In that case, only 100 percent reserve backing (or access to lenders who have or can create those reserves) will allow government to avoid default.

We repeat that convertibility is not necessary to ensure demand for the domestic currency. As discussed earlier, so long as government can impose and collect taxes it can ensure at least some demand for a nonconvertible currency. All it needs to do is to insist that taxes be paid in its own currency. This "promise to accept in tax payment" is sufficient to create a demand for the currency: taxes drive money.

Private IOUs denominated in the domestic currency

Similarly, private issuers of IOUs also promise to accept their own liabilities. For example, if a household has a loan with its bank, it can always pay principle and interest on the loan by writing a check on its deposit account at the bank. In this case, the bank accepts its own IOU in payment.

Indeed, modern banking systems operate a check clearing facility so that each bank accepts checks drawn on all other banks in the country. This allows anyone with a debt due to any bank in the country to present a check drawn on any other bank in the country for payment of the debt. The check-clearing facility then operates to settle accounts among the banks. (More on this in the next section.)

The important point is that banks accept their own liabilities (checks drawn on deposits) in payments on debts due to banks (the loans banks have made), just as governments accept their own liabilities (currency) in payments on debts due to government (tax liabilities).

Leveraging

There is one big difference between government and banks, however. Banks normally do promise to convert their liabilities to something. You can present a check to your bank for payment in currency – what is normally called "cashing a check" – or you can simply withdraw cash at the Automatic Teller Machine (ATM) from one of your bank accounts. In either case, the bank IOU is converted to a government IOU. Banks normally promise to make these conversions either "on demand" (in the case of "demand deposits", which are normal checking accounts) or after a specified time period (in the case of "time deposits", including savings accounts and certificates of deposits – known as CDs – often with a penalty for early withdrawal).

Banks hold a relatively small amount of currency in their vaults to handle these conversions; if they need more, they ask the central bank to send an armored truck. Banks don't want to keep a lot of cash on hand, nor do they need to do so in normal circumstances. Lots of cash could increase the attractiveness to bank robbers, but the main reason for minimizing holdings is because it is costly to hold currency. The most obvious cost is the vault and the security guards, however, more important to banks is that holding reserves of currency does not earn profits. Banks would rather hold loans as assets, because debtors pay interest on these loans. For this reason, banks *leverage* their currency reserves, holding a very tiny fraction of their assets in the form of reserves against their deposit liabilities. (See Section 3.4 for analysis of bank balance sheets.)

So long as only a small percentage of their depositors try to convert deposits to cash on any given day, this is not a problem. However, in the case of a *bank run* in which a large number of depositors tries to convert on the same day, the bank will have to obtain currency from the central bank.

This can even lead to a *lender of last resort* action by the central bank that lends currency reserves to a bank facing a run. In such an intervention, the central bank lends its own IOUs to the banks in exchange for their IOU – the bank gets a reserve credit from the central bank (an asset for the bank) and the central bank holds the bank's IOU as an asset. When cash is withdrawn from the bank, its reserves at the central bank are debited, and the bank debits the depositor's account at the bank. The cash then held by the (former) depositor is the central bank's liability, offset by the bank's liability to the central bank.

In the next section we will begin with an analysis of how banks clear accounts among themselves, by using central bank reserves. This also leads to a discussion of "pyramiding": in modern economies that leverage liabilities, it is common to make one's own IOUs convertible to those higher in the debt pyramid. Ultimately, all roads lead back to the central bank.

Box: Frequently asked questions

Q: Can't the Fed just control money and inflation by raising required reserve ratios? What about a 100 percent reserve requirement?

A: As discussed in a bit more detail below, required reserve ratios do not control bank lending. To hit its interest rate target, the central bank must accommodate the demand for reserves – whether the ratio is 1 percent (about where it was in the United States on average against all deposits, until the financial crisis and Quantitative Easing) or 10 percent (the ratio usually used in textbooks to simplify math). (Note: the required reserve ratio in Canada is a big zip, zero! That is actually the most advanced way to run the system.) Since it would not control lending there is little reason to believe raising ratios would affect inflation. Also note that raising the ratio does not affect the overnight rate (fed funds rate in the United States) – since that is the policy variable.

Higher ratios do act like a tax on banks – they must hold a very low earning asset. If the ratio is 1 percent they hold 1 percent of their assets (more or less; close enough for this analysis) in an asset that earns a very low interest rate (the support rate paid by the central bank on reserves). They need to cover their costs and make profits by earning more than that on the rest of their assets (99 percent). Raising the ratio to 10 percent means they only have 90 percent of their assets potentially earning higher returns. And so on. Will that affect lending rates earned (what they charge borrowers) and deposit rates paid (what they pay depositors)? Banks earn revenue on the spread between those two; that is how they cover costs and make profits. So, yes, raising ratios might cause them to raise loan rates and lower deposit rates – not a good thing for borrowers or depositors.

Finally, what about 100 percent reserves? There is a good book by Ronnie Phillips (1995) on the Fisher-Simons-Friedman proposal to do just that. However, this is usually presented as a way to make banks "safe": they'd hold only reserves or treasuries against their demand deposits, on the idea that with safe assets, the deposits are always safe (so you do not need deposit insurance, that is, FDIC in the United States). That sounds fine so far as it goes. Someone else has to do the lending since the banks are not allowed to do it, so it isolates "narrow banks" from lending risk, but others will do the lending and create IOUs that are not backed by 100 percent reserves. It is not clear that the proposal would in any way reduce the creation of "money", defined as IOUs denominated in the money of account.

Q: Does a lack of sufficient reserves constrain loans?

A: No. Don't take my word for it. The former Fed's Senior Vice President, Federal Reserve Bank of New York, Alan Holmes, explained why the then faddish Monetarist policy of controlling inflation by controlling the growth of base money (reserves plus cash) had failed, saying that it suffered from "a naive assumption" that the banking system only expands loans after the (Federal Reserve) System (or market factors) have put reserves in the banking system. In the real world, banks extend credit, creating deposits in the process, and look for the reserves later. The question then becomes one of whether and how the Federal Reserve will accommodate the demand for reserves. In the very short run, the Federal Reserve has little or no choice about accommodating that demand. This is for two main reasons: first, the central bank operates with an overnight interest rate target (when banks are short they bid the market rate above the target, triggering reserve provision by the central bank), and second, the central bank stands by to ensure checks clear at par (it needs to debit reserves of the bank the check is drawn against, so lends reserves if the bank is short).

Q: Where do banks keep their money? In their vaults? Or at the central bank?

A: Banks don't really keep money at the central bank or in their vaults, indeed, banks do not really "have" money. Willie Sutton

(Google him) was wrong; when asked why he robbed banks, he reportedly responded "because that's where the money is". Don't bother robbing banks, because that is NOT where the money is. Banks have an electronic account at the Fed – numbers on a hard drive. In addition, banks have a very small amount of "vault cash" in their vaults. Believe me, they are not worth robbing. If you really want to rob banks, my colleague Bill Black says the best way to rob a bank is to own one. Then you simply credit your own bank account with bonuses. Where will you get the millions of dollars to credit your account once you own a bank? Keystrokes! We'll examine that later, but it is much like the keystroke entries onto the scoreboard at the football game. So, really, "bank money" consists of the "keystroke" entries they make to their depositor's accounts!

Box: The central bank balance sheet

The balance sheet of any central bank looks more or less like this:

Central bank balance sheet

Assets	Liabilities and Net Worth
A1: Credit market instruments (securities) A2: Loans to domestic banks (advances of reserves to domestic banks) A3: Gold, foreign exchange, and SDR certificates A4: Treasury Currency (coins held by the central bank) A5: Other assets (buildings, furniture, etc.)	L1: Vault Cash and Cash in Circulation (central banknotes held by banks and the public) L2: Reserve balances (a checking account due to banks) L3: Checking Account due to Treasury and Banknotes held by Treasury L4: Checking Account due to Foreigners and others and Banknotes Held by Foreigners and others L5: Other liabilities (including net worth)

Banknotes (called Federal Reserve notes in the United States) and Checking Accounts at the central bank are liabilities of the central bank, but they are an asset for everybody else. Note that there are no domestic monetary instruments on the asset side of the central bank (except a few coins if the treasury is in charge of minting them as in the United States).

L1 and L2 are approximately equal to what is called the monetary base (coins in circulation have to be added to get the full amount of the monetary base). Their sum represents the amount of central bank money things that are held either by the public (in the form of banknotes) or by banks (in the form of banknotes and reserves, a checking account at the central bank; the sum of which is counted as bank reserves).

It is common to take the items in the central bank's balance sheet to write what is known as the "monetary base" or "high-powered money" equation. This gets a little wonky and squeamish readers can skip this part. From the balance sheet we know that:

$$L_1 + L_2 = A_1 + A_2 + A_3 + A_4 + A_5 - L_3 - L_4 - L_5$$

Hence, changes to these items will increase or decrease the monetary base. For example:

Source of injections: increase in assets held by central bank, which buys them by issuing liabilities

Increase in assets of the central bank:

- Higher A1: Buying securities (T-bills, T-bonds, etc.) (Open Market Operations)
- Higher A2: Advances of Federal Funds (Discount Window Operations)
- Higher A3: Buying gold
- Higher A5: Buying a pizza, a building, or a service from someone
- Source of removal/leakages: Reverse of injection

Decrease in assets of the central bank:

- Sell Securities
- Repayment of Advances by banks and others

Let us see how the monetary base changes. For example, assume the central bank buys T-Bills worth $100 from banks:

Change in Assets	Change Liabilities and NW
$\Delta A1 = +\$100$ T-bills	$\Delta L2 = +\$100$ Reserves

You have just witnessed the creation of some monetary base: The central bank credited the account of banks (it could also have printed central bank notes instead: $\Delta L1 = +\$100$)

Where did the Federal Reserve get the funds it provided? From nowhere; the reserves are the liabilities of the central bank so it can create an unlimited amount of them. The central bank does not need gold, does not needs tax revenue or anything else to create its IOUs. Chairman Bernanke made the following comment in a CBS TV interview on March 12, 2009:

Pelley: Is it tax money that the Fed is spending?
Bernanke: It's not tax money. The banks have accounts with the Fed, much the same way that you have an account in a commercial bank. So, to lend to a bank, we simply use the computer to mark up the size of the account that they have with the Fed.

He is right. As shown above, the Federal Reserve just keystroked a bookkeeping entry on its balance sheet. This is done in a matter of seconds. It has nothing to do with taxes.

What would be the impact of people paying their taxes? Say Mr. X needs to pay his taxes due of $1,000. The impact is to debit his bank account at Bank A by $1,000. At the same time, the reserves of Bank A would be reduced by $1,000 ($\Delta L2 = -\$1,000$) and the treasury account at the central bank would rise by $1,000 ($\Delta L3 = +\$1,000$):

Central bank balance sheet

Change in Assets	Change Liabilities and NW
	$\Delta L2 = -\$1000$ $\Delta L3 = +\$1000$

You have just witnessed the destruction of some monetary base (because the treasury's deposit at the central bank is not counted as part of the monetary base): Tax payments destroy monetary base ($L_1 + L_2$ declined), that is, the amount of central bank money things held by the public and banks.

3.2 Clearing and the pyramid of liabilities

Previously we discussed denomination of government and private liabilities in the state money of account: the Dollar in the United States, the Yen in Japan, and so on. We also introduced the concept of *leverage*, for example, the practice of holding a small amount of government currency in reserve against IOUs denominated in the state's unit of account while promising to convert those IOUs to currency. This also led to a discussion of a "run" on private IOUs, demanding conversion. Since the reserves held are not nearly sufficient to meet the demand for conversion, the central bank must enter as *lender of last resort* to stop the run by lending its own IOUs to allow the conversions to take place. Now we examine bank clearing and the notion of a "pyramid" of liabilities with the government's own IOUs at the top of that pyramid.

Clearing accounts extinguishes IOUs

Banks clear accounts using government IOUs, and for that reason either keep some currency on hand in their vaults, or, more importantly, maintain reserve deposits at the central bank. Further, they have access to more reserves should they ever need them, both through borrowing from other banks (called the interbank overnight market; this is the fed funds market in the United States), or through borrowing them from the central bank.

All modern financial systems have developed procedures that ensure banks can get currency and reserves as necessary to clear accounts among themselves and with their depositors. When First National Bank receives a check drawn on Second National Bank, it asks the central bank to debit the reserves of Second National and to credit its own reserves. This is now handled electronically. Note that while Second National's assets will be reduced (by the amount of reserves debited), its liabilities (checking deposits) will be reduced by the same amount. Similarly, when a depositor uses the ATM machine to withdraw currency, the bank's assets (cash reserves) are reduced, and its IOUs to the depositor (the liabilities in the deposit account) are reduced by the same amount.

Other business firms use bank liabilities for clearing their own accounts. For example, the retail firm typically receives products from wholesalers on the basis of a promise to pay after a specified time period (usually 30 days). Wholesalers hold these IOUs until the end of the period, at which time the retailers pay by a check drawn on their bank account (or, increasingly, by an electronic transfer from their account to the account of the wholesaler). At this point the retailer's IOUs held by the wholesalers are destroyed.

Alternatively, the wholesaler might not be willing to wait until the end of the period for payment. In this case the wholesaler can sell the retailer's IOUs at a *discount* (for less than the amount that the retailer promises to pay at the end of the period). The discount is effectively *interest* that the wholesaler is willing to pay to get the funds earlier than promised.

Usually it will be a financial institution that buys the IOU at a discount called "discounting" the IOU (this is where the term "discount window" at the central bank comes from: the US Fed would buy commercial paper – IOUs of commercial firms – at a discount). In this case the retailer will finally pay the holder of these IOUs (perhaps a financial institution) at the end of the period, which effectively earns interest (the difference between the amount paid for the IOUs and the amount paid by the retailer to extinguish the IOUs). Again, the retailer's IOU is cancelled by delivering a bank liability (the holder of the retailer's IOU receives a credit to her own bank account).

Pyramiding currency

Private financial liabilities are not only denominated in the government's money of account, but they also are, ultimately, convertible into the government's currency.

As we have discussed previously, banks explicitly promise to convert their liabilities to currency (either immediately in the case of demand deposits, or with some delay in the case of time deposits). Other private firms mostly use bank liabilities to clear their own accounts. Essentially this means they are promising to convert their liabilities to bank liabilities, "paying by check" on a specified date (or according to other conditions specified in the contract). For this reason, they must have deposits, or have access to deposits, with banks to make the payments.

Things can get even more complex than this, because there is a wide range of financial institutions (and even nonfinancial institutions that offer financial services) that can provide payment services. These can make payments for other firms, with net clearing among these "nonbank financial institutions" (also called "shadow banks") occurring using the liabilities of banks. Banks, in turn, clear accounts using government liabilities.

There could thus be "six degrees of separation" (many layers of financial leveraging) between a creditor and a debtor involved in clearing accounts, ultimately with net clearing on the books of the central bank.

We can think of a *pyramid* of liabilities, with different layers according to the degree of separation from the central bank. See the Figure below. Perhaps the bottom layer consists of the IOUs of households held by other households, by firms engaged in production, by banks, and by other financial institutions. The important point is that households usually clear accounts by using liabilities issued by those higher in the debt pyramid, usually financial institutions.

The next layer up from the bottom consists of the IOUs of firms engaged in production, with their liabilities held mostly by financial institutions higher in the debt pyramid (although some are directly held by households and by other firms), and who mostly clear accounts using liabilities issued by the financial institutions.

At the next layer we have nonbank financial institutions, which in turn clear accounts using the banks whose liabilities are higher in the pyramid. Just below the apex of the pyramid, banks use government liabilities for net clearing.

Finally, the government is highest in the pyramid – with no liabilities higher than its inconvertible IOUs.

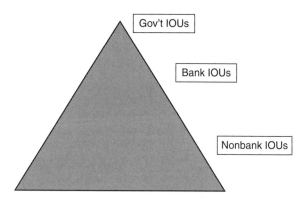

The shape of the pyramid is instructive for two reasons. First, there is a hierarchical arrangement whereby liabilities issued by those higher in the pyramid are generally more acceptable. In some respects this is due to higher creditworthiness (the sovereign government's nonconvertible liabilities are free from credit risk; as we move down the pyramid through bank liabilities, toward nonfinancial business liabilities, and finally to the IOUs of households, risk tends to rise – although this is not a firm and fast rule).

Second, the liabilities at each level typically *leverage* the liabilities at the higher levels. In this sense the whole pyramid is based on leveraging of (a relatively smaller number of) government IOUs. There are typically far more liabilities lower in the pyramid than there are high in the pyramid, at least in the case of a financially developed economy.

Note however that in the case of a convertible currency, the government's currency is not at the apex of the pyramid. Since it promises to convert its currency on demand and at a fixed exchange rate into something else (gold or foreign currency), that "something else" is at the top. The consequences have been addressed previously: government must hold or at least have access to the thing into which it will convert its currency. That can constrain its ability to use policy to achieve some goals such as full employment and robust economic growth, a topic for Chapter 5.

Of course, the pyramid above is very simple – we could divide banks into different categories, and for most purposes it would be useful to divide "nonbanks" into firms and households. In fact, it is rather arbitrary where we put the dividing line between bank IOUs and IOUs of "other" financial institutions. Perhaps the most useful way is to distinguish between those types of institutions that have direct access to the central bank, and those that do not.

That also brings up the following point: what happens if something goes wrong nearer the bottom of the pyramid (say, in the shadow banks that do not have access to the central bank)? That is indeed what happened in the global financial crisis (GFC). Typically those lower in the pyramid issue IOUs that are convertible on some conditions to bank IOUs, that in turn are convertible to government (central bank reserve) IOUs. When something goes wrong, the nonbanks and shadow banks turn to banks for finance (lending against the nonbank's IOUs); the banks in turn go to the central bank. But when expectations turn ugly, the banks won't lend, so the nonbanks cannot make good on promises. That led to the liquidity crisis; the US Fed eventually decided to lend to virtually everyone, including investment banks and the rest of the "shadow" banking sector, and even to nonfinancial firms like Harley Davidson, as well as to foreign central banks.

Additionally, the pyramid is useful for thinking about whose IOUs one can use to make payments on one's own IOUs. You cannot repay your IOU with your own IOU (you'd still owe); only sovereign governments can do that (as we discussed, if you present a five-Pound note to the Queen, she gives you another; she still owes. But so what – you'll never get anything else out of her even if you go to court!). You use someone else's IOU to retire your own, what we call a second-party or third-party IOU (not first, which is yours; second would be using your creditor's own IOU; third would be using the IOU of someone unrelated). Normally those lower in the pyramid use bank IOUs; banks in turn use government IOUs (central bank reserves) to "clear" their own IOUs.

Box: Frequently asked questions

Q: What about settlement of Eurodollars?

A: Note: Eurodollars are deposit accounts denominated in Dollars that are issued by banks outside the United States. (We won't go into the history of these, but they were created in part to get around US regulations and supervision of banks.) Really this is the same story as clearing by banks within the United States. Ultimate clearing in Eurodollars is at the Fed since these "leverage" US Dollars. (Note: I am simplifying, there are also private settlement services. Banks with offsetting claims on one another can use a private settlement system; they only need to go to the central bank for net clearing, as only the central bank can create reserves.)

Q: Where does the Fed borrow from and is there a limit? And wouldn't it be better to spend the money to bail out Main Street? Didn't Chairman Bernanke admit he bailed out the banks with keystrokes?

A: Yes to the last two questions. The Fed "keystroked" trillions of reserves into existence, lending and buying Treasuries and toxic waste MBSs. Calling this "borrowing" by the Fed is misleading, which is why I do not use that term. The Fed is indebted, dollar for dollar, for every one of those keystrokes since reserves are Fed IOUs. So you could call that "borrowing" and the banks with the reserves could be called "lenders" since they are the creditors. But this is nothing like you or me borrowing to buy a car. We are truly limited in how much we can borrow. The Fed has no limit to keystrokes, and the reserves do not exist until the Fed keystrokes them into existence. The Fed spent (buying assets) and lent a total of $29 trillion to rescue the financial system after the global financial collapse (there are a number of pieces tallying up the total at www.levy.org). Wouldn't it be better to spend a fraction of that to rescue Main Street and the unemployed? I think so. Probably most Americans would agree.

Q: What is meant by the term "inside money"?

A: "Inside money" is the money-denominated IOUs of the non-government sector – what I often call private money things. "Outside money" is the money-denominated IOUs of the government sector (cash plus reserves; we can also include treasuries since those are just reserves that pay higher interest). Note it is outside money that is at the top of the pyramid.

3.3 Central bank operations in crisis: lender of last resort

In a crisis, an important role played by the central bank is to operate as a "lender of last resort", providing reserves on demand to financial institutions. Originally this was to stop a "bank run" – depositors trying to exchange their deposits for cash. That type of run is now rare. Most take the form of uninsured creditors refusing to "roll over" short-term bank liabilities. When the global financial crisis hit, banks could not refinance their positions in assets because their creditors demanded payment as liabilities matured. The US Fed had to step in to provide the refinancing.[1] In this section we will look at US Fed operations, both "normal" lending and "lender of last resort" lending in crisis. Other central banks follow similar practices (except for the European Central Bank since individual members were supposed to be responsible for their own banks; but, as we'll see later, the crisis in Euroland forced the ECB to intervene).

First, the most common role of Fed lending on a typical day is through intraday overdrafts, which banks are required to clear by the end of the day. Really this is just like "overdraft" protection you might have on your checking account. Prior to the problems encountered by Lehman Brothers (which set off the global financial crisis), this lending by the Fed was averaging about $50 billion every minute of the day, with peak settlement periods of about $150 billion per minute. So there is a lot of lending going on by the Fed (however, after the crisis, banks held so many excess reserves this type of lending slowed to a trickle). Note by the end of the day the bank should clear its overdrafts by borrowing reserves "overnight". When a bank is short it borrows in the private "fed funds" market; if no funds are available, the Fed routinely provides temporary lending of reserves by discounting eligible assets (discounting just means the assets are presented as collateral).

Second, the Fed has always attached a stigma to its overnight or discount-window lending. Its stated purpose has always been to get banks to clear overdrafts among themselves by the end of the day. Several other central banks do this in their own way without stigmatizing such lending, so the Fed is rather unique as it provides most reserves to markets through open market purchases of Treasuries. Further complicating this is that unlike most other interbank systems, the US system is highly decentralized, which means it's not unusual for the Fed's open market activities to be insufficient for: (a) offsetting all changes to the Fed's balance sheet, and (b) reserve balances in circulation to make it to every bank desiring them. Combine these two – stigma along with complications associated with the US system – and you get a greater likelihood of rates rising even well above the Fed's overnight target to dislodge banks from lending their excess reserves instead of borrowing from the Fed.

In a crisis these characteristics make things worse, as banks are wary of one another, so the overnight rate spikes can be way above the target. Note, though, that this doesn't change the fact that the Fed is acting as a lender of last resort (LOLR). What happens is that the Fed's LOLR actions are occurring both in normal and crisis times but at a higher price (higher interest rate relative to the target rate) than would be desirable. During the crisis, recognizing more needed to be done, the Fed offered several more types of standing facilities to carry out a massive LOLR effort. There was little or no stigma associated with these non-conventional standing facilities, unlike the traditional discount window. We won't go into the details, but the Fed "auctioned" reserves rather than providing them through loans at the discount window. The Fed would announce, say, it was willing to provide $100 billion of reserves through a new special facility, essentially lending against eligible assets (in some cases this could be what is called a repurchase agreement, with the Fed temporarily buying an asset and the selling bank promising to buy it back at a slightly higher price in the future. The difference in the sell/buy prices would be the interest charged.

Box: Frequently asked questions

Q: What does the central bank lend against? How does a bank get cash?

A: The central bank lends against qualifying assets. It's the boss and can decide. Usually, central banks lend against treasuries (IOUs of the treasury); they can lend against "real bills" (short-term commercial loans made by banks to good customers); and they can lend against toxic waste MBSs (those subprime mortgage-backed securities that triggered the global financial crisis – maybe a bad idea?). It can use collateral requirements as a way to supervise/regulate banks since the central bank can encourage them to make only safe loans by narrowing what it accepts as collateral.

When you go to the ATM to withdraw cash, your bank has a bit of cash on hand – that counts as part of its reserve base. If everyone goes tomorrow to withdraw cash, obviously the bank runs out quickly. It orders more from the central bank – shipped in armored trucks – and the central bank debits the bank's reserves, and when that is insufficient it lends the cash (a loan of reserves) against collateral. The central bank holds the bank's IOU as an asset; it is of course a liability of the bank.

Q: What happens if a borrower goes bankrupt? Banks can be illiquid but not insolvent?

A: We'll look in more detail at how banks "work" later, but here's a brief description. Banks can become illiquid, and they can become insolvent. They've got assets on one side of their balance sheet and liabilities plus capital on the other. When the assets go bad, the capital is reduced (shareholders lose); once the capital is wiped out, the losses come out of the other liabilities, so bank creditors lose. Since governments often insure depositors (in the United States this is the role of the FDIC), if losses are big enough to hit deposits, government covers those. A liquidity problem is different: the assets might be perfectly good, but if they cannot be quickly marketed without losing value, then a bank facing withdrawals cannot cover them by selling assets. Instead, the central bank lends reserves to solve liquidity problems, lending against collateral. Banks do become insolvent, as discussed above. They then must be "resolved"; there are a variety of methods but it comes down to selling the assets, covering insured depositors first and then other creditors, and the shareholders take the loss.

3.4   Balance sheets of banks, monetary creation by banks, and interbank settlement

The balance sheet of a typical bank looks like this:

Table 3.1   Balance sheet of a typical bank

Assets	Liabilities and NW
Advances (Loans) Securities Reserves Other Assets	Checking accounts Savings accounts Other liabilities Net Worth

Where are the money things? They are the checking and savings accounts on the balance sheet. Note that they are the IOUs of banks. The bank promises to convert deposits in a checking account (and deposits in most savings accounts) into cash on demand.

Say that Bank A starts with the following very simple balance sheet:

Table 3.2   Bank A balance sheet

Assets	Liabilities and NW
Building = $200	Net Worth = $200

It has not engaged in any banking activity yet; its owners have paid-in capital to buy a building. Now Mr. X comes into the bank and says that he would like to borrow $200 to finance the purchase of a car. His bank checks his creditworthiness (asks for income tax returns, proof of assets, credit history, etc.). If Mr. X is approved then the following occurs on the bank's balance sheet.

Bank A balance sheet

Assets	Liabilities and NW
Loan to Mr. X = $200 Building = $200	Checking Account of Mr. X = $200 Net Worth = $200

Note that the bank's total assets and total liabilities are now $400 each. The bank just created $200 of money things (deposits in the checking account of Mr. X in return for Mr. X's IOU, or promise to pay $200). We will move on later to Mr. X's spending of his deposit. But first let us examine this balance sheet carefully.

Where did the bank get the money thing it created?

- It did not get it from anywhere: a checking account was created *ex nihilo*, that is, from nothing, by entering a number (200) in a computer. In the past banks could also issue their own banknotes, but generally only central banks can do that now.
- The bank did not need any prior deposits, or any cash in its vault. In fact the bank did not have any cash in its vault, nor any deposits in its account at the central bank.
- The bank is not lending anything it has, it just creates money things – bank deposits – at will
- Those money things are its liabilities/IOUs.
- By creating those bank IOUs the bank promises to:
  - convert deposits into cash on demand;
  - accept any of those IOUs in payment of debts owed to the bank.

The checking account is just a legal promise to convert to cash on demand, and to accept payment in the form of the bank's own IOUs. The bank does not have to have any cash now.

Think of a coupon for a free pizza that you receive in the mail. The coupon was created before the pizza was made and the pizza company did not have to have any pizza ready before it printed the coupon and mailed it to you. The pizza will be made only if you present the coupon at the pizzeria, at which time it will be made. In our analogy the cash is the pizza and the coupon is the checking account. It turns out that most people are satisfied with just having a deposit in the checking account and rarely ask for cash. As shown below, if people want cash, banks can get it very easily. The problem is that it may be costly to get it (like it may be costly to make a pizza if flour happens to become expensive).

The success of the banking operation (lending by accepting an IOU, and creation of a demand deposit) depends on:

- The capacity of Mr. X to repay (creditworthiness)
  - If Mr. X has problems making timely payments on his debts, this affects the value of the bank's assets and its own income

inflows and ultimately affects the net worth of the bank, the bank's capital ratio, and the shareholders' return on equity.
- The bank's capacity to acquire reserves at low cost if
  - Mr. X wants to withdraw cash
  - If the bank needs to pay debts to other banks: interbank settlement
  - The bank needs to settle tax payments made by Mr. X to the government

If these conditions are not satisfied the bank gets in trouble; it can become insolvent or illiquid. The first means its net worth falls to or below zero; the second means it cannot meet cash withdrawals or clearing. Thus, even though banks can create unlimited amounts of money, they have no incentive to do so because it may be unprofitable.

So what happens if now Mr. X pays $200 to a car dealer who happens to have a bank account at another bank called Bank B? The balance sheet of the bank looks like this:

Table 3.3   Bank A balance sheet

Change in Assets	Change in Liabilities and NW
	Checking Account of Mr. X = −$200 Reserve due to Bank B = +$200

Bank B balance sheet

Change in Assets	Change in Liabilities and NW
Claim on Bank A Reserves = +$200	Checking Account of Car Dealer = +$200

Bank A owes $200 of reserves to Bank B but it doesn't have any. Where does it get the reserves?

Bank A will get the reserves via the source that is the least costly. It may sell assets (in our example, Bank A only has a building so it would be very costly to get reserves that way, but it could sell bonds if it had any) or it may borrow reserves from other banks, other economic units (domestic or foreign), or the central bank. A common way to get the reserves is to borrow from the central bank who is the monopoly supplier of reserves so we have:

Bank A balance sheet

Change in Assets	Change in Liabilities and NW
Reserve = +$200	Debt to Federal Reserve = +$200

Federal Reserve balance sheet

Change in Assets	Change in Liabilities and NW
Reserve Loan to Bank A = +200	Reserve = +$200

Now that Bank A has the reserves it needs to settle its debt with Bank B.

Bank A balance sheet

Change in Assets	Change in Liabilities and NW
Reserves = –$200	Reserves due to Bank B = –$200

Bank B balance sheet

Change in Assets	Change in Liabilities and NW
Claim on Bank A = –$200 Reserves = +$200	

That is it! The debt between the two banks was settled. The final balance sheets of Bank A, Bank B, and the central bank look like this:

Bank A balance sheet

Assets	Liabilities and NW
Advance of Funds to Mr. X = $200 Building = $200	Debt to Federal Reserve = $200 Net Worth = $200

Bank A makes money as long as the interest it receives on the advance to Mr. X is higher than the interest it pays to the Federal Reserve.

The balance sheet of Bank B looks like this (assuming it did not have any reserves before):

Bank B balance sheet

Assets	Liabilities and NW
Reserves = $200	Checking Account of Car Dealer = $200

And the balance sheet of the central bank is (assuming that it did not provide any advances to banks or any cash):

Federal Reserve balance sheet

Assets	Liabilities and NW
Reserve Loan to Bank A = $200	Reserves = $200

Note that all these operations did not involve any transfer of physical cash – it was all bookkeeping entries through keystrokes to computers. Also note we only show the assets and liabilities directly related to our examples. Of course, private banks and the central bank have many other assets and liabilities, as well as net worth on their balance sheets.

In practice, the central bank will usually not advance reserves to the bank directly in the form of an unsecured advance; instead it will ask for collateral (usually a treasury security) in exchange and will provide funds for less than the value of the collateral. So, if Bank A has a $300 bond, it surrenders it to the Federal Reserve in exchange for reserves. The Fed will usually give only, say, $285 if the discount is 5 percent.

Box: Frequently asked questions

Q: What is the relation between the accounting of debits and credits and the financial uses and sources approach? In my business school accounting classes I learned this a bit differently.

A: In this Primer we use "T accounts" that are presented in every money and banking textbook. Bank loans are on the asset side of the bank's balance sheet; demand deposits are on the liability side. Reverse that for the borrower. For the wonkier with a bit of business school education behind them, I strongly recommend this article: Ritter, "The Flow-of-Funds Accounts: A New Approach" (*Journal of Finance*, May 1963) which goes through the balance sheet, the financial uses and sources approach, treatment of real and financial, and integration into flow of funds accounts. Conceptually the two approaches lead to the same result; the T Accounts approach is simpler.

3.5 Exogenous interest rates and quantitative easing

In economics the distinction between endogenous and exogenous is used in three different senses: control, theoretical, and statistical. Only econometricians care about the last one – which has to do with the independence of variables from the error term – so we'll skip over that. In the control sense exogeneity means the government can "control" the variable, for example, can control the money supply, control the interest rate, or control the price level, and so on.

MMT shares with the "endogenous money" or "horizontalist" approaches the view that the central bank cannot control the money supply or bank reserves. Instead the central bank must accommodate the demand for reserves (however, as noted below, things changed with QE). (See Moore 1988 for more on Horizontalism.) On the other hand, the central bank's target interest rate is clearly exogenous in the control sense: the central bank can set its target at 25 basis points, or raise it to 150 basis points. Finally, the control sense and the theoretical sense are related but not identical. Let us say a country has a fixed exchange rate and uses the interest rate policy to hit the peg. We can say the interest rate is exogenously controlled (set by the central bank) but it is not theoretically exogenous because the overriding policy is to peg the exchange rate. In the theoretical sense, the central bank's concern is to hit the exchange rate target so that it has surrendered control of the interest rate (it uses the interest rate as a tool to hit the targeted exchange rate). On the other hand, let us say that the central bank targets full employment and uses the interest rate to achieve that target. Again we would say the interest rate is exogenous in the control sense, but not in the theoretical sense because it is used to target full employment.

Above we stated that we normally take the overnight interest rate as exogenous in the control sense, but reserves are taken as endogenous because the central bank accommodates demand for reserves in order to hit the interest rate target. That is the "endogenous money, horizontal reserve" approach popularized since about 1980. However, this theory was formulated back when the interest rate paid on reserves was zero in the United States, while the Fed's target overnight interest rate was nonzero. In that situation, excess reserves drove the market rate (fed funds rate) below target so the Fed would have to drain reserves by selling Treasuries. But in the aftermath of the global financial crisis, the Fed adopted a near zero interest rate target (like Japan) so it could leave excess reserves in the system and pay 25 basis points on them. In that case, no matter how many excess reserves banks hold, the market rate remains near 25 basis points (any bank can get 25 basis points on excess reserves from the Fed so there is no point in lending them in the fed funds market at a rate below that).

So with what is called Quantitative Easing the Fed "exogenously" increases bank reserves. There is an asymmetry, though, because the Fed can leave banks full of excess reserves but cannot leave them short reserves, which would drive the market rate above the target. That would trigger an open market purchase of Treasuries by the Fed to add reserves and move the fed funds rate back to the target.

3.6   The technical details of central bank and treasury coordination: the case of the Fed[2]

Previously we discussed the general case of government spending, taxing, and bond sales. To briefly summarize, we saw that when a government spends, there is a simultaneous credit to someone's bank deposit and to the bank's reserve deposit at the central bank; taxes are simply the reverse of that operation: a debit to a bank account and to bank reserves. Bond sales are accomplished by debiting a bank's reserves.

For the purposes of the simplest explication, it is convenient to consolidate the treasury and central bank accounts into a "government account". To be sure, the real world is more complicated: there is a central bank and a treasury, and there are specific operational procedures adopted. In addition there are constraints imposed on those operations. Two common and important constraints are: a) the treasury keeps a deposit account at the central bank, and must draw upon that in order to spend, and b) the central bank is prohibited from buying bonds directly from the treasury and from lending to the treasury (which would directly increase the treasury's deposit at the central bank).

The United States is an example of a country that has both of these constraints. In this section we will go through the complex operating procedures used by the Fed and US Treasury. Scott Fullwiler is perhaps the most knowledgeable economist on these matters, and this discussion draws very heavily on his exposition cited below. Readers who want even more detail should go to his paper, which uses a stock-flow consistent approach to explicitly show results.

First, however, let us do the simple case, beginning with a consolidated government (central bank plus treasury) and look at the consequences of its spending. Then we will look at the real-world example of the United States today. I am using some simple T accounts here. It might take some readers a bit of patience to work through this, but it will help to study previous examples using balance sheets. (Note: these are partial balance sheets; I am only entering the minimum number of entries to show what is going on.)

Let us assume government buys a bomb and imposes a tax liability. This is shown as Case 1a:

Government	
Asset	Liability
+Bomb	+Reserve
+Tax Liability	+Net Worth

Private Bank		Private Nonbank Entity	
Asset	Liability	Asset	Liability
+Reserve	+DD	+DD	+Tax Liability
		−Bomb	−Net Worth

Figure 3.1 Case 1a: Government imposes a tax liability and buys a bomb by crediting an account at a private bank

The government gets the bomb, the private seller gets a demand deposit. Note that the tax liability reduces the seller's net worth and increases the government's (after all, that is the purpose of taxes – to move resources to the government). The private bank gets a reserve deposit at the government.

Now the tax is paid by debiting the taxpayer's deposit and the bank's reserves:

Government	
Asset	Liability
−Tax Liability	−Reserves

Private Bank			Private Nonbank Entity	
Asset	Liability		Asset	Liability
−Reserves	−DD		−DD	−Tax Liability

Government			Private Nonbank Entity	
Asset	Liability		Asset	Liability
+Bomb	+Net Worth		−Bomb	−Net Worth

Figure 3.2 Final position, Case 1a

The implication of "balanced budget" spending and taxing by the government is to move the bomb to the government sector, reducing the private sector's net worth. Government uses the monetary system to accomplish the "public purpose": to get resources such as bombs.

Now let us see what happens when government deficit spends. (Don't get confused – we are not arguing that taxes are not needed; remember "taxes drive money" so there is a tax system in place but government decides that this week it will buy a bomb without imposing an additional tax.)

Government	
Asset	Liability
+Bomb	+Reserves

Private Bank		Private Nonbank Entity	
Asset	Liability	Asset	Liability
+Reserves	+DD	−Bomb +DD	

Figure 3.3 Case 1b: government deficit spends, which creates private net wealth

Here the bomb is moved to the government, but the deficit spending allows net financial assets to be created in the private sector (the seller has a demand deposit equal to the government's financial liability – reserves). However, the bank is holding more reserves than desired. It would like to earn more interest, so government responds by selling a bond (bonds are sold as part of monetary policy, to allow the government to hit its overnight interest rate target):

Government		Private Bank	
Asset	Liability	Asset	Liability
	−Reserves +Bond	−Reserves +Bond	

Government	
Asset	Liability
+Bomb	+Bond

Private Bank		Private Nonbank Entity	
Asset	Liability	Asset	Liability
+Bond	+DD	−Bomb +DD	

Figure 3.4 Final position, Case 1b

The net financial asset remains, but in the form of a treasury rather than reserves. Compared with Case 1a, the private sector is much happier! Its total wealth is not changed, but the wealth was converted from a real asset (bomb) to a financial asset (claim on government).

Ah, but that was too easy. Government decides to tie its hands behind its back by requiring it sell the bond before it deficit spends. Here's the first balance sheet, with the bank buying the bond and crediting the government's deposit account:

Government		Private Bank	
Asset	Liability	Asset	Liability
+DD	+Bond	+Bomb	+DD Gov.

Figure 3.5 Case 2: government must sell bond before it can deficit spend

Government	
Asset	Liability
−DD +Bomb	

Private Bank		Private Nonbank Entity	
Asset	Liability	Asset	Liability
	−DD Gov. +DD Private	−Bomb +DD	

Figure 3.6 Government buys bomb, writing check on private bank

The bank debits the government's deposit and credits the seller's. The final position is as follows:

Government

Asset	Liability
+Bomb	+Bond

Private Bank		Private Nonbank Entity	

Asset	Liability	Asset	Liability
+Bond	+DD	−Bomb +DD	

Figure 3.7 Final position, Case 2

Note it is exactly the same result as Case 1b: selling the bond before deficit spending has no impact on the result, so long as the private bank is able to buy the bond and the government can write a check on its deposit account.

That, too, is too simple. Let's tie the government's shoes together: it can only write checks on its account at the central bank. So in the first step it sells a bond to get a deposit at a private bank.

Treasury		Private Bank	

Asset	Liability	Asset	Liability
+DD Private Bank	+Bond	+Bond	+DD Treasury

Figure 3.8 Case 3: treasury can write checks only on its central bank account

Treasury		Central Bank	

Asset	Liability	Asset	Liability
−DD Private Bank +DD Central Bank		+Loaned Reserves	+DD Treasury

Private Bank

Asset	Liability
	−DD Treasury +Borrowed Res.

Figure 3.9 Treasury moves deposit to central bank account

We have assumed the bank had no extra reserves to be debited when the treasury moved its deposit, hence the central bank had to lend reserves to the private bank (temporarily, as we will see). Now the treasury has its deposit at the central bank, on which it can write a check to buy the bomb.

Government			Central Bank	
Asset	Liability		Asset	Liability
−DD +Bomb			−Loaned Reserves	−DD Treasury

Private Bank			Private Nonbank Entity	
Asset	Liability		Asset	Liability
	+DD −Borrowed Res.		−Bomb +DD	

Figure 3.10   Treasury buys bombs

When the treasury spends, the private bank receives a credit of reserves, allowing it to retire its short-term borrowing from the central bank (looking to the private bank's balance sheet, we could show a credit of reserves to its asset side, and then that is debited simultaneously with its borrowed reserves; I left out the intermediate step to keep the balance sheet simpler). The private bank credits the bomb seller's account. The final position is as follows:

Government	
Asset	Liability
+Bomb	+Bond

Private Bank			Private Nonbank Entity	
Asset	Liability		Asset	Liability
+Bond	+DD		−Bomb +DD	

Figure 3.11   Final position, Case 3

What do you know, it is exactly the same as Case 2 and Case 1b! Even if the government ties its hands behind its back and its shoes together, it makes no difference.

OK, admittedly these are still overly simple thought experiments. Let's see how it is really done in the United States – where the Treasury really does hold accounts in both private banks and the Fed, but can write checks only on its account at the Fed. Further, the Fed is prohibited from buying Treasuries directly from the Treasury (and is not supposed to allow overdrafts on the Treasury's account). The Treasury's deposits in private banks come (mostly) from tax receipts, but Treasury cannot write checks on those deposits. So the Treasury needs to move those deposits from private banks before spending. And it must sell bonds to obtain deposits when tax receipts are too low. So let us go through the actual steps taken. Warning: it gets wonky.

3.7 Treasury debt operations

The Federal Reserve Act now specifies that the Fed can only purchase Treasury debt in "the open market," though this has not always been the case. This necessitates that the Treasury have a positive balance in its account at the Fed (which, as set in the Federal Reserve Act, is the fiscal agent for the Treasury and holds the Treasury's balances as a liability on its balance sheet). Therefore, prior to spending, the Treasury must replenish its own account at the Fed either via balances collected from tax (and other) revenues or debt issuance to "the open market".

Given that the Treasury's deposit account is a liability for the Fed, flows to/from this account affect the quantity of reserve balances. For example, Treasury spending will increase bank reserve balances while tax receipts will lower reserve balances. Normally, increases or decreases to banking system reserves impact overnight interest rates. Consequently, the Treasury's debt operations are inseparable from the Fed's monetary policy operations related to setting and maintaining its target rate. Flows to/from the Treasury's account must be offset by other changes to the Fed's balance sheet if they are not consistent with the quantity of reserve balances required for the Fed to achieve its target rate on a given day. As such, the Treasury uses transfers to and from thousands of private bank deposit (both demand and time) accounts – usually called tax and loan accounts – for this purpose.

Prior to fall 2008, the Treasury would attempt to maintain its end-of-day account balance at the Fed at $5 billion on most days, achieving this through "calls" from tax and loan accounts to its account at the Fed (if the latter's balance were below $5 billion) or "adds" to the tax and loan accounts from the account at the Fed (if the latter were above $5 billion). (The global financial crisis and the Fed's response, especially "quantitative easing" has led to some rather abnormal situations that we will mostly ignore here.)

In other words, *timeliness* in the Treasury's debt operations requires consistency with both the Treasury's management of its own spending/revenue time sequences and the time sequences related to the Fed's management of its interest rate target. As such, under normal, "pre-global financial crisis" conditions for the Fed's operations in which its target rate was set above the rate paid on banks' reserve balances (which had been set at zero prior to October 2008, but is now set above zero as the Fed pays interest on reserves), there were six financial transactions required for the Treasury to engage in deficit spending.

The six transactions for Treasury debt operations for the purpose of deficit spending in the base case conditions are the following:

A. The Fed undertakes repurchase agreement operations with primary dealers (in which the Fed purchases Treasury securities from primary dealers with a promise to buy them back on a specific date) to ensure sufficient reserve balances are circulating for settlement of the Treasury's auction (which will debit reserve balances in bank accounts as the Treasury's account is credited) while also achieving the Fed's target rate. It is well known that settlement of Treasury auctions are "high payment flow days" that necessitate a larger quantity of reserve balances circulating than other days, and the Fed accommodates the demand.

B. The Treasury's auction settles as Treasury securities are exchanged for reserve balances, so bank reserve accounts are debited to credit the Treasury's account, and dealer accounts at banks are debited.

C. The Treasury adds balances credited to its account from the auction settlement to tax and loan accounts. This credits the reserve accounts of the banks holding the credited tax and loan accounts.

D. (Transactions D and E are interchangeable; that is, in practice, transaction E might occur before transaction D.) The Fed's repurchase agreement is reversed, as the second leg of the repurchase agreement occurs in which a primary dealer purchases Treasury securities back from the Fed. Transactions in A above are reversed.

E. Prior to spending, the Treasury calls in balances from its tax and loan accounts at banks. This reverses the transactions in C.

F. The Treasury deficit spends by debiting its account at the Fed, resulting in a credit to bank reserve accounts at the Fed and the bank accounts of spending recipients.

The analysis is much the same in the case of a deficit created by a tax cut instead of an increase in spending. That is, with a tax cut the Treasury's spending is greater than revenues just as it is with proactive deficit spending.

Note also that the end result is exactly as stated above using the example of a consolidated government (treasury and central bank): government deficit spending leads to a credit to someone's bank account and a credit of reserves to a bank which are then exchanged for a treasury to extinguish the excess reserves. However, with the procedures actually adopted, the transactions are more complex and the sequencing is different. But the final balance sheet position is the same: the government has the bomb, and the private sector has a treasury.

The implications of this for understanding the "self-imposed constraint" described above are highly significant. Recognize that only reserve balances can settle Treasury auctions via Fedwire. Note, though, that the only sources of reserve balances over time (that is, aside from various short-term effects from autonomous changes to the Fed's balance sheet) are loans from the Fed or the Fed's purchases of financial assets either outright or in repurchase agreements. Further, the Fed normally purchases Treasury securities or requires Treasury securities as collateral for repurchase agreements. (In the aftermath of the global crisis, the Fed has engaged in highly unusual purchases of a wider variety of assets, and has lent against various kinds of assets.) Since existing Treasury securities were issued as a result of a previous government budget deficit, it is the case that the reserve balances required to purchase Treasury securities are the result of a previous government deficit or a loan from the Fed to the nongovernment sector. This is true even though the Treasury must have a positive balance in its account before it can spend, and even though the Fed is legally prohibited from providing the Treasury with overdrafts in its account.

Finally, note that:

1. If interest is paid on reserve balances at the Fed's target rate and substantial excess reserve balances are left circulating – as was the case after the crisis when the Fed engaged in several phases of "quantitative easing" – the analysis is unchanged. While the Fed would not have to actively engage in operations specifically related to Treasury auctions for the purpose of achieving and maintaining its target rate, the reserve balances already circulating were created via Fed lending to the private sector (or purchases of private sector securities) or previous deficits.

2. Overall, adding the rule that the Treasury must finance its operations in the open market to the need to achieve timeliness in the Fed's operations results in the six transactions described above for the Treasury's debt operations. The added complexity in the Treasury's operations that results is unnecessary since it does not change the facts that (1) reserve balances must be provided via previous deficits or Fed loans to the private sector in order for Treasury auctions to settle, and (2) deficits accompanied by new issues of Treasury securities do not result in fewer deposits circulating than without such security issuance. Further, the rule itself and the added complexity can be counterproductive if they influence policymakers' decisions regarding options available in times of macroeconomic difficulty.

In sum: even after adding the self-imposed constraints and going through the minute details of Fed–Treasury operations, we find that the basic claims made in the much simplified model hold. Government deficit spending adds to the bank deposits of the recipient. Initially, bank reserves are created, but excess reserves are (normally) exchanged for Treasuries. Net financial assets held in the private sector are increased by the amount of the deficit (bank deposits held are equal to bank deposits owed by banks, so the net financial assets are equal to the Treasuries held by banks, plus any additional reserves or cash retained). (See also Chapter 6 for discussion of the debt limit debate – another self-imposed constraint.)

Box: Frequently asked questions

Q: *My understanding of domestic government budget surpluses is that they merely destroy the dollars that earlier government spending created. Isn't it meaningless to suggest that a sovereign government "saves" its own fiat currency?*

A: In practical terms, yes. In the United States during the Clinton boom there was a projection that all outstanding US Treasury debt would be retired. This led to a mad rush at the Fed to figure out how the federal government could continue to run surpluses if there were no government IOUs out there to "destroy". If we ever did get to that point, the only way the private sector could continue to run deficits against the government would be to surrender assets (rather than government IOUs) in payment. You'd have to turn over your car, house, bank account, and children to the government to pay taxes! That is the logical result of a government surplus carried to infinity: government would accumulate infinite claims on the private sector. And, yes, you are correct that sovereign government does not – cannot – "save" its own currency!

4
Fiscal Operations in a Nation That Issues Its Own Currency

In this chapter we will begin to examine our next topic: government spending, taxing, interest rate setting, and bond issue – that is, we will examine fiscal policy for a government that issues its own currency. Note that it is not possible to completely separate fiscal policy from monetary policy, especially in the area of the issue of treasury debt. We will therefore include in this chapter interest-targeting operations by the central bank.

We will bear in mind that the exchange rate regime chosen does have implications for the operation of domestic policy. We will distinguish between operational procedures and constraints that apply to all currency-issuing governments and those that apply only to governments that allow their currency to float. Over the previous discussion we have touched on much of this, but now it is time to get down to "brass tacks", to look at some of the nitty-gritty. As always, we are trying to stay true to the purposes of a "Primer": a fairly general analysis that can be applied to all nations that issue their own currency. We will note where the results only apply to specific exchange rate regimes. And we will get into some of the procedures adopted that effectively "tie shoelaces together": self-imposed constraints. In Chapter 5 we explore in more detail the implications of alternative exchange rate regimes.

4.1 Introductory principles

Statements that do not apply to a currency issuer

Let us begin with some common beliefs that actually are false, that is to say, the following statements do NOT apply to a sovereign currency-issuing government.

- Governments have a budget constraint (like households and firms) and have to raise funds through taxing or borrowing
- Budget deficits are evil, a burden on the economy except under some special circumstances (such as a deep recession)
- Government deficits drive interest rates up, crowd out the private sector and lead to inflation
- Government deficits take away savings that could be used for investment
- Government deficits leave debt for future generations; government needs to cut spending or tax more today to diminish this burden
- Higher government deficits today imply higher taxes tomorrow, to pay interest and principle on the debt that results from deficits

While these statements are consistent with the conventional wisdom, and while several of them are more-or-less accurate if applied to the case of a government that does not issue its own currency, they do not apply to a currency issuer.

Principles that apply to a currency issuer

Let us replace these false statements with propositions that are true of any currency-issuing government, even one that operates with a fixed exchange rate regime.

- The government names a unit of account and issues a currency denominated in that unit;
- the government ensures a demand for its currency by imposing a tax liability that can be fulfilled by payment of its currency;
- government spends by crediting bank reserves and taxes by debiting bank reserves;
- in this manner, banks act as intermediaries between government and the nongovernment sector, crediting depositors' accounts as government spends and debiting them when taxes are paid;
- government deficits mean net credits to banking system reserves and also to deposits at banks;
- the central bank sets the overnight interest rate target; it adds/drains reserves as needed to hit its target rate;

- the overnight interest rate target is "exogenous", set by the central bank; but the quantity of reserves is "endogenous", determined by the needs and desires of private banks;
- the "deposit multiplier" is simply an ex post ratio of reserves to deposits – it is best to think of deposits as expanding endogenously as they "leverage" reserves, but with no predetermined leverage ratio;
- the treasury coordinates operations with the central bank to ensure its checks don't bounce and that fiscal operations do not move the overnight interest rate away from the target;
- the treasury cooperates with the central bank, providing new bond issues to drain excess reserves, or with the central bank buying treasuries when banks are short of reserves;
- for this reason, bond sales are not a borrowing operation (in the usual sense of the term) used by the sovereign government, instead they are a tool that helps the central bank to hit interest rate targets;
- and the treasury can always "afford" anything for sale in its own currency, although government always imposes constraints on its spending.

Some of these statements will seem cryptic at this point, although many have already been covered. We will clarify further in the following sections. Here we are setting out the general principles that will be discussed later in order to contrast them with the "conventional wisdom" that likens a government's budget to a household budget.

Let us be careful to acknowledge that these principles do not imply that government *ought to* spend without constraint. Nor does the statement that government can "afford" anything for sale in its own currency imply that government *should* buy everything for sale in its currency. And if things are for sale only in a foreign currency, then government cannot buy them directly using its own currency, so "affordability" concerns do apply in such a case.

These principles also do not deny that too much spending by government would be inflationary. Further, there can be exchange rate implications: if government spends too much, or if it sets its interest rate target too low, this might set off pressure to depreciate the currency. This means that the government's interest-setting policy as well as its budget policy will be mindful of possible impacts on exchange rates and/or inflation rates; in that sense, interest-rate-setting and fiscal policy are "constrained" by government's desire to influence the exchange rate or the inflation rate.

This brings us to the exchange rate regime: while the principles above do apply to governments that peg their exchange rates, they must operate fiscal and monetary policy with a view to maintaining the peg. For this reason, while these governments can "afford" to spend more, they might choose to spend less to protect their exchange rates. And while government can "exogenously" lower its interest rate target, this might conflict with its exchange rate target. For that reason, it might choose to keep its interest rate target high if it is pegging its exchange rate.

In the next section we will begin to examine in more detail the government's budget when it is the issuer of the currency.

Box: Frequently asked questions

Q: Don't you pay taxes with demand deposits?

A: You write a check to the tax collection agency (in the Treasury; in the United States it is the Internal Revenue Service) but your bank pays the taxes for you using reserves, since the agency sends the check on to the central bank, which debits the bank's reserves (and increases the treasury's deposit).

Q: Why does government need to borrow its own IOUs and pay interest? And why pay interest on "fiat money"?

A: Good questions! Government cannot really borrow its own IOUs. Neither can you! If you give an IOU to your neighbor for a cup of borrowed sugar, you do not go back and ask if you can borrow it. That would be a senseless operation.

As we'll see, government offers treasuries as a higher interest paying IOU, exchanged for reserves. At your bank, you can exchange your demand deposit for a saving deposit on which you earn higher interest. That is really all that a government bond sale is: a substitution of a demand deposit at the central bank for a time deposit; the first is a liability of the central bank; the second is a liability of the treasury.

Note that cash ("fiat money") does not pay interest. A loan shark might lend you cash at 140 percent interest. Why? You are desperate. He gets compensated for the risk that you will run with the money. Of course there is a substantial penalty for nonpayment (he sends his goons with clubs). But why would the treasury pay interest on its bonds, and why would the central bank pay interest on reserves? There is no need to do that. We'd accept cash and banks would accept reserves without interest; there is no default risk (on sovereign government IOUs on a floating exchange rate), and we need them to pay taxes. As we know from earlier discussion, government doesn't sell treasuries to "borrow" its own currency. But it is nice to get interest, isn't it? Think of it as a government transfer payment, a form of charity. It might be a bad idea, but it is common practice – a topic for later.

4.2   Effects of sovereign government budget deficits on saving, reserves, and interest rates

Let us now begin to examine in more detail the government's budget and impacts on the nongovernment sector. In this section we will look at the relation between budget deficits and saving, and the effects of budget deficits on bank reserves and interest rates. The discussion that follows is of a general nature; we will examine operational constraints and other details later.

Budget deficits and saving

Recall from earlier discussions in the Primer that it is the deficit spending of one sector that generates the surplus (or saving) of the other; this is because the entities of the deficit sector can in some sense decide to spend more than their incomes, while the surplus entities can decide to spend less than their incomes only if those incomes are actually generated. In Keynesian terms this is simply another version of the twin statements that "spending generates income" and "investment generates saving". Here, however, the statement is that the government sector's deficit spending generates the nongovernment sector's surplus (or saving).

Obviously this reverses the orthodox (conventional wisdom) causal sequence because the government's deficit "finances" the nongovernment's saving in the sense that the deficit spending by government provides the income that allows the nongovernment sector to run a surplus. Looking to the stocks, it is the government's issue of IOUs that allows the nongovernment to accumulate financial claims on government.

While this seems mysterious, the financial processes are not hard to understand. Government spends (purchasing goods and services or making "transfer" payments such as Social Security and welfare) by crediting bank accounts of recipients; this also leads to a credit to their bank's reserves at the central bank. Government taxes by debiting taxpayer accounts (and the central bank debits reserves of their banks). Deficits over a period (say, a year) mean that more bank accounts have been credited than debited. The nongovernment sector realizes its surplus initially in the form of these net credits to bank accounts.

All of this analysis is reversed in the case of a government surplus: the government surplus means the nongovernment sector runs a deficit, with net debits of bank accounts (and of reserves). The destruction (net debiting) of nongovernment sector net financial assets of course equals the government's budget surplus.

Effects of budget deficits on reserves and interest rates

Budget deficits initially increase bank reserves by the same amount. This is because treasury spending leads to a simultaneous credit to the bank deposit account of the recipient and to that bank's reserve account at the central bank.

Let us first examine a system like the one that existed in the United States until recently, in which the central bank does not pay interest on reserves. Deficit spending that creates bank reserves will (eventually) lead to excess reserves: banks will hold more reserves than desired. Their immediate response will be to offer to lend reserves in the overnight interbank lending market (called the fed funds market in the United States).

If the banking system as a whole has excess reserves, the offers to lend reserves will not be met at the going overnight interbank lending rate (often called the bank rate, but in the United States this is called the fed funds rate). Hence the banks with excess reserve positions will offer to lend at ever-lower interest rates. This drives the actual "market" rate below the central bank's target rate for overnight funds.

Once the rate has fallen sufficiently far away from the target, the central bank will intervene to remove the excess reserves. Since the demand for reserves is fairly interest-inelastic, lowering the offered lending rate will not increase the quantity of reserves demanded by very much. In other words, it is difficult to eliminate a position of system-wide excess reserves by lowering the overnight rate. Instead, the central bank must remove them.

The way that it does this is by selling from its stock of treasury bonds. That is called an open market sale (OMS). An OMS leads to a substitution of bonds for excess reserves: the central bank's liabilities (reserves) are debited, and the purchasing bank's reserves are also debited. At the same time, the central bank's holding of treasuries is debited and the bank's assets are increased by the amount of treasuries purchased.

Since the bank's reserves decline by the same amount that its holdings of treasuries are increased, this is effectively just a substitution of assets. However, it now holds a claim on the treasury (bonds) instead of a claim on the central bank (reserves); and the central bank holds fewer assets (bonds) but owes fewer liabilities (reserves). The bank is happy because it now receives interest on the bonds.

It is easy to see that the same process would be triggered even if the central bank paid interest on reserves, as is now done in the United States and has been done for a long time in Canada. Once banks have accumulated all the reserves they want, they will try to substitute for higher-earning treasuries. They will not push the overnight rate below the central bank's "support rate" (what it pays on reserves) since no bank would lend to another at a rate below what it can receive from the central bank. Instead banks with undesired reserves will immediately go into the treasuries market to seek a higher return.

The impact, then, will be to push rates on treasuries down. In this second case, the central bank need not do anything; it does not need to sell bonds since it maintains its overnight interest rate by paying interest on reserves.

In practice, a central bank that adopts this second procedure usually pays a slightly lower rate on reserves than it charges to lend reserves. For example, in the United States and Canada today the central bank lends "at the discount window" and at the "discount rate" (other terms are also used, such as bank rate or overnight rate).

It might charge 25 basis points (0.25 percentage points) more on its lending than it pays on reserves. For example, it might charge 2 percent on loans and pay 1.75 percent on reserves at the central bank. The "market" interest rate on interbank lending (in the United States, called the fed funds rate) will remain approximately within that band since a bank needing reserves has the option of borrowing at the central bank at 2 percent, while a bank having extra reserves can earn 1.75 percent simply by holding them at the central bank.

Complications and private preferences

There are often two objections to the claim that government spending effectively takes place by simultaneously crediting the recipient's bank account as well as the bank's reserves: a) it must be more complicated than this; and b) what if the private sector's spending and portfolio preferences do not match the government's budget outcome? In this section we will deal with the first question: it must be more complicated. In the next section we will deal with the second in more detail.

The first of these objections has been carefully dealt with in a long series of published articles and working papers (by Bell [a.k.a. Kelton]; Bell and Wray; Wray, Fullwiler, and Rezende who look at actual operating procedures in the United States, Canada, and Brazil; see Section 3.6 for details, references, and links). In practice, the treasury typically cannot directly credit bank accounts when it wants to spend since banks do not hold accounts at the treasury.

Rather, a complex series of steps is required that involve the treasury, the central bank, and private banks each time the treasury spends or taxes. The central bank and the treasury develop such procedures to ensure that government is able to spend, that taxpayer payments to treasury do not lead to bounced checks, and – most importantly – that undesired effects on banking system reserves do not occur. While the end result is exactly as described above (treasury spending leads to bank credits, taxes lead to debits, and budget deficits mean net credits to both demand deposits and bank reserves), it is more complicated. (Readers who want the details can return to Section 3.6.)

This often generates another sub-question: what if the central bank refused to cooperate with the treasury? The answer is that the central bank would miss its overnight interest rate target (and eventually would endanger the payments system because checks would start bouncing). Readers are referred to the substantial literature surrounding the coordination and to Section 3.6. Nonspecialists can be assured that the simple explanation above is sufficient: the conclusion from close analysis is that government deficits do lead to net credits to reserves, and if undesired excess reserves are created they are drained through bond sales to maintain the central bank's target interest rate.

The operational impact of bond sales is to substitute government bonds for reserves; it is like providing banks with a savings account at the central bank (government bonds) instead of a checking account (central bank reserves). This is done to relieve downward pressure on the overnight interest rate.

With regard to the second objection, we first must notice that if the government's fiscal stance is not consistent with the desired saving of the nongovernment sector, then spending and income adjust until the fiscal outcome and the nongovernment sector's balance are consistent. For example, if the government tried to run a deficit larger than the desired surplus of the nongovernment sector, then some combination of higher spending by the nongovernment sector (lower nongovernment saving and lower budget deficit), greater tax receipts (thus lower budget deficit and lower saving), or higher nongovernment sector income (so greater desired saving equal to the higher deficit) is produced.

Since tax revenues (and some government spending) are endogenously determined by the performance of the economy, the fiscal stance is at least partially determined endogenously; by the same token, the actual balance achieved by the nongovernment sector is endogenously determined by income and saving propensities. By accounting identity (the three sectors balance was presented earlier) it is not possible for the nongovernment's balance to differ from the government's balance (with the sign reversed: one has a deficit and the other a surplus); this also means it is impossible for the aggregate saving of the nongovernment sector to be less than (or greater than) the budget deficit.

In the next section we look in more detail at the private saving decision so that we can finish our answer the second objection.

Box: Frequently asked questions

Q: *The central bank sets the overnight interest rate but what about other interest rates? What if markets react against budget deficits, so the bond market "vigilantes" demand higher rates?*

A: As discussed, the central bank can set the overnight rate, plus the rate on any other financial assets it stands ready to buy and sell. It can peg the 10-year government bond rate, or the 30-year bond rate. In the United States, the Fed actually did that in World War II. But now the Fed usually does not do that. Even under Quantitative Easing (which was supposed to lower longer term interest rates) the Fed used a rather roundabout method to try to bring down long rates on Treasuries. It tried to use quantities rather than prices to hit a price target! That is, it would announce how much it would spend buying Treasuries, hoping that would lower rates sufficiently; a much more efficient method would have been to announce it was going to buy a sufficient quantity to lower the rate on long-term Treasuries to its target (and then stand ready to buy as many as necessary).

Any rates the Fed does not target are set complexly; some more complexly than others. In the United States, policy used to set the saving and demand deposit rates. (This was called Regulation Q, which imposed a zero interest rate on demand deposits and a 5.25 or 5.5 percent maximum rate on savings deposits, depending on type of institution.) US policy also set some loan rates. Leaving to the side government-managed interest rates, others are set by a complex of factors: markups and markdowns over the regulated rates, credit and liquidity risks, expectations of central bank policy, expected exchange rate movements, and so on. Interest rate theory is too complicated to discuss in more detail here. Bond vigilantes? Don't sell them the bonds if they demand higher rates than government wants to pay. Sovereign government *never* needs to sell bonds, as it can just leave the reserves in the banks instead. The central bank can pay zero interest on reserves, or whatever support rate it chooses. That actually was J. M. Keynes's recommendation, which he called "euthanasia of the rentier".

Q: *What if the budget deficit is too low to satisfy net financial saving desires by the private (and foreign) sectors?*

A: In that case, the private (and/or foreign) sector reduces spending (trying to raise saving), causing the budget deficit to widen.

Now, to be clear, causation is complex. There can be many slips between lip and cup. As private sector spending falls, its income falls (sales fall, people get laid off) and that could either intensify the desire to save, or reduce it as people must dip into saving to avoid starvation. But we do know that the identity must hold, so when all is said and done it will be true that the government deficit will equal the sum of the private sector balance and the external sector balance. All three of these balances are to some extent endogenously determined; each one can adjust. We only know for sure that after adjustments, their identity holds.

4.3   Government budget deficits and the "two-step" process of saving

In the previous section we have shown that government budget deficits take the form of net credits to bank reserves at the central bank and as well to the deposit accounts of those who receive net government spending. Normally this leads to excess reserves that are drained through the offer of government bonds, sold either by the central bank or by the treasury. Hence budget deficits normally result in net positive acquisition of treasuries. But even if they do not, the nongovernment sector ends up with net saving in the form of claims on government.

To put it as simply as possible: government deficit spending creates nongovernment sector saving in the form of domestic currency (cash, reserves, and treasuries). This is because government deficits necessarily mean the government has credited more accounts through its spending than it debited through its taxes.

We need to make clear that we are talking about net saving in the domestic currency. The domestic nongovernment sector can also net save in foreign currency assets. And some members of the nongovernment sector can save in the form of claims on other members of the domestic nongovernment sector, but that all nets to zero (as we said, that is "inside wealth").

Let us return to the two objections raised in the previous section to our claim that government spending effectively takes place by simultaneously crediting the recipient's bank account as well as the bank's reserves: a) it must be more complicated than this; and b) what if the private sector's spending and portfolio preferences do not match the government's budget outcome? In the previous section as well as in Section 3.6 we dealt with the first. Now it is time to respond to the second.

As argued above, the nongovernment savings in the domestic currency cannot preexist the budget deficit, so we should not imagine that a government that deficit spends must first approach the nongovernment sector to borrow its savings. Rather, we should recognize that government spending conceptually comes first; it is accomplished by credits to bank accounts. Further, we recognize that both the resulting budget deficit as well as the nongovernment's savings of net financial assets (budget surplus) are in this sense residuals and are equal.

More generally, as Keynes argued, saving is actually a two-step process: given income, how much will be saved; and then given saving, in what form will it be held. Thus many who proffer the second objection – that nongovernment portfolio preferences can deviate from government spending plans – have in mind the portfolio preferences (that is, the second step) of the nongovernment sector. How can we be sure that the budget deficit that generates accumulation of claims on government will be consistent with portfolio preferences, even if the final saving position of the nongovernment sector is consistent with saving desires? The answer is that interest rates (and thus asset prices) adjust to ensure that the nongovernment sector is happy to hold its saving in the existing set of assets. Here we must turn to the role played by government interest-earning debt ("treasuries", or bills and bonds) to gain an understanding.

For the purposes of this discussion, we can assume that anyone who sold goods and services to government did so voluntarily (no "forced" sales); we can also assume that any recipient of a government "transfer" payment (such as Social Security) was happy to receive the deposit. Recipients of government spending then can hold receipts in the form of a bank deposit, can withdraw cash, or can use the deposit to spend on goods, services, or assets.

In the first case, no further portfolio changes by the saver occur. In the second case, bank reserves and deposit liabilities are reduced by the same amount (this can generate further actions if it reduces aggregate banking system reserves below desired or required levels, but bank desires are always accommodated by the central bank to the extent that attempts by banks to adjust reserve holdings cause the targeted interest rate to move away from the target). In the third case, the deposits shift to the sellers (of goods, services, or assets). Only cash withdrawals or repayment of loans can reduce the quantity of bank deposits – otherwise only the names of the account holders change.

Still, these processes can affect prices – of goods, services, and, most importantly, of assets. If deposits and reserves created by government deficit spending are greater than desired at the aggregate level, then the "shifting of pockets" bids up prices of goods and services and asset prices, lowering interest rates. The attempt by the nongovernment sector to shift out of bank deposits will stop once the prices of goods, services, and assets adjust sufficiently so that all the deposits are willingly held.

Modern central banks operate with an overnight interest rate target, so if overnight rates are moved away from the target, the central bank responds. For example, when excess reserves cause banks to bid the actual overnight rate below the target, this triggers an open market sale of government bonds that drains excess reserves.

Remember that reserves are on the asset side of the bank's balance sheet while deposits are on the liability side. When government makes a payment, both sides go up – the bank's reserves at the central bank are credited, and the recipient's demand deposit is credited. Most of those additional reserves will be excess reserves (details on this are complicated as reserve requirements are calculated after a lag, but let us ignore those details for now). Banks make a portfolio decision: let's buy something that earns a higher interest rate. First they can lend reserves in the overnight market, pushing that rate down. Next they can buy a close substitute, treasuries (government bonds), and then diversify into other assets. (Note: unless they buy treasuries from the treasury or central bank, this simply shifts reserves among banks but does not reduce aggregate reserves.) Since central banks target an interest rate (i.e. the fed funds rate in the United States) they will react once the interest rate falls below the target. They will begin to sell treasuries. That eliminates the excess reserves and the downward pressure on interest rates. (As discussed earlier, we modify this if the target interest rate is zero, or if the central bank pays a support rate below which excess reserves cannot push market rates.)

So the answer to the second objection about inconsistency of portfolio preferences is really quite simple: asset prices/interest rates adjust to ensure that the nongovernment's portfolio preferences are aligned with the quantity of reserves and deposits that result from government spending, and if the central bank does not want short-term interest rates to move away from its target, it intervenes in the open market. (Note: asset prices and interest rates move in opposite directions. As the price of a bond goes up, its yield – interest rate – goes down. If banks have excess reserves, they bid up bond prices as they try to get a better return than the rate paid on reserves and that lowers the effective yield on bonds. An open market sale of bonds by the central bank stops bond prices from rising and rates from falling.)

It is best to think of the net saving of the nongovernment sector as a consequence of the government's deficit spending, which creates income and savings. These savings cannot preexist the deficits, since the net credits by government create the savings. Hence the savings do not really "finance" the deficits, but rather the deficits create an equal amount of savings. Still, as emphasized throughout this Primer, it takes two to tango and the adjustment processes can be complex.

Finally, the fear that government might "print money" if the supply of finance proves insufficient is exposed as unwarranted. All government spending generates credits to private bank accounts, which could be counted as an increase of the money supply (initially, deposits and reserves go up by an amount equal to the government's spending). However, the portfolio preferences of the nongovernment sector will determine how many of the created reserves will be transformed into bonds, and incremental taxes paid will determine how many of the created reserves and deposits will be destroyed.

Bond sales provide an interest-earning alternative to reserves

We can say that short-term treasury bonds are an interest-earning alternative to bank reserves (as discussed earlier, reserves at the central bank often do not pay any interest; if they do pay interest, then government bonds are a higher-earning substitute). When they are sold either by the central bank (open-market operations) or by the treasury (new issues market), the effect is the same: reserves are exchanged for treasuries. This is to allow the central bank to hit its overnight interest rate target, thus whether the bond sales are by the central bank or the treasury they should be thought of as a monetary policy operation.

Reserves are nondiscretionary from the point of view of the government. (In the literature, this is called the "accommodationist" or "horizontalist" position.) If the banking system has excess reserves, the overnight interbank lending rate falls below the target (so long as that is above any support rate paid on reserves), triggering bond sales; if the banking system is short, the market rate rises above target, triggering bond purchases. The only thing that is added here is the recognition that no distinction should be made between the central bank and the treasury on this score; the effect of bond sales/purchases is the same.

There is a surprising result, however. Since a government budget deficit leads to net credits to bank deposits and to bank reserves, it will likely generate an excess reserve position for banks. If nothing is done, banks will bid down the overnight rate. In other words, the initial impact of a budget deficit is to lower (not raise) interest rates. Bonds are then sold by the central bank and the treasury to offer an interest-earning alternative to excess reserves. This is to prevent the interest rate from falling below target. If the central bank pays a support rate on reserves (pays interest on reserve deposits held by banks), then budget deficits tend to lead banks gaining reserves to bid up prices on treasuries (as they try to substitute into higher interest bonds instead of reserves), lowering their interest rates. This is precisely the opposite of what many believe: budget deficits push interest rates down (not up), all else equal.

Central bank accommodates demand for reserves

Also following from this perspective is the recognition that the central bank cannot "pump liquidity" into the system if that is defined as providing reserves in excess of banking system desires. The central bank cannot encourage/discourage bank lending by providing/denying reserves. Rather, it accommodates the banking system, providing the amount of reserves desired. Only the interest rate target is discretionary, not the quantity of reserves.

If the central bank "pumps" excess reserves into the banking system and leaves them there, the overnight interest rate will fall toward zero (or toward the central bank's support rate if it pays interest on reserves). This is what happened in Japan for more than a decade after its financial crisis, and what happened in the United States when the Fed adopted "quantitative easing" in the aftermath of the financial crisis that began in 2007. In the United States, so long as the Fed pays a small positive interest rate on reserves (for example, 25 basis points), then the "market" (fed funds rate) will remain close to that rate if there are excess reserves.

Central banks now operate with an explicit interest rate target – although many of them allow the overnight rate to deviate within a band – and intervene when the market rate deviates from the target by more than what the central bank is willing to tolerate. In other words, modern central banks operate with a price rule (target interest rate), not a quantity rule (reserves or monetary aggregates).

In the financial crisis, bank demand for excess reserves grew considerably, and the US Fed learned to accommodate that demand. While some commentators were perplexed that Fed "pumping" of "liquidity" (the creation of massive excess reserves through quantitative easing) did not encourage bank lending, it has always been true that bank lending decisions are not restrained by (or even linked to) the quantity of reserves held.

Banks lend to creditworthy borrowers, creating deposits and holding the IOUs of the borrowers. If banks then need (or want) reserves, they go to the overnight interbank market or the central bank's discount window to obtain them. If the system as a whole is short, upward pressure on the overnight rate signals to the central bank that it needs to supply reserves through open market purchases.

Government deficits and global savings

Many analysts worry that financing of national government deficits requires a continual flow of global savings (in the case of the United States, especially Chinese savings to finance the persistent US government deficit); presumably, if these prove insufficient, it is believed, government would have to "print money" to finance its deficits, which is supposed to cause inflation. Worse, at some point in the future, government will find that it cannot service all the debt it has issued so that it will be forced to default.

For the moment, let us separate the issue of foreign savings from domestic savings. The question is whether national government deficits can exceed nongovernment savings in the domestic currency (domestic plus rest-of-world savings). From our analysis above, we see that this is not possible. First, a government deficit by accounting identity equals the nongovernment's surplus (or savings). Second, government spending in the domestic currency results in an equal credit to a bank account. Taxes then lead to bank account debits, so that the government deficit exactly equals net credits to bank accounts. As discussed, portfolio balance preferences then determine whether the government (central bank or treasury) will sell bonds to drain reserves. These net credits (equal to the increase of cash, reserves, and bonds) are identically equal to net accumulation of financial assets denominated in the domestic currency and held in the nongovernment sector.

Those who claim that the US government must borrow Dollars from thrifty Chinese don't understand basic accounting. The Chinese do not issue Dollars – the United States does. Every Dollar the Chinese "lend" to the United States came from the United States. In reality, the Chinese receive Dollars (reserve credits at the Fed) from their export sales to the United States (mostly), then they adjust their portfolios as they buy higher-earning Dollar assets (mostly Treasuries). The US government *never* borrows from the Chinese to *"finance"* its budget deficit. Actually, the US current account deficit provides Dollar claims to the Chinese, and the US budget deficit ensures these are in the form of "currency" (broadly defined to include cash, reserves, and Treasuries).

We conclude: since government deficits create an equivalent amount of nongovernment savings it is impossible for the government to face an insufficient supply of savings.

We'll look at foreign bond holding in more detail in the next section.

4.4 What if foreigners hold government bonds?

Previously we have shown that government deficits lead to an equivalent amount of nongovernment savings. The nongovernment savings created will be held as claims on government. Normally, the nongovernment sector prefers to hold some of that savings in government IOUs that promise interest, rather than in nonearning IOUs like cash. Further, we have shown that budget deficits create an equivalent amount of reserves. And banks prefer to hold higher-earning assets than reserves that pay almost nothing (until recently, they paid zero in the United States). Hence both savers as well as banks would rather have government bonds. We thus find that in normal times, government will offer interest-earning bonds in an amount almost equal to its deficits (the difference is made up by bank accumulation of reserves and private sector accumulation of currency).

However, when government deficit spends, some of the claims on government will end up in the hands of foreigners. Does this matter? Yes, according to many. At one extreme we have many commentators worrying that the US government might run deficits but will find that the Chinese desire to "lend to" the US government is insufficient to absorb bond issues. Others argue that while Japan can run up government debt-to-GDP ratios equal to 200 percent of GDP this is only because more than 90 percent of all that debt is held domestically. The United States, it is said, cannot run up debts that great because so much of its "borrowing" is from foreigners, who might "go on strike". Others worry about the ability of the US government (for example) to pay interest to foreigners. And what if foreigners demand more interest? And what about effects on exchange rates? We now begin to look at such issues.

Foreign holdings of government debt

Government deficit spending creates equivalent nongovernment savings (dollar for dollar and yen for yen). However, some of the savings created will accumulate in the hands of foreigners, since they can also accumulate the government's domestic currency-denominated debt.

In addition to actually holding the currency including both cash and reserves (indeed, it is likely that foreigners hold most US Dollar-denominated paper currency), they can also hold government bonds. These usually just take the form of an electronic entry on the books of the central bank of the issuing government. Interest is paid on these "bonds" in the same manner, whether they are held by foreigners or by domestic residents, simply through a "keystroke" electronic entry that adds to the nominal value of the "bond" (itself an electronic entry). The foreign-holder portfolio preferences will determine whether they hold bonds or reserves, with higher interest on the bonds. As discussed in previous sections, shifting from reserves to bonds is done electronically, and is much like a transfer from a "checking account" (reserves) to a "savings account" (bonds).

There is a common belief that it makes a great deal of difference whether these electronic entries on the books of the central bank are owned by domestic residents versus foreigners. The reasoning is that domestic residents are far less likely to desire to shift to assets denominated in other currencies. Further, interest payments to residents increase domestic income and thus government tax revenue supposedly making it easier to service debt.

Let us presume that for some reason foreign holders of a government's debt decide to shift to debt denominated in some other currency. In that case, they either let the bond mature (refusing to roll over into another instrument) or they sell it. The fear is that this could have interest rate and exchange rate effects: as debt matures government might have to issue new debt at a higher interest rate, and selling pressure could cause the exchange rate to depreciate. Let us look at these two possibilities separately.

a) Interest rate pressure. Let us presume that sizable amounts of a government's bonds are held externally, by foreigners. Assume foreigners decide they would rather hold reserves than bonds – perhaps because they are not happy with the low interest rate paid on bonds. Can they pressure the government to raise the interest rate it pays on bonds?

A shift of portfolio preferences by foreigners against this government's bonds reduces foreign purchases. It would appear that only higher interest rates promised by the government could restore foreign demand.

However, recall from previous discussions that bonds are sold to offer an interest-earning alternative to reserves that pay little or no interest. Foreigners and domestic residents buy government bonds when they are more attractive than reserves. Refusing to "roll over" maturing bonds simply means that banks taken globally will have more reserves (credits at the issuing government's central bank) and less bonds. Selling bonds that have not yet matured simply shifts reserves about – from the buyer to the seller.

Neither of these activities will force the hand of the issuing government; there is no pressure on it to offer higher interest rates to try to find buyers of its bonds. From the perspective of government, it is perfectly sensible to let banks hold more reserves while issuing fewer bonds.

Or it could offer higher interest rates to sell more bonds (even though there is no need to do so) but this means that keystrokes are used to credit more interest to the bond holders. Government can always "afford" larger keystrokes, but markets cannot force the government's hand because it can simply stop selling bonds and thereby let markets accumulate reserves instead.

b) Exchange rate pressure. The more important issue concerns the case where foreigners decide they do not want to hold either reserves or bonds denominated in some currency.

When foreign holders decide to sell off the government's bonds, they must find willing buyers. Assuming they wish to switch currencies, they must find holders of other currency-denominated reserve credits willing to exchange these for the bonds offered for sale. It is possible that the potential buyers will purchase bonds only at a lower exchange rate (measured as the value of the currency of the government bonds that are offered for sale relative to the currency desired by the sellers).

For this reason it is true that foreign sales of a government's debt can affect the exchange rate. However, so long as a government is willing to let its exchange rate "float" it need not react to prevent a depreciation.

We conclude that shifting portfolio preferences of foreign holders can indeed lead to a currency depreciation. But so long as the currency is floating, the government does not have to take further action if this happens.

Current accounts and foreign accumulation of claims

Just how do foreigners get hold of reserves and bonds denominated in a government's domestic currency?

As we have shown in previous pages, our macroeconomic sectoral balance ensures that if the domestic private sector balance is zero, then a government budget deficit equals a current account deficit. That current account deficit will lead to foreign net accumulation of financial assets in the form of the government's debt. This is why, for example, the US government typically runs deficits and issues government debt that is accumulated in China and elsewhere.

Of course, in the case of the United States, for many years (during the Bill Clinton and George W. Bush presidencies) the domestic private sector was also running budget deficits, so foreigners also accumulated net claims on American households and firms. The US current account deficit guarantees – by accounting identity – that Dollar claims will be accumulated by foreigners.

After the crisis, the US domestic sector balanced its budget and actually started to run a surplus. However, the current account deficit remained. The US government budget deficit grew; by identity it was equal to the current account deficit plus the private sector surplus. Given that the US government became the only net source of new Dollar-denominated financial assets (the US private sector was running a surplus), foreigners must – by accounting identity – have accumulated US government debt.

Some fear – as discussed earlier – that suddenly the Chinese might decide to stop accumulating US government debt. But it must be recognized that we cannot simply change one piece of the accounting identity, and we cannot ignore the stock-flow consistency that follows from it.

For the rest of the world to stop accumulating Dollar-denominated assets, it must also stop running current account surpluses against the United States. Hence the other side of a Chinese decision to stop accumulating Dollars must be a decision to stop net exporting to the United States. It could happen, but the chances are remote.

Further, trying to run a current account surplus against the United States while avoiding the accumulation of Dollar-denominated assets would require that the Chinese offload the Dollars they earn by exporting to the United States, trading them for other currencies. That, of course, requires that they find buyers willing to take the Dollars. This could – as feared by many commentators – lead to a depreciation of the value of the Dollar. That in turn would expose the Chinese to a possible devaluation of the value of their US Dollar holdings – reserves plus Treasuries that total over $2 trillion.

Depreciation of the Dollar would also increase the dollar cost of their exports, imperiling their ability to continue to export to the United States. For these reasons, a sudden run by China out of the Dollar is quite unlikely. A slow transition into other currencies is a possibility, and more likely if China can find alternative markets for its exports.

Next we will look to the frequent claim that the United States is "special" – while it might be able to run persistent government deficits and trade deficits, other countries cannot.

Box: Frequently asked questions

Q: What about the Chinese or others buying US assets with the Dollars they have credited to their accounts? Couldn't they then control US firms, households, and government?

A: I recall the same arguments in the 1980s when the Japanese were "buying up" Hawaii and New York City. However, once they buy US assets they are subject to US laws. If US voters don't like what they are doing with "their" property, the voters change the laws. In any case, most of the "Chinese Dollars" are safely locked up at the Fed, either in the form of reserves or US Treasuries. The Chinese get no obvious control over the United States from that ownership except whatever advantages the United States decides to give to them.

Q: When foreign central banks purchase U.S. dollars, how does the accounting go from their perspective?

A: Typical case: a country (say, China) exports goods to the United States. Its exporters earn Dollars but need domestic currency, RMB (to pay workers, buy raw materials, service debt). Their bank credits their deposit account with RMB, and the central bank of China credits the bank's reserves in RMB. So the Dollar reserves end up at the Bank of China (an asset of the Bank of China, a liability of the Fed). The Bank of China knows its reserve deposits at the Fed earn no interest, so it buys US Treasuries. The Fed debits their reserves and credits the Bank of China with Treasuries. Impact in the United States: some US bank's reserves are debited; Bank of China's reserves are credited; no change of total reserves until the Bank of China buys Treasuries. At that point the reserves disappear, the Fed's liability to China is reduced, and the US Treasury's liability to China is increased. There is no necessary impact on the dollar/RMB exchange rate since the exports sold and imports bought were voluntary, and China only exported because she wanted Dollars (initially in the form of reserves, then exchanged for Treasuries). The next question always is: but what if China decides to run out of the Dollar and dumps Treasuries? OK, if that happened there could be depreciation pressure on the Dollar, in which case China loses since its Dollar assets decline in value relative to RMB. Fortunately, China does not want the Dollar to crash. It will not run out of Dollars in part because it wants the Dollar to hold its value so that Americans buy Chinese exports.

Q: To what extent do foreign countries other than China hold US Dollars as a way to protect their own currencies? If the Dollar were to be suddenly devalued for whatever reason, is there any other stable currency that could plausibly be used instead by countries that now use US Dollars to protect their own?

A: Yes, many nations hold Dollars to enable them to manage or peg their currencies. Holdings increased after the Asian Tigers' crisis, when nations came to realize they need an unassailable reserve to successfully peg. Does that increase demand for Dollars? Yes. Is there any alternative to the Dollar now? Not really. You can't get safe Euro debts in sufficient quantity – Euroland as a whole is a (small) net exporter. Besides, you need safe Euro-denominated Treasuries, and markets are wary of most Euro nations – and especially of the ones that are running budget deficits and trade deficits (which are the nations that are issuing lots of Euro debt). Germany is a net exporter and the model of fiscal rectitude, so it does not issue much Euro debt. What about China's RMB? Again, the supply is too low as she is a better Germany than Germany is – a big net exporter. Japanese Yen? As both China and Japan are exporters they create sufficient domestic saving to absorb their own government debt. TINA: there is no alternative to the Dollar, today. This will likely change, but not for some time.

Q: Can we confirm that the high rates of domestic saving in Japan are the result of large government deficits and little of this 'leaks' abroad due to their current account surpluses? And can we surmise from this that Japanese savings rates are largely determined BY the government deficits? Hence, it's the deficits that 'cause' the savings and not the savings that "allow" the deficits?

A: Exactly! Japanese government deficits + current account surpluses = large domestic savings. By identity, Yen for Yen. Indeed, the causation goes from spending to income to saving, or from injections to leakages, in the normal Keynesian way. Japan's "two lost decades" – slow growth – have generated very large budget deficits that are sufficient to prevent complete collapse of the economy as the budget deficit plus trade surplus satisfy the domestic net savings desires. To be sure, it always takes two to tango. By construction, the modern government budgetary outcome is accommodative: taxes fall and spending rises in a downturn. The downturn, in turn, can be thought of as resulting from inadequate aggregate demand which leads to a reluctance to spend. That in turn results from a preference for saving, especially in liquid form. Ergo: the private sector wants to net save in government IOUs, so it won't spend, generating a budget deficit to satisfy the saving desire. To be sure, causation is always complex but that is a rough and ready explanation. Japan has an inadequate safety net in conjunction with two decades of sluggish growth. That makes it perfectly rational to save, which generates low growth and hence a budget deficit. However, since the saving cannot occur unless the budget deficit occurs (and trade surplus) it makes sense to say the deficits allow the desired saving to be realized.

4.5 Currency solvency and the special case of the US Dollar

In previous sections we've been looking at sovereign government issues of bonds. We have argued that this is not really a "borrowing" operation, but rather bond issues offer a (higher) interest-earning alternative than do reserve deposits at the central bank. We also have argued that it makes little practical difference whether the government bonds are held domestically or by foreigners.

However, it is true that in a floating currency regime foreigners who hold reserves or government bonds could decide to "run" out of them, impacting the exchange rate. By the same token, countries that want to run net exports with, say, the United States, are interested in accumulating Dollar claims – often because their domestic demand is too low to absorb potential output and because they want to peg their currencies to the Dollar. For that reason, a "run" is unlikely.

This then leads to the objection that the US is surely a special case. Yes, it can run budget deficits that help to fuel current account deficits without worry about government or national insolvency precisely because the rest of the world wants Dollars. But surely that cannot be true of any other nation. Today the US Dollar is the international reserve currency, making the United States special. Let us examine this argument.

Isn't the United States special?

Yes and no. Accounting identities are identities; they are true for all nations. If a nation runs a current account deficit, by identity there must be a demand for its assets (real or financial) by someone. (A foreigner could either demand the nation's currency for "foreign direct investment" that includes buying property or plant and equipment, or the foreigner could demand financial assets denominated in that currency.) If that demand for assets declines, then the current account deficit must also decline.

There is little doubt that US Dollar-denominated assets are highly desirable around the globe; to a lesser degree, the financial assets denominated in UK Pounds, Japanese Yen, European Euros, and Canadian and Australian Dollars are also highly desired. Often assets denominated in these currencies are held in diversified portfolios of insurance and pension funds. This makes it easier for these nations to run current account deficits by issuing domestic-currency-denominated liabilities. They are thus "special", at least to varying degrees.

Many developing nations will not find a foreign demand for their domestic currency liabilities. Indeed, some nations could be so constrained that they must issue liabilities denominated in one of these more highly desired currencies in order to import. This can lead to many problems and constraints – for example, once such a nation has issued debt denominated in a foreign currency, it must earn or borrow foreign currency to service that debt. These problems are important and not easily resolved.

If there is no foreign demand for IOUs (government currency or bonds, as well as private financial assets) issued in the currency of a developing nation, then its foreign trade becomes something close to barter: it can obtain foreign produce only to the extent that it can sell something abroad. This could include domestic real assets (real capital or real estate) or, more likely, produced goods and services (perhaps commodities, for example). It could either run a balanced current account (in which case revenues from its exports are available to finance its imports) or its current account deficit could be matched by foreign direct investment.

Alternatively, it can issue foreign currency-denominated debt to finance a current account deficit. The problem with this option is that the nation must then generate revenues in the foreign currency to service debt. This is possible if today's imports allow the country to increase its productive capacity to the point that it can export more in the future, servicing the debt out of foreign currency earned on net exports. However, if such a nation runs a continuous current account deficit without enhancing its ability to export, it will almost certainly run into debt service problems. (Another alternative is to rely on charity by foreigners.)

The United States, of course, does run a persistent trade deficit. This is somewhat offset by a positive flow of net profits and interest (US investments abroad earn more than do foreign investments in the United States). But the two main reasons why the US can run persistent current account deficits are: a) virtually all its foreign-held debt is in Dollars; and b) external demand for Dollar-denominated assets is high, for a variety of reasons already discussed.

The first of these implies that servicing the debt is done in Dollars – easier for indebted American households, firms, and governments to obtain. The second implies that foreigners are willing to export to the United States to obtain Dollar-denominated assets, meaning that a trade deficit is sustainable so long as the rest of the world wants Dollar assets.

What about government that borrows in foreign currency?

What about nations that issue foreign currency-denominated assets? Returning to a nation that does issue debt denominated in a foreign currency, what happens if the debtors cannot obtain the foreign currency they need to service the debt?

We have thus far left to the side questions about who is typically issuing foreign currency-denominated debt. If it is a firm or household, then failure to earn the foreign currency needed to service the debt can lead to default and bankruptcy. This would be handled in the courts (typically, when debt is issued it is subject to the jurisdiction of a particular court) and by itself poses no insurmountable problem. If the debt is too large, bankruptcy results and the debt must be written off.

Sometimes, however, governments intervene to protect domestic debtors by taking over the debts. (Ireland in the aftermath of the global financial crisis is a good example.) Alternatively, governments sometimes issue foreign currency debt directly. In either case, default by government on foreign currency debt is usually more difficult – both because bankruptcy by sovereign government is a legally problematic issue and because sovereign default is a politically charged issue.

In practice, sovereign default (especially on foreign currency debt) is not uncommon, often chosen as the less painful alternative to continuing to service debt. Sovereign governments typically choose when to default; they almost always could have continued to service debt for some time (for example, by imposing austerity to increase exports, or by turning to international lenders). Apparently, they decide that the benefits of default outweigh the costs. However, this can lead to political repercussions. Still, history is littered with government defaults on foreign currency debt.

Governments sometimes issue foreign currency debt on the belief that this will lower borrowing costs since interest rates in, say, the US Dollar are lower than those in the domestic currency. However, foreign currency debt carries default risk. Still, it is not uncommon for governments to try to play the interest differentials, issuing debt in a foreign currency that has a lower interest rate. Unfortunately, this can be a mirage; markets recognize the higher default risk in foreign currency, eliminating any advantage.

Further, as discussed earlier, for a sovereign government, the domestic interest rate (at least the short-term interest rate in the domestic money of account) is a policy variable. If the government is spending domestically in its own currency, it can choose to leave reserves in the banking system or it can offer bonds. In other words, it does not have to pay high domestic interest rates if it does not want to, for it can instead let banks hold low (or zero) interest rate reserves. This option is available to any currency-issuing government – so long as its spending is in domestic currency.

As discussed earlier, government will be limited to purchasing what is for sale in its currency, and if it is constrained in its ability to impose and collect taxes then the domestic demand for its currency will be similarly limited. So we do not want to imply that government spending is not constrained, even in a sovereign country that issues its own currency. It can only buy what is for sale in its currency.

But if a national government issues foreign currency-denominated IOUs, the interest rate it pays is "market determined" in the sense that markets will take the base interest rate in the foreign currency and add a markup to take care of the risk of default on the foreign currency obligations. It is likely that the borrowing costs in foreign currency will turn out to be higher than what government would pay in its own currency to get domestic (and foreign) holders to accept the government's IOUs.

This is usually not understood because the domestic currency interest rate on government debt is a policy variable – usually set by the central bank – but policymakers believe they must raise domestic rising interest rates when the budget deficit rises. This is done to fight inflation pressures or downward pressure on exchange rates that policymakers believe to follow on from budget deficits. In truth – as discussed above – if a country tries to peg its exchange rate, then a budget deficit could put pressure on the exchange rate, so there is some justification for attempting to counteract budget deficits with tighter monetary policy (higher domestic interest rates to keep the exchange rate from falling).

But the point is that government sets the domestic interest rate on overnight funds, which then closely governs the interest rate on short-term government bonds. So if government wants lower rates on its debt, it can always use domestic monetary policy to achieve that goal. Unfortunately, this is not widely understood, hence governments issue foreign currency-denominated debt and then take on risk of default because they actually must get hold of foreign currency to service the debt. Thus it is almost always a mistake for government to issue foreign currency bonds.

Conclusion on US exceptionality

So, yes, the United States (and other developed nations to varying degrees) is special, but all is not hopeless for the nations that are "less special". To the extent that the domestic population must pay taxes in the government's currency, the government will be able to spend its own currency into circulation. And where the foreign demand for domestic currency assets is limited, there still is the possibility of nongovernment borrowing in foreign currency to promote economic development that will increase the ability to export.

There is also the possibility of international aid in the form of foreign currency. Many developing nations also receive foreign currency through remittances (workers in foreign countries sending foreign currency home). And, finally, foreign direct investment provides an additional source of foreign currency.

Next we will turn to impacts of government policy in an open economy: trade deficits and exchange rate effects.

Box: Frequently asked questions

Q: What is MMT's view of the reserve currency?

A: Well, today it is the Dollar; a century ago it was the Pound. MMT principles apply: it is a sovereign currency issued through keystrokes. The issuer of the reserve currency can either float (in which case the issuer does not promise to convert at a fixed exchange rate) or it can fix. As I have argued, fixing reduces domestic policy space. Reserve status increases external demand for the nation's currency, which is used for international clearing. To satisfy that demand, the reserve currency issuer (the United States today) either supplies the currency through the capital account (lending) or the current account (trade deficit, for example).

Many believe this allows the nation that issues the reserve currency to "get something for nothing", often called "seigniorage". This is largely false. Did American consumers get free goods and services over the past decade as the United States ran current account deficits? No, of course not. They are left with a mountain of debt. Did the US government get "something for nothing"? Well, perhaps – but all sovereign governments can be said to get something for nothing, since they purchase by keystrokes.

But that is not seigniorage; it results from the fact that sovereign government imposes liabilities on its population: taxes, fees, and fines. The United States does it; but so does Turkey. Sovereign government first puts its population in debt, then it uses keystrokes to move resources to the public sector and its keystrokes create its IOUs which provide the means through which taxpayers can retire their tax debt. The sovereign's currency can circulate outside the country to varying degrees, but that is ultimately because the sovereign's citizens need it to pay taxes domestically, since foreigners are not normally subject to the tax.

So in principle the issuer of the reserve currency is not unique, although the external demand for the reserve currency is greater.

4.6   Sovereign currency and government policy in the open economy

Government policy and the open economy

A government deficit can contribute to a current account deficit if the budget deficit raises aggregate demand, resulting in rising imports.

The government can even contribute directly to a current account deficit by purchasing foreign output. A current account deficit means the rest of the world is accumulating claims on the domestic private sector and/or the government. This is recorded as a "capital inflow".

Exchange rate pressure might arise from a continual current account deficit. While the usual assumption is that current account deficits lead more-or-less directly to currency depreciation, the evidence for this effect is not clear-cut. Still, that is the usual fear, so let us presume that such pressure does arise.

Implications of this depend on the currency regime. According to the well-known trilemma, government can choose only two out of the following three: independent domestic policy (usually described as an interest rate peg), fixed exchange rate, and free capital flows. A country that floats its exchange rate can enjoy domestic policy independence and free capital flows. A country that pegs its exchange rate must choose to regulate capital flows or must abandon domestic policy independence. If a country wants to be able to use domestic policy to achieve full employment (through, for example, interest rate policy and by running budget deficits), and if this results in a current account deficit, then it must either control capital flows or it must drop its exchange rate peg.

Floating the exchange rate thus gives more domestic policy space. Capital controls offer an alternative method of protecting an exchange rate while pursuing domestic policy independence.

Obviously such policies must be left up to the political process, but policymakers should recognize accounting identities and trilemmas. Most countries will not be able to simultaneously pursue domestic full employment, a fixed exchange rate, and free capital flows. The exception is a country that maintains a sustained current account surplus, as do several Asian nations. Because they have a steady inflow of foreign currency reserves, they are able to maintain an exchange rate peg even while pursuing domestic policy independence and (if they desire) free capital flows.

In practice, many of the trade surplus nations have not freed their capital markets. By controlling capital markets and running trade surpluses, they are able to accumulate a huge "cushion" of international reserves to protect their fixed exchange rate. To some extent, this was a reaction to the exchange rate crisis suffered by the "Asian Tigers" when foreign exchange markets lost confidence that they could maintain their pegs because their foreign currency reserves were too small. The lesson learned was that massive reserves are necessary to fend off speculators.

Do floating rates eliminate "imbalances"?

In the global economy, every current account surplus must be offset by a current account deficit somewhere. The counterpart to the accumulation of foreign currency reserves is accumulation of indebtedness by the current account deficit nations. This can create what is called a deflationary bias to the global economy. Countries desiring to maintain a trade surplus will keep domestic demand in check in order to prevent rising wages and prices that could make their products less competitive in international markets.

At the same time, countries with trade deficits might cut domestic demand to push down wages and prices in order to reduce imports and increase exports. With both importers and exporters attempting to keep demand low, the result is insufficient demand globally to operate at full employment (of labor and plant and equipment). Even worse, such competitive pressure can produce trade wars – nations promoting their own exports and trying to keep out imports. This is the downside to international trade, and it is made worse to the extent that nations try to peg exchange rates.

Some economists (notably, Milton Friedman) had argued in the 1960s that floating exchange rates would eliminate trade "imbalances" – each nation's exchange rate would adjust to move it toward a current account balance. When the Bretton Woods system of fixed exchange rates collapsed in the early 1970s, much of the developed world did move to floating rates – and yet current accounts did not move to balance (indeed, "imbalances" increased).

The reason is because those economists who had believed that exchange rates adjust to eliminate current account surpluses and deficits had not taken into account that an "imbalance" is not necessarily out of balance. As discussed previously, a country can run a current account deficit so long as the rest of the world wants to accumulate its IOUs. The country's capital account surplus "balances" its current account deficit.

It is thus misleading to call a current account deficit an "imbalance"; by definition it is "balanced" by the capital account flows. In that sense, it "takes two to tango": a nation cannot run a current account deficit unless someone wants to hold its IOUs. We can even view the current account deficit as resulting from a rest-of-the-world desire to accumulate net savings in the form of claims on the country. Certainly for the US Dollar that would be an appropriate way to look at it. The rest of the world (ROW) wants to accumulate Dollar assets, so exports to the United States. Even if the United States were to try to deflate its economy to reduce its trade deficit, that is not likely to work because the ROW would make adjustments to continue to net export to the United States.

Sovereign versus nonsovereign currencies

It is important to recognize the difference between a fully sovereign, nonconvertible currency and a nonsovereign, convertible currency. A government that operates with a nonsovereign currency, using a foreign currency or a domestic currency convertible to foreign currency (or to precious metal at a fixed exchange rate), faces solvency risk. However, a government that spends using its own floating and nonconvertible currency cannot be forced into default. This is something that is recognized – at least partially – by markets and even by credit raters. This is why a country like Japan can run government debt-to-GDP ratios that are more than twice as high as the "high debt" Euro nations (the "PIIGS": Portugal, Ireland, Italy, Greece, and Spain) while still enjoying extremely low interest rates on sovereign debt.

By contrast, US states, or nations like Argentina that operate currency boards (as it did in the late 1990s), and Euro nations (that adopted the Euro, essentially a foreign currency for them) face downgrades and rising interest rates with deficit ratios much below those of Japan or the United States . This is because a nation operating with its own currency can always spend by crediting bank accounts, and that includes spending on interest. Thus there is no risk of involuntary default. However, a nation that pegs or operates a currency board can be forced to default – much as the US government abrogated its commitment to gold in 1933.

We will explore the Euro in more detail in the next chapter, but briefly the problem with the Eurozone is that the nations gave up their sovereign currencies in favor of the Euro. For individual nations, the Euro is a foreign currency. It is true that the individual national governments still spend by crediting bank accounts of sellers and this results in a credit of bank reserves at the national central bank. The problem is that national central banks have to get Euro reserves at the ECB for clearing purposes. The ECB in turn is prohibited from directly buying public debt of governments. The national central banks can get reserves only to the extent the ECB will lend them or has created them by purchasing national government debt in secondary markets. And note that the ECB frowns on the practice of continual purchase of government debt by the central banks of member states.

What this means is that although national central banks can facilitate "monetization" to enable governments to spend, the clearing imposes constraints. This is somewhat analogous to the situation of individual states in the United States, which really do need to tax or borrow in order to spend. Similarly, because a nation like Greece is integrated into the Eurozone, if its government runs deficits then the central bank of Greece is likely to face a continual drain of reserves from its ECB account. This is replenished through sale of Greek government bonds in the rest of the Eurozone, reversing the flow of reserves in favor of the Greek central bank. The mechanics of this are somewhat different for US states (which, of course, do not operate with their own central banks) but the implications are similar: Euro national governments and US states really do need to borrow and thus are subject to market interest rates.

By contrast, a sovereign nation like the United States, Japan, or the United Kingdom does not borrow its own currency. It spends by crediting bank accounts. When a country operates with sovereign currency, it doesn't need to issue bonds to "finance" its spending. Issuing bonds is a voluntary operation that gives the public the opportunity to substitute their zero- or low-interest-earning government liabilities, currency, and reserves at the central bank, into higher-interest-earning government liabilities, treasury bills, and bonds, which are credit balances in securities accounts at the same central bank. If one understands that bond issues are a voluntary operation by a sovereign government, and that bonds are nothing more than alternative accounts at the same central bank operated by the same government, it becomes irrelevant for matters of solvency and interest rates whether there are takers for government bonds and whether the bonds are owned by domestic citizens or foreigners.

(Of course, as we discussed before, government can impose rules on its own behavior, for example, rules that require it to sell treasuries and obtain deposits in its account at the central bank *before* it cuts a check. Once it has adopted such a rule, you could say it has "no choice". This is much like the Jack Nicholson character in the movie *As Good As It Gets* who had self-imposed a series of actions he had to take before he could open a door. These are matters perhaps better addressed by behavioral psychologists than by economists.)

Box: Frequently asked questions

Q: What is it that makes a country's currency desirable to foreigners?

A: Typically it is because foreigners want to buy output produced by the country, to visit as tourists, or to buy financial assets denominated in that currency. For example, the demand for the Australian Dollar expanded when global pension funds and other managed money decided to allocate a portion of their portfolios to Oz Dollars. Of course the commodities boom also helped; the rest of the world (ROW) wanted Oz's commodities. We should be realistic, however. Many countries in the world do not now produce goods and services the ROW wants, and their assets are deemed too risky even if interest rates were to be kept high. Unfortunately many nations then see the way to increase interest in their goods and assets is to "dollarize" (typically, pegging an exchange rate, or better yet adopting a currency board). But that won't help much. At best it adds default risk in place of currency risk (the country might not be able to keep the promise to convert to dollars, so even though the exchange rate is fixed, the country's assets are risky). And it can encourage foreign vacations and shopping sprees by its own well-heeled citizens. There is no easy answer to this. There are lots of other risks involved in holding assets denominated in developing country currencies – most of them probably are not economic. Obviously political risk matters and, in some cases, corruption. I would suggest that it is far better to look inward: develop the nation's own capacity to produce and to consume its own products.

Q: Wouldn't a weaker Dollar be good for the US economy because it'd make it less attractive to export American jobs and possibly even bring some back? Would the positive effects of this offset the negative effects of more expensive oil and imports?

A: Estimates of trade benefits of Dollar depreciation are almost certainly overstated. First, many of America's trading partners "peg" to the Dollar; depreciation has no direct effect if they hold the peg. Second, those that don't peg are willing to take lower profits (hold Dollar prices steady) to keep market share (this has been the strategy of some exporters to the United States). Third, exports are a cost, imports a benefit, so trying to maximize a trade surplus is a net cost maximizing strategy (see Section 6.9). Fourth, it is not likely that many of those factory jobs will return to the United States. Today low-wage workers in developing nations take them; tomorrow they'll mostly be done by robots who don't mind hard work without wages. Fifth, the inevitable march of progress means that labor productivity in manufacturing rises so that fewer workers are needed. There is a better alternative: create jobs in the United States (see Chapter 7 on the job guarantee below).

Q: It seems to me that the current system is set up so that net exporting nations always "win" the international trade game and they do that by sucking liquidity out of the target nation, depressing the domestic economy because the domestic government is too scared to replace the liquidity with new liabilities.

A: They "win" the accounting game and "lose" the real game. Exports are a cost! This is a matter of not understanding what an economy is for. But I agree – many countries operate their economies this way.

4.7   What about a country that adopts a foreign currency?

A country might choose to use a foreign currency for domestic policy purposes. Even the US government accepted foreign currencies in payment up to the mid-nineteenth century, and it is common in many nations to use foreign currencies for at least some purposes. Here, however, we are examining a nation that does not issue a currency at all. In this section we will examine the case in which a nation adopts a foreign currency, abandoning its own.

Let us say that some national government adopts the US Dollar as the official currency, accepted at public pay offices, with taxes and prices denominated in the Dollar. Banks make loans and create deposits in Dollars. Government spends in Dollars. While the nation cannot create US Dollars, it is clear that households, firms, and government can create IOUs denominated in Dollars. These IOUs are part of the debt pyramid, leveraging actual US Dollars. Some of the IOUs (such as bank deposits) are directly convertible to US Dollars. The currency in circulation is the US Dollar (US coins and notes), but many or most payments will be done electronically. Check clearing will be done at the country's central bank, by shifting central bank reserves that are denominated in Dollars, debiting one bank's reserves and crediting another.

Note, however, that withdrawals from banks are made in the form of actual US Dollars. Further, international payments will be made in Dollars (a current account deficit will require transfer of Dollars from the country to a foreign country). How is that accomplished? The domestic central bank will have a Dollar account at the US Fed. When payment is made to a foreigner, the central bank's account is debited, and the account of some other foreign central bank's account is credited (unless, of course, the payment is made to the United States).

Because this nation does not issue Dollars, but rather *uses* Dollars, it must obtain them to ensure it can make these international payments and can meet domestic cash withdrawals so that Dollar currency can circulate in its economy. It obtains Dollars in the same way that any nation obtains foreign currency because the Dollar really is a foreign currency in terms of ability to obtain cash and Dollar reserves. Hence it can obtain Dollars through exports, through borrowing, through asset sales (including foreign direct investment), and through remittances.

It is apparent that adoption of a foreign currency is equivalent to running a very tight fixed exchange rate regime – one with no wiggle room at all because there is no way to devalue the currency. It provides the least policy space of any exchange rate regime. This does not necessarily mean that it is a bad policy. But it does mean that the nation's domestic policy is constrained by its ability to obtain the "foreign currency" Dollar. In a pinch, it might be able to rely on US willingness to provide foreign aid (transfers or loans of Dollars). Or it might be able to borrow Dollars from foreign banks with access to them. But that will depend on "the market's" perception of risk of lending to this nation.

Solvency questions and Ponzi finance in a nonsovereign currency

There is a further consideration. When a private entity goes into debt, its liabilities are another entity's asset. Netting the two, there is no net financial asset creation. When a sovereign government issues debt, it creates an asset for the private sector without an offsetting private sector liability. Hence government issuance of debt results in net financial asset creation for the private sector. Private debt is debt but government debt is financial wealth for the private sector.

A buildup in private debt should raise concerns because the private sector can reach a point at which it cannot service its debt. But the sovereign government as the monopoly issuer of its own currency can always make payments on its debt by crediting bank accounts – and those interest payments are nongovernment income, while the debt is nongovernment assets. When a private debtor cannot service debt out of income flows it must go further into debt, borrowing to pay interest. This is called Ponzi finance and it is usually dangerous because outstanding debt grows. (This is the term popularized by economist Hyman Minsky, named after Charles Ponzi, a fraudster who ran a "pyramid scheme." A more recent pyramid scheme was run by Bernie Madoff. In Minsky's terminology, Ponzi means that a debtor must borrow just to pay interest, which means debt grows, typically in an unsustainable manner.) For government with a sovereign currency, there is no imperative to borrow, hence it is never in a Ponzi position as it can always service debt using keystrokes.

Sovereign governments do not face financial constraints in their own currency (except those they impose on themselves, through budgeting, debt limits, or operating procedures) as they are the monopoly issuers of that currency. They make any payments that come due, including interest payments on their debt and payments of principal by crediting bank accounts, meaning that operationally they are not constrained in terms of how much they can spend. As bond issues are voluntary, a sovereign government doesn't have to let the markets determine the interest rate it pays on its bonds either. They do not really borrow their own currency.

On the other hand, nonsovereign governments like Greece that give up their monetary sovereignty, do face financial constraints and are forced to borrow from capital markets at market rates to finance their deficits. As the Greek debt crisis shows, this monetary arrangement allows the markets and rating agencies (or other countries in case of Greece) to dictate domestic policy to a politically sovereign country. Nonsovereign governments can become Ponzi; unable to service existing debt out of tax revenue, they must go to markets to borrow to pay interest.

Clearly such debt dynamics severely constrain the nonsovereign government. As it borrows more, markets demand higher interest rates to compensate for the rising risk of insolvency. The government can easily get into a vicious spiral as it must borrow ever more to pay ever higher interest rates. Markets will cut off credit, probably even before a true Ponzi position is reached. Orange County, California (one of the richest counties in the United States) got caught in a situation in which markets refused to lend. While Euro nations like Greece have not quite got to that point (as of Spring 2012), they have required intervention by the ECB (as well as other entities that have helped provide a series of quasi bailouts).

A nation that adopts foreign currency cedes a significant degree of its sovereign power. In the next chapter we turn to alternative exchange rate regimes and visit the situation in Europe.

Box: Frequently asked questions

Q: When a developing country adopts or pegs to the US Dollar, doesn't it get to enjoy a lower interest rate?

A: Of course this is related to default risk. If you look at the experience of Argentina (which adopted a currency board based on the Dollar), its interest rate remained about the same as its neighbor Brazil's rate (which did not Dollarize), and that was much higher than the US Dollar interest rate. Why? Eliminating exchange rate risk was completely offset by adding on default risk as markets worried Argentina could not hold the peg. (I won't go into it in detail, but Keynes's interest rate parity theorem holds reasonably well: a nation's interest rate must compensate for expected exchange rate movements, so to the base interest rate we add the risk premium and also expected exchange rate movements. For that reason, unless a nation has unassailable Dollar reserves, the risk that it cannot hold the peg offsets the advantage of adopting the Dollar.)

5
Modern Money Theory and Alternative Exchange Rate Regimes

The previous discussions were quite general and apply to all countries that use a domestic currency. It does not matter whether these currencies are pegged to a foreign currency or to a precious metal, or whether they are freely floating – the principles are the same. In this chapter we will examine the implications of exchange regimes for our analysis.

Let us first deal with the case of governments that do not promise to convert their currencies on demand into precious metals or anything else. When a $5 note is presented to the US Treasury, it can be used to pay taxes or it can be exchanged for five $1 notes (or for some combination of notes and coins to total $5) – but the US government will not convert it to anything else.

Further, the US government does not promise to maintain the *exchange rate* of US Dollars at any particular level. We can designate the US Dollar as an example of a *sovereign currency* that is *nonconvertible,* and we can say that the United States operates with a *floating exchange rate*. Examples of such currencies include the US Dollar, the Australian Dollar, the Canadian Dollar, the UK Pound, the Japanese Yen, the Turkish Lira, the Mexican Peso, the Argentinean Peso, and so on.

In the following sections we will distinguish between these sovereign nonconvertible floating currencies and currencies that are *convertible* at *fixed exchange rates*.

5.1 The gold standard and fixed exchange rates

A century ago, many nations operated with a *gold standard* in which the country not only promised to redeem its currency for gold, but also promised to make this redemption at a *fixed exchange rate*. An example of a fixed exchange rate is a promise to convert thirty-five US Dollars to one ounce of gold. For many years, this was indeed the official US exchange rate. Other nations also adopted fixed exchange rates, pegging the value of their currency either to gold or, after WWII, to the US Dollar. For example, the official exchange rate for the UK Pound was $2.80 US. In other words, the government of the United Kingdom would provide $2.80 (US currency) for each UK Pound presented for conversion. With an international fixed exchange rate system, each currency will be fixed in value relative to all other currencies in the system.

In order to make good on its promises to convert its currency at fixed exchange rates, the UK had to keep a reserve of foreign currencies (and/or gold). If a lot of UK Pounds were presented for conversion, the UK's reserves of foreign currency could be depleted rapidly. There were a number of actions that could be taken by the UK government to avoid running out of foreign currency reserves, but none of them was very pleasant. The choice mostly boiled down to three types of actions: a) *depreciate* the Pound; b) *borrow* foreign currency reserves; or c) *deflate* the economy.

In the first case, the government changes the conversion ratio to, say, $1.40 (US currency) per UK Pound. In this manner it effectively doubles its reserve because it only has to provide half as much foreign currency (or gold) in exchange for the Pound. Unfortunately, such a move by the UK government could reduce confidence in the UK government and in its currency, which could actually increase the demands for redemption of Pounds.

In the second case, the government borrows foreign currencies to meet demanded conversions. This requires willing lenders, and puts the UK into debt on which interest has to be paid. For example, it could borrow US Dollars but then it would be committed to paying interest in Dollars – a currency it cannot issue.

Finally, the government can try to *deflate,* or slow, the economy. There are a number of policies that can be used to slow an economy – together called "austerity measures" – but the idea behind them is that slower economic growth in the United Kingdom will reduce imports of goods and services relative to exports. This could allow the United Kingdom to run a surplus budget on its foreign account, accumulating foreign currency reserves. The advantage is that the United Kingdom obtains foreign currency without going into debt. The disadvantage, however, is that domestic economic growth is lower, which usually results in lower employment and higher unemployment.

Note that a *deflation* of the economy can work in conjunction with a currency *depreciation* to create a net export surplus. This is because a currency depreciation makes domestic output cheap for foreigners (they deliver less of their own currency per UK Pound) while foreign output is more expensive for British residents (it takes more Pounds to buy something denominated in a foreign currency).

Hence, the United Kingdom might use a combination of all three policies to meet the demand for conversions while increasing its holding of Dollars and other foreign currencies.

Box: Frequently asked questions

Q: How do countries obtain the foreign exchange reserves they use to peg their currencies?

A: For the most part, they run current account surpluses (selling goods and services abroad, or earning factor incomes in foreign currency or receiving foreign remittances) or they borrow them. How do those reserves end up at government? Because the exporters who earn – let us say – US Dollars need to cover their own domestic expenses in the domestic currency. The central bank offers exchange services to its banks – it creates domestic currency reserves and buys the foreign currency reserves. The central bank then typically exchanges Dollar reserves at the Fed for US Treasuries because it wants to earn interest. That is why there is a very close link between US current account deficits and foreign accumulation of Treasuries.

5.2 Floating exchange rates

Since the early 1970s, the United States, as well as most developed nations, has operated on a *floating exchange rate* system, in which the government does not promise to convert the Dollar. Of course, it is easy to convert the US Dollar or any other major currency at private banks and at kiosks in international airports. Currency exchanges do these conversions at the current exchange rate set in international markets (less fees charged for the transactions). These exchange rates change day-by-day, or even minute-by-minute, fluctuating to match demand (from those trying to obtain Dollars) and supply (from those offering Dollars for other currencies).

The determination of exchange rates in a floating exchange rate system is exceedingly complex. The international value of the Dollar might be influenced by such factors as the demand for US assets, the US trade balance, US interest rates relative to those in the rest of the world, US inflation, and US growth relative to that in the rest of the world. So many factors are involved that no model has yet been developed that can reliably predict movements of exchange rates.

What is important for our analysis, however, is that on a floating exchange rate, a government does not need to fear that it will run out of foreign currency reserves (or gold reserves) for the simple reason that it does not convert its domestic currency to foreign currency at a fixed exchange rate. Indeed, the government does not have to promise to make any conversions at all.

In practice, governments operating with floating exchange rates do hold foreign currency reserves, and they do offer currency exchange services for the convenience of their financial institutions. However, the conversions are done at current market exchange rates, rather than to keep the exchange rate from moving. Governments can also intervene in currency exchange markets to try to nudge the exchange rate in the desired direction. They will also use macroeconomic policy (including monetary and fiscal policy) in an attempt to affect exchange rates. Sometimes this works, and sometimes it does not.

The point is that on a floating exchange rate, attempts to influence exchange rates are *discretionary*. By contrast, with a fixed exchange rate, government *must* use policy to try to keep the exchange rate from moving. The floating exchange rate ensures that the government has greater freedom to pursue other goals – such as maintenance of full employment, sufficient economic growth, and price stability.

As we continue this discussion in coming sections, we will argue that a *floating* currency provides more *policy space* – the ability to use domestic fiscal and monetary policy to achieve policy goals. By contrast, a *fixed exchange rate* reduces policy space. That does not necessarily mean that a government with a fixed exchange rate cannot pursue domestic policy. It depends. One important factor will be whether it can accumulate sufficient foreign currency (or gold) to defend its currency.

Next, however, we will take a brief diversion to examine so-called commodity money. The fixed exchange rate based on a gold standard has been a reality only in relatively recent times. During much of the past two millennia, governments issued coins with silver and gold content. Many equate these with "commodity money" – a monetary system supposedly based on precious metal; indeed, one in which money derives value from embodied gold or silver.

We will come to a surprising conclusion, however. Even coins made of gold and silver are really IOUs stamped on metal. They are not examples of commodity money. They are sovereign currencies.

Box: Frequently asked questions

Q: Floating exchange rates provide more domestic policy space. But don't fixed exchange rates remove a lot of uncertainty?

A: The belief is that fixed rates provide more certainty – you know what the Dollar will be worth relative to the Pound. That makes it easier to write (non-hedged) contracts. However, the uncertainty is shifted to the ability of government to maintain the peg. That is especially problematic in the post-Bretton Woods era in which countries that peg are essentially "going it alone".

Many also (paradoxically) believe that fixed exchange rates reduce the chance of speculative attacks. That is counterfactual as well as counterintuitive. Remember the Pound? George Soros brought it down and supposedly made a billion Dollars in a day betting the United Kingdom could not defend the fix. Would you rather short a currency that is fixed, or one that floats minute by minute? In which of those two cases could you make a billion a day? Would you rather try to hit a moving target, or one that is stationary?

Now it is true that daily fluctuation of pegged rates might be nil for long periods of time, in contrast to floating rates that might vary all the time. But when pegged rates do move, they can generate currency crises because when the peg is broken, that is equivalent to a default. If I promise to you to convert my Dollar IOUs to a foreign currency (or gold) at a fixed rate, and then I tell you that I'll only give you half the promised amount of foreign currency, I have just defaulted. That causes havoc in markets.

So, yes, fixed rates can in some cases provide greater certainty – until they are abandoned. To ensure the fixed rate will be maintained, the country will need access to substantial foreign currency reserves. A country like China or Taiwan today can provide a believable promise of conversion at fixed exchange rates. Most nations cannot.

5.3 Commodity money coins? metalism versus nominalism, from Mesopotamia to Rome

At the end of the previous section I asserted that coins have never been a form of commodity money; rather they have always been the IOUs of the issuer. Essentially, a gold coin is just the state's IOU that happens to have been stamped on gold. It is just a "token" of the state's indebtedness – nothing but a record of that debt. The state must take back its IOU in payments made to itself. "Taxes drive money" – these "money things" are accepted because there are taxes "backing them up", not because they have embodied gold. In this section I will begin to try to dispel the view that coins used to be commodity monies. In the next section I will finish up the discussion.

In this primer I do not want to go deeply into economic history – we are more interested here with how money "works" today. However, that does not mean that history does not matter, nor should we ignore how our stories about the past affect how we view money today. For example, a common belief (accepted by most economists) is that money first took a commodity form. Our ancient ancestors had markets, but they relied on inconvenient barter until someone had the bright idea of choosing one commodity to act as a medium of exchange. At first it might have been pretty sea shells, but through some sort of evolutionary process, precious metals were chosen as a more efficient money commodity.

Obviously, metal had an intrinsic value – it was desired for other uses. It is typically argued that the intrinsic value imparted value to coined metal. This helped to prevent inflation – that is, a decline in the purchasing power of the metal coin in terms of other commodities – since the coin could always be melted and sold as bullion. There are then all sorts of stories about how government debased the value of the coins (by reducing precious metal content), causing inflation.

According to this story, government later issued paper money (or base metal coins of very little intrinsic value) but promised to redeem it for the metal. Again, there are many stories about government defaulting on its promise. And then finally we end with today's "fiat money", with nothing "real" standing behind it. And that is how we supposedly get the modern examples of the Weimar Republics and the Zimbabwes – with nothing really backing the money it now is prone to causing hyperinflation as government prints up too much of it. Which leads us to the goldbug's lament: if only we could go back to a "real" money standard: gold.

In this discussion, we cannot provide a detailed historical account to debunk the traditional stories about money's history. Let us instead provide an overview of an alternative.

First we need to note that the money of account is many thousands of years old – at least four millennia old and probably much older. (The "modern" in "modern money theory" comes from Keynes's claim that money has been state money for the past 4,000 years "at least".) We know this because we have, for example, the clay tablets of Mesopotamia that record values in money terms, along with price lists in that money of account.

We also know that money's earliest origins are closely linked to debts and recordkeeping, and that many of the words associated with money and debt have religious significance: debt, sin, repayment, redemption, "wiping the slate clean", and Year of Jubilee. In the Aramaic language spoken by Christ, the word for "debt" is the same as the word for "sin". The "Lord's Prayer" that is normally interpreted to read "forgive us our trespasses" could be just as well translated as "our debts" or "our sins" – or as Margaret Atwood says, "our sinful debts".[1]

Records of credits and debits were more akin to modern electronic entries – etched in clay rather than on computer tapes. And all known early money units had names derived from measures of the principal grain foodstuff – how many bushels of barley equivalent were owed, owned, and paid. All of this is more consistent with the view of money as a unit of account, a representation of social value, and an IOU rather than as a commodity. Or, as we MMTers say, money is a "token", like the cloakroom "ticket" that can be redeemed for one's coat at the end of the operatic performance. However, government's IOUs are "redeemed" for taxes.

Indeed, the "pawn" in pawnshop comes from the word for "pledge", as in the collateral left, with a token IOU provided by the shop that is later "redeemed" for the item left. St. Nick is the patron saint of pawnshops (and, appropriately, for thieves who pawn their stolen goods), while "Old Nick" refers to the devil (hence, the red suit and chimney soot – and "to nick" means to steal) to whom we pawn our souls. The Tenth Commandment's prohibition on coveting thy neighbor's wife (which goes on to include male or female slave, or ox, or donkey, or anything that belongs to your neighbor) originally had nothing to do with sex and adultery but rather with receiving them as pawns for debt. By contrast, Christ is known as "the Redeemer" – the "Sin Eater" who steps forward to pay the debts we cannot redeem, a much older tradition behind which lies the practice of human sacrifice to repay the gods (Atwood 2008).

We all know Shakespeare's admonition "neither a borrower nor a lender be", as religion typically views both the "devil" creditor and the debtor who "sells his soul" by pawning his wife and kids into debt bondage as sinful – if not equally then at least simultaneously tainted, united in the awful bondage of debt. Only "redemption" can free us from humanity's debts owing to Eve's original sin. Of course, for most of humanity today, it is the original sin/debt to the tax collector, rather than to Old Nick, that we cannot escape. The Devil kept the first account book, carefully noting the purchased souls and only death could "wipe the slate clean" as "death pays all debts". Now we've got our tax collector, who, like death, is one of the two certain things in life. In between the two, we had the clay tablets of Mesopotamia recording debits and credits in the temple's unit of account, and then the palace's money of account for the first few millennia after money was invented as a universal measure of our multiple and heterogeneous sins.

The first coins were created thousands of years later, in the greater Greek region (so far as we know, in Lydia in the seventh century BC). And in spite of all that has been written about coins, they have rarely been more than a very small proportion of the "money things" involved in finance and debt payment. For most of European history, for example, tally sticks, bills of exchange, and "bar tabs" did most of that work. (Bar tabs were kept with chalk upon slate behind the bar – again, the reference to "wiping the slate clean" is revealing, something that might not be done for a year or two at the pub, where the alewife kept the accounts.)

Until recent times, most payments made to the Crown in England were in the form of tally sticks (the King's own IOU, recorded in the form of notches in hazelwood) – whose use was only discontinued well into the nineteenth century – with a catastrophic result: the Exchequer had them thrown into the stoves with such zest that Parliament was burnt to the ground by those devilish tax collectors! In most realms, the quantity of coin was so small that it could be (and was) frequently called in to be melted for re-coinage. (If you think about it, calling in all the coins to melt them for re-coinage would be a very strange and pointless activity if coins were already valued by embodied metal!)

So what were coins and why did they contain precious metal? To be sure, we do not know. Money's history is "lost in the mists of time when the ice was melting... when the weather was delightful and the mind free to be fertile of new ideas – in the islands of the Hesperides or Atlantis or some Eden of Central Asia" as Keynes put it. We have to speculate.

One hypothesis about early Greece (the presumed mother of both democracy and coinage – almost certainly the two are linked in some manner) is that the elites had nearly monopolized precious metal, which was important because their social circles were tied together by "hierarchical gift exchange". They were above the *agora* (marketplace) and hostile to the rising *polis* (democratic city-state government). According to Classical scholar Leslie Kurke, the *polis* first minted coin to be used in the *agora* to "represent the state's assertion of its ultimate authority to constitute and regulate value in all the spheres in which general-purpose money operated. ... Thus state-issued coinage as a universal equivalent, like the civic *agora* in which it circulated, symbolized the merger in a single token or site of many different domains of value, all under the final authority of the city."[2] The use of precious metals was a conscious thumbing-of-the-nose against the elite who placed great ceremonial value on precious metal. By coining their precious metal, for use in the *agora's* houses of prostitution by mere common citizens, the *polis* sullied the elite's hierarchical gift exchange by appropriating precious metal, and with its stamp asserting its ultimate authority.

As the *polis* used coins for its own payments and insisted on payment in coin, it inserted its sovereignty into retail trade in the *agora*. At the same time, the *agora* and its use of coined money subverted hierarchies of gift exchange, just as a shift to taxes and regular payments to city officials (as well as severe penalties levied on officials who accepted gifts) challenged the "natural" order that relied on gifts and favors. As Kurke argues, since coins are really nothing more than tokens of the city's authority, they could have been produced from any material. However, because the aristocrats measured a man's worth by the quantity and quality of the precious metal he had accumulated, the *polis* was required to mint high quality coins, unvarying in fineness. (Note that gold is called the noble metal because it remains the same through time, like the king; coined metal needed to be similarly unvarying.) The citizens of the *polis*, by their association with high quality, uniform coin (and in the literary texts of the time, the citizen's "mettle" was tested by the quality of the coin issued by his city) gained equal status; by providing a standard measure of value, coinage rendered labor comparable and in this sense coinage was an egalitarian innovation.

From that time forward, coins commonly contained precious metal. Rome carried on the tradition, and Kurke's thesis is consistent with the statement of St. Augustine, who declared that just as people are Christ's coins, the precious metal coins of Rome represent a visualization of imperial power – inexorably doing the emperor's bidding just as the reverent do Christ's. ("He said, 'Why tempt ye Me, ye hypocrites; show Me the tribute money,' that is, the impress and superscription of the image. Show me what ye pay, what ye get ready, what is exacted of you. And 'they showed Him a *denarius*;' and 'He asked whose image and superscription it had.' They answered, 'Caesar's.' So Caesar looks for his own image. It is not Caesar's will that what he ordered to be made should be lost to him, and it is not surely God's will that what He hath made should be lost to Him. Caesar, my Brethren, did not make the money; the masters of the mint make it; the workmen have their orders, he issues his commands to his ministers. His image was stamped upon the money; on the money was Caesar's image. And yet he requires what others have stamped; he puts it in his treasures; he will not have it refused him. Christ's coin is man. In him is Christ's image, in him Christ's Name, Christ's gifts, Christ's rules of duty." (From St. Augustine on the Sermon on the Mount, Harmony of the Gospels and Homilies on the Gospels: Nicene and Post-Nicene Fathers of the Christian Church, Part 6" (Sermon XL) ; available here: http://www.synaxis.org/cf/volume15/ECF00038.htm. A commentator also noted: "People as coins" might also be a Rabbinic allusion: "When Caesar puts his image on a thousand coins, they all look alike. But when God puts His image on a thousand people, they all come out different.")

Note, again, the link between money and religion. That brings us up to Roman times. In the next section we examine coinage from Rome through to modern times.

Box: Frequently asked questions

Q: Didn't use of gold coins reduce forgery?

A: Undoubtedly, since gold was relatively hard to get hold of. But it then led to clipping, weighing, Gresham's Law dynamics, and so on as discussed in the next section. So the advantages of use of gold were offset by all the problems. Note also that sovereigns had long known about other methods of reducing forgery. The clay shubati tablets were put in "cases" that repeated the main information recorded on the encased tablets. To get to all the details, you had to break the case, so that was done only on the date of final settlement. That prevented alteration of the tablet. Or the better known example is the tally stick: notches were cut across the stick to indicate so many currency units. Then the stick was split, into "stock" and "stub". The creditor got one, the debtor the other. The one held by the creditor would circulate as a means of payment. When finally "redeemed" by presentation to the debtor, the stock and stub would be matched – and the notches ensured a good match. Of course, we still do that with ticket "stock and stub", matching numbers. So there were much better ways to prevent forgery. Later, as coin stamping techniques improved, it became harder to counterfeit – and precious metal was not needed.

5.4 Commodity money coins? metalism versus nominalism, after Rome[3]

In the last section, we examined the origins of coins, arguing that coinage is a relatively recent development. From the beginning, coins did have precious metal content. We examined a hypothesis for that, because from the MMT view, the "money thing" is simply a "token" or record of debt. If that is true, why "stamp" the record on precious metal? For thousands of years before and after the invention of coins, debts were recorded on clay or wood or paper. Why the switch? We argued that the origins of coins in ancient Greece must be placed in the specific historical context of that society. Use of precious metal was not a coincidence, but the origin of coinage also was not consistent with the commodity money view. While it is true that use of precious metal was important and perhaps even critical, this was for social reasons and was tied to the rise of the democratic *polis*. We now examine coinage from Roman times to the present in Western society.

Roman coins also contained precious metal. But Roman law adopted what is called "nominalism" – the nominal value of the coin is determined by the authorities, not by the value of embodied metal in the coin (termed "metalism"). The coin system was well-regulated and, although precious metal content changed across coinages, there was no significant problem with debasement or inflation.

In Roman law, one could deposit a sack of particular coins (*in sacculo*) and when repaid demand the same coins to be returned (*vindication*). However, if one were owed a sum of money (rather than specific coins), one had to accept in payment any combination of coins tendered that were "money of the realm" – officially sanctioned coins with payment enforced in court (*condictio*).

This practice continued through the early modern period, in which one deposited for safekeeping either sealed sacks of coins (and could demand exactly the same coins back in the still-sealed bag) or loose coins (in which case, any legal coins had to be accepted). Hence, "nominalism" prevailed in the general case although what appears to be a form of "metalism" applied to specific coins *in sacculo.*

In reality, it had more to do with the view that coins were a "moveable chattel", something the owner had a property interest in. However, once the owner's loose coins were mixed with other coins, there was "no earmark" – no way of determining specific owner-ship and hence the claimant only had a claim to be repaid in legal money – the *legalis moneta Angliae*, for example, in England, which was stipulated to be a sum of "sterlings". There was no sterling coin (indeed, England did not even coin the Pound at that time, its money of account), rather, the debt was paid up by providing the appropri-ate sum of coins declared lawful money by the Crown – this could include foreign coins – at the nominal value dictated by the King.

The authorities that issued coins were free to change the metal content at each coinage; penalties for refusing to accept a sovereign's coin in payment at the value stated by the sovereign were severe (often, death). Still, there is the historical paradox that when the King was paid in coin (in fees, fines, and taxes), he would have them weighed – and reject or accept at lower value the coins that were low weight. If coins were really valued nominally, why bother weighing them? Why did the issuer – the King – appear to have a double stand-ard, one nominalist, one metalist?

In private circulation, sellers also favored "heavy" coins – those that weighed more, or that were of higher fineness (i.e., that had more precious metal content). They certainly did not want to find themselves in the situation of trying to make payments to the Crown with low-weight coins. Hence, a "Gresham's Law" (the "bad" forces the "good" out of circulation) would operate: everyone wanted to pay in "light" coins, but to be paid in "heavy coins". There was thus obvious concern with the metal content of coins, and fairly accurate (and quite tiny) scales were manufactured and sold to weigh coins individually. This makes it appear to modern historians (and econo-mists) that "metalism" reigned: the value of coins appears to have been determined by metal content.

And yet we see, in court rulings, indications that the law favored a nominalist interpretation: any legal coin had to be accepted. And we see Kings who imposed long prison terms, or death, for refusing any coin deemed legal. It all appears so confusing! Was it nominal or was it metal? (The sentence was usually to serve "at the King's pleasure" – a nice way of putting it! One can just imagine the King's pleasure at holding indefinitely those who refused his coins.)

The final piece of the puzzle appears to be this: until modern mint-ing techniques were invented (including milling and stamping), it was relatively easy to "clip" coins – cut some of the metal off the edge. They could also be rubbed to collect grains of the metal. (Even normal wear and tear rapidly reduced metal content; gold coins in particular were soft. For that reason they were particularly ill-suited as an "efficient medium of exchange" – yet another reason to doubt the metalist story.)

This is why the King had them weighed to test for clipping. (As you can imagine, the penalty for clipping was also severe, including death – but it was hard to catch.) If he did not, he would be the victim of Gresham's Law; each time he recoined he would have less precious metal to work with. But because he weighed the coins, everyone else also had to avoid being on the wrong side of Gresham's Law (or be accused of clipping). Far from being an "efficient medium of exchange", we find that use of precious metals set up a destructive dynamic of clipping, weighing, and punishing that would only finally be resolved with the move to paper money! (Actually, even paper is less than ideal; perhaps some readers have experienced problems getting older paper money accepted – as I did even in Italy before it adopted the Euro – due to Gresham Law dynamics. Thank goodness for computers and keystrokes and LEDs to record money values that cannot be clipped, ripped, or ruined in the washing machine.)

A King sometimes made those dynamics worse – by recanting his promise to accept his old coined IOUs at previously agreed upon values. This was the practice of "crying down" the coins. Until recent times, coins did not have the nominal value stamped on them – they were worth what the King said they were worth at his "pay houses". (Take a look at early coins: they bore mythical figures or the King's likeness, but no indication of nominal value.) To effectively double the tax burden, he could announce that all the outstanding coins were worth only half as much as their previous value. Since this was the prerogative of the sovereign, holders could face some uncertainty over the nominal value. This was another reason to accept only heavy coins – no matter how much the King cried down the coins, the floor value would be equal to the value of the metallic content. Normally, however, the coins would circulate at the higher nominal value set by the sovereign, and enforced by the court and the threat of severe penalties for refusing to accept the coins at that value.

There is also one more aspect to the story. With the rise of the regal predecessors to our modern state, there were the twin and related phenomena of mercantilism and foreign wars. Within an empire or state, the sovereign's IOUs are sufficient "money things": so long as the sovereign takes them in payment, its subjects or citizens will also accept them. Any "token" will do – it can be metal, paper, or electronic entries. But outside the boundaries of the authority, mere tokens might not be accepted at all. In some respects, international trade and international payments are more akin to barter unless there is some universally accepted "token" (like the US Dollar today).

Put it this way: why would anyone in France want the IOU of France's sworn enemy, the King of England? Outside England, the King of England's coins might circulate only at the value of the precious metal contained in them. Metalism as a theory might well apply as a sort of floor to the value of a King's IOU: at worst, it cannot fall in value much below gold content as it can be melted for bullion.

And that leads us to the policy of mercantilism, and also to the conquest of the New World. Why would a nation want to export its output, only to have silver and gold return to fill the King's coffers? And why the rush to the New World to get gold and silver? Because the gold and silver were needed to conduct the foreign wars, which required the hiring of mercenary armies and the purchase of all the supplies needed to support those armies in foreign lands. (England did not have huge aircraft to parachute the troops and supplies into France – instead they hired mainland mercenary troops and bought the supplies from the local outfitters.) There was a nice vicious circle in all this: the wars were fought both by and for gold and silver!

And it made for a monetary mess in the home country. The sovereign was always short of gold and silver, hence had a strong incentive to debase the currency (to preserve metal to fund the wars), while preferring payment in the heaviest coins. The population had a strong incentive to refuse the light coins in payment, while hoarding the heavy coins. Or, sellers could try to maintain two sets of prices – a lower one for heavy coins and a high one for light coins. But that meant toying with the gallows. What a monetary mess!

The mess was resolved only very gradually with the rise of the modern nation state, a clear adoption of nominalism in coinage, and – finally – with abandonment of the long practiced phenomenon of including precious metal in coins. And with that we finally got our "efficient media of exchange": pure IOUs recorded electronically. Precious metal coins were always records of IOUs, but they were imperfect. And they certainly have misled historians and economists!

Admittedly, I have not yet made a thorough case that money *must* be an IOU, not a commodity. We need some more building blocks first before we can make the *logical* argument that money cannot be a precious metal commodity. However, these two sections should provide sufficient reason to reject the "commodity money" view of coinage.

Box: Frequently asked questions

Q: Was crying down coins inflationary or did it lead to hoarding and thus was deflationary?

Answer: As discussed, there would be some Gresham's Law dynamics: you hoard heavy coins and push the light ones in payment. Any coins cried down would be pushed (not hoarded). At the public pay offices (where you paid fees, fines, and taxes) you would experience inflation (deliver more coins to pay your tax debt). From what I understand, the impact on prices in "markets" would not be quite one-to-one. In other words, prices would not necessarily rise fully to take account of the lower value at the public pay offices. But I would say that these historical reports are not conclusive. Still, we can surmise that the coins that were cried down probably would fall in value so we would see some market price inflation in terms of these coins. And "velocity" of them would probably increase as everyone tried to offload them. Coins that were not cried down would get hoarded. But that effect was probably not huge – the historical reports are that crying down was well understood and even more-or-less accepted as a legitimate means of increasing the tax burden. The story is that the population accepted it so long as it was not done too often. Finally, recall that coins had no nominal value printed on them – so the crown had to announce the value at which they'd be accepted. And recall that entire coinages would frequently be called in for re-coinage. In any case, it is misleading to focus so much on coins. They were rarely important. Most taxes were paid in tallies (which could not be cried down since the nominal value was cut into stock and stub) and most private transactions took place in bills of exchange or as credits and debits (bar tallies, for example) – again all nominal.

Q: But doesn't the gold standard prevent inflation?

A: Yes, if you play by the rules on a gold standard, the quantity of gold constrains coin issue. However there are also tricks to get around these constraints. You can call in gold (jewelry, family heirlooms, etc.), you can raise the price for gold paid at the mint, you can put less gold in your coins, and you can use hazelwood tally sticks and bar tabs and paper money supposedly backed by gold. All of the above were done. As even Milton Friedman argued, although the gold standard looks good in theory as a way to avoid inflation, in practice governments "cheat". So he actually supported a floating exchange rate, but with money growth rules. Note however, that a strict gold standard works by constraining government spending; it is a fiscal constraint. Government must get hold of gold to spend. So unless there is a new discovery of gold, government's spending is largely constrained by the gold it receives in tax payments. So this is not a monetary constraint in the normal use of that term – it is not like the central bank controlling the money supply. It is more like a balanced budget amendment.

5.5 Exchange rate regimes and sovereign defaults

Let's quickly look at three examples of exchange rate regimes. In the next section we will take an extended look at the case of the Euro, in which members of the European Monetary Union went "whole hog" and essentially adopted a "foreign currency" – the Euro. That is the most constraining of pegged systems. In this section we will look at three unusual cases: a country that pegs its exchange rate but has plenty of domestic policy space; a country that pegged and defaulted on its sovereign debt; and a country that floats but is experiencing problems with its government debt.

Let's begin with China, which has a loose peg – a tightly managed exchange rate system. To be sure, China has let its currency gradually appreciate, but at the pace it chooses. This has led to charges of "currency manipulation", especially by US officials. Ostensibly this is because Washington thinks China is keeping its exchange rate too low, obtaining an advantage for its exports. In my view the charge is not justified for two reasons. First, it is not likely that even with very substantial appreciation of the Yuan (or RMB – China's currency) it would make much difference with respect to America's current account deficit with China. China's wages are currently very low relative to American wages, and most of China's exports are low-value-added products. China typically performs some of the intermediate assembly processes that are labor-intensive. If the Yuan did appreciate sufficiently for China to lose the jobs, they'd probably go elsewhere in Asia, rather than to the United States.

Second, the argument that exchange rates ought to be floating seems to me to be weak. Recall that until the early 1970s the United States and other developed nations adopted fixed exchange rates. True, they have since recognized that such a policy is not in their interests. But it is unjustified for the developed nations now to insist that developing nations must free their exchange rates. Exchange rate policy, like interest rate policy and fiscal policy, should be left to domestic policymakers. It should be clear from the arguments made in the primer that I believe that floating rates usually *are* in the national interest because they free up domestic policy space. But many nations around the world, especially the developing countries, adopt pegged rates in what they perceive to be their own self-interest. This is a matter to be left to each nation, in my view. At this stage of its development, China perceives it to be in its interest to carefully manage its own exchange rate.

However, given that I have argued that pegged rates reduce policy space and are inherently risky, since they invite speculation, the question is: why does China seem to perform so well even with pegged (but periodically adjusted) rates? The answer is pretty simple: trillions of Dollars of foreign exchange reserves! No one is going to bet against China's ability to peg its exchange rate. So, yes, there are exceptions to the rule that pegged exchange rates reduce policy space. China's huge foreign currency reserves enable it to operate with plenty of domestic policy space even as it pegs its currency; and this will continue for the foreseeable future because China is still able to run a current account surplus (although that will likely turn around at some point).

China's growth and transformation is really quite unprecedented. It will soon become the biggest economy in the world, and its per capita GDP is likely to grow sufficiently that it will join the world's wealthy nations. As its productive capacity grows and its wages grow, it will rely less and less on exports. Eventually it will probably run current account deficits that will drain foreign currency reserves. At that point it will probably choose to float the currency so that it can retain domestic policy space. And it is possible that China's currency will replace the Dollar as the international reserve currency. I expect that is some decades into the future.

Let's turn to another example, Russia. Of course, Russia had been part of the Soviet Union and was already relatively developed and wealthy. However, dissolution of the USSR generated economic and political problems that we will not go into. In 1998 Russia shocked financial markets by defaulting on its government debt. Many people believe that Russia's default is contrary to the MMT position that there is no default risk on sovereign government debt. It is clear that the debt was denominated in Rubles, the currency issued by the government. What went wrong? The key is its fixed exchange rate – a peg to the Dollar.

Warren Mosler has direct knowledge of the Russian fiasco as a hedge fund manager who held some positions linked to its sovereign debt. He wrote the following explanation: "In August 1998, the Ruble was convertible into $US at the Russian Central Bank at the rate of 6.45 Rubles per $US. The Russian government, desirous of maintaining this fixed exchange rate policy, was limited in its *willingness* to pay by its holdings of $US reserves, since even at very high interest rates holders of rubles desired to exchange them for $US at the Russian Central Bank. Facing declining $US reserves, and unable to obtain additional reserves in international markets, convertibility was suspended around mid-August, and the Russian Central Bank had no choice but to allow the ruble to float. Throughout this process, the Russian Government had the *ability* to pay in rubles. However, due to its choice of fixing the exchange rate at a level above 'market levels' it was not, in mid-August, *willing* to make payments in rubles. In fact, even after floating the ruble, when payment could have been made without losing reserves, the Russian Government, which included the Treasury and Central Bank, continued to be *unwilling* to make payments in rubles when due, both domestically and internationally. It defaulted on ruble payment *by choice*, as it always possessed the *ability* to pay simply by crediting the appropriate accounts with rubles at the Central Bank." (All emphasis in the original. See http://www.epicoalition.org/docs/flawed_logic.htm for his discussion.)

Why Russia made this choice is the subject of much debate. However, there is no debate over the fact that Russia had the *ability* to meet its notional ruble obligations but was *unwilling* to pay and instead *chose* to default. As best I can determine, it was a political decision. We cannot completely ignore politics. A similar case was the US Congressional debate over the federal government's debt limit in 2011. Yes, Congress could have decided not to raise the debt limit. Default on commitments appeared to be quite close. There was no good economic reason to do it – but politics can lead to some crazy results.

So we conclude that in the case of Russia there were two related factors at work that led to a default on its own sovereign currency debt: a pegged exchange rate and then a political decision to default.

Finally, let us look at the case of Hungary at the beginning of 2012. Hungary floats its currency, the Forint. As it is a currency issuer and does not promise to convert the currency to metal or foreign currency, it should have maximum domestic policy space to serve the public purpose (see Chapter 6 for a discussion of the public purpose). It should be able to buy anything for sale in Forints simply through "keystrokes". And it does not need to "borrow" its own currency – although it might choose to issue bonds, that is more properly seen as part of its monetary goal of hitting an overnight interest rate target. And yet it currently is experiencing serious problems with its government debt. How can that be?

Bill Mitchell explains the problem (here: Bilbo.economicoutlook. net/blog?p=17645). Hungary's economy was hit hard by the global financial crisis, with growth turning sharply negative as it slipped into a deep recession. This hit the government's budget, as you would expect, because tax revenues plummeted and social needs increased. However, Hungary has been trying to meet the Maastricht criteria in order to join the EMU (see the following sections) – which set limits to budget deficits and debt ratios. Hence, rather than ramping up fiscal policy to deal with the crisis, the government allowed the economy to slump. Its floating currency also depreciated, and to stop that its central bank actually has hiked interest rates (to try to induce foreigners to buy Forint-denominated assets that promise high interest rates).

The currency depreciation plus rising domestic rates hit Hungarian debtors hard. A lot of the debtors had actually issued IOUs denominated in foreign currency, but their incomes are in Forints. As the Forint depreciates, the burden of servicing foreign currency debt rises (it takes more Forints to make the payments). And if their debts are in Forints, the higher domestic interest rates also increase debt service. So borrowers are hurt whether they are indebted in foreign currency or domestic Forints.

But here's the real problem. The government also borrowed in foreign currency – just about half of its outstanding debt is in foreign currency. The only sources of foreign currency to service both government and private debt denominated in foreign currency are exports or more borrowing from foreigners, or exchanging ever-more Forints to obtain the foreign currency. And, of course, there really is default risk on all of this debt since Hungary's government cannot simply keystroke foreign currency into existence. As markets worry about Hungary's ability to service the debt, interest rates rise further; a vicious cycle can be generated in which credit ratings agencies downgrade the debt, increasing interest rates and debt service costs more, which then leads to more downgrades.

To top it all off, Hungary's government has imposed on itself various rules regarding deficits and debt that constrain its ability to react to the crisis through fiscal stimulus.

As Bill concludes: "Life in Hungary will get very difficult because it is now so exposed to movements in its currency. The private sector will experience significant reductions in its real standards of living as they struggle to service foreign-currency denominated debt with a declining domestic income. The government will also be pushed towards default by a slowing economy, the massive revaluations of its foreign-currency denominated debt as the currency falls and the declining capacity of the economy to generate export growth (as the rest of Europe slows). It is a very dire situation and the bond markets are reacting to the increased risk of default. The lesson is that Hungary does not provide a case against the insights provided by MMT. Budget deficits in a sovereign, floating currency never entail solvency risk. Sovereign government can always 'afford' whatever is for sale in terms of its own currency. It is never subject to 'market discipline'. A sovereign government spends by crediting bank accounts, and it can never 'run out' of such credits."

These three examples show us the problems of pegging a currency (unless the nation can accumulate huge foreign currency reserves), the probably rare but costly problems associated with defaulting on sovereign debts for political reasons, and the very real risks of default on foreign-currency denominated debts. Far better to adopt a sovereign currency with no promise to convert at a fixed exchange rate, and to avoid issuing foreign-currency denominated debt.

Let us now turn to perhaps the biggest experiment of the past few centuries in trying to run economies without a sovereign currency – the Euro.

5.6   The Euro: the set-up of a nonsovereign currency

Let us return to the question of a fixed versus a floating exchange rate currency. Above I argued that a floating exchange rate provides the greatest domestic policy space, while a fixed exchange rate normally reduces that space – unless, like China, sufficient foreign currency reserves are accumulated to remove any doubt that the peg can be maintained. There are different ways to fix an exchange rate; the most extreme is to simply adopt some other country's currency. There are several countries that have adopted the US Dollar – or created their own Dollar that exchanges one-for-one against the US Dollar. These are small exceptions to the "one nation, one currency" rule that we usually observe. However, there is one huge exception: the creation of the European Monetary Union – those European nations that dropped their own currencies and adopted the Euro. In this section we will examine this case. Note that the EMU is facing a crisis and it is not at all clear that it will survive – by the time this book is published, the crisis might be resolved or the entire EMU might be dissolved. It is very hard to say right now which is more likely. (See the following discussion for some speculation on the "end game".) This section will instead focus on what is wrong with the set-up. I have long argued that it was a system "designed to fail". For a long time, such a position was ignored or even derided. Now many commentators recognize the design flaws.

The Euro

The analysis in this primer so far (with the exception of the previous subsection) has concerned the typical case of "one nation, one currency". Until the development of the European Monetary Union (EMU), examples of countries that share a currency have been rare. They were usually limited to cases such as the Vatican in Italy (while nominally separate, the Vatican is located in Rome and used the Italian Lira), or to former colonies or protectorates. However,

Europe embarked on a grand experiment, with those nations that join the EMU abandoning their own currencies in favor of the Euro. Monetary policy is set at the center by the European Central Bank (ECB) – this means that the overnight interbank interest rate is the same across the EMU. The national central banks are no longer independent – they are much like the regional US Federal Reserve Banks, which are essentially subsidiaries of the Federal Reserve's Board of Governors that sets interest rates (in meetings of the Federal Open Market Committee in Washington).

There is one difference, however, in that the individual national central banks still operate clearing facilities among banks and between banks and the national government. This means they are necessarily involved in facilitating domestic fiscal policy. But while monetary policy was in a sense "unified" across the EMU in the hands of the ECB, fiscal policy remained in the hands of each individual national government. Thus, to a significant degree, fiscal policy was separated from the currency.

We can think of the individual EMU nations as "users" not "issuers" of the currency; they are more like US states (or, say, provinces of Canada). They tax and spend in Euros, and they issue debt denominated in Euros, much as US states tax and spend and borrow in Dollars.

Comparison with US States

In the United States, the states are required to submit balanced budgets (48 states actually have constitutional requirements to do so; this does not necessarily mean that at the end of the fiscal year they have achieved a balanced budget – revenues can come in lower than anticipated, and spending can be higher). This does not mean they do not borrow – when a US state government finances long-lived public infrastructure, for example, it issues Dollar-denominated bonds. It uses tax revenue to service that debt. Each year it includes debt service as part of its planned spending, and aims to ensure that total revenues cover all current expenditures including debt service. (Technically, the constitutional requirements require balancing the current account that includes interest on debt.)

When a US state ends up running a budget deficit, it faces the possibility that credit raters will downgrade its debt – meaning that interest rates will go up. This could cause a vicious cycle of interest rate hikes that increase debt service costs, resulting in higher deficits and more downgrades. Default on debt becomes a real possibility – and there are examples in the United States in which state and local governments have either come close to default, or actually were forced to default (Orange County – one of the richest counties in the United States – did default). Economic downturns – such as the crisis that began in 2007 – cause many state and local governments to experience debt problems, triggering credit downgrades. This then forces the governments to cut spending and/or raise taxes.

To reduce the possibility of such debt problems among EMU nations, each agreed to adopt restrictions on budget deficits and debt issue – the guidelines were that nations would not run national government budget deficits greater than 3% of GDP and would not accumulate government debt greater than 60% of GDP. In reality, virtually all member nations persistently violated these criteria.

EMU nations are users, not issuers of the currency

For the nations that have adopted the Euro, their currency is not sovereign in the sense adopted throughout this primer. It is as if they had adopted a foreign currency – something like "dollarization" of a country that chooses to operate with a currency board based on the US Dollar. It is not quite that extreme because the formation of the European Union has ensured some willingness of member states to come to the rescue of states in financial trouble (something that has been witnessed since the Global Financial Crisis first touched Euroland after 2008).

Further, the existence of the European Central Bank (ECB) that has the ability to act as "lender of last resort" provides some flexibility for individual nations. When a country – say, Argentina – adopts a currency board based on a foreign currency, it has no assurance (and perhaps no expectation) that the issuer of that currency (say, the United States) will come to its rescue. And while the Maastricht criteria had appeared to erect strong barriers to financial rescues of troubled states, there always was some expectation that "bailouts" would be provided in an emergency.

While the followers of MMT had long predicted that the structure of Euroland would not permit it to deal with a financial crisis, the problems did not become apparent until Greece faced a collapse in the aftermath of the Global Financial Crisis. Only scrambling by other member nations and the ECB forestalled a collapse of the market for Greek government debt. As of Spring 2012, the crisis continues to roll across Euroland because no permanent solution has been found to the problems raised by use of a nonsovereign currency. Let us look at the crisis in some detail.

Box: Frequently asked questions

Q: Can a Euro-using nation like Greece issue net financial assets to its nation?

A: Ignore for a second the government and foreign sectors. Within the domestic private sector, many economic units issue IOUs held by other economic units as their assets. Clearly for every debt there is an asset – they net to zero. Now add the government sector. It has claims on the domestic private sector, and it issues claims on itself. The private sector meets its obligations to government by delivering the government's own IOUs (i.e., currency broadly defined, although in practice taxes are ultimately paid using reserves – a transaction performed by banks that have accounts at the central bank). As we know from previous sections, deficit spending by government leads to net credits. So the private sector will have net financial assets in the form of claims on government. And in practice those net claims will be bank reserves at the central bank. Government can then sell treasuries as a higher-interest-earning alternative – treasuries which are bought through debits to reserve accounts. The question is whether these reserves or treasuries are net financial assets for the domestic private sector. Surely they are.

Let's now add the foreign sector to the analysis. Presume the government is operating with what amounts to a fixed peg – either it makes its currency convertible one-to-one against a foreign currency, or it actually adopts a foreign currency (say, the Euro). Its central bank opens a reserve account at the central bank that issues the currency, in this case at the ECB. It accumulates claims on foreign (other EMU national) central banks (its financial assets) and foreigners accumulate claims on it (its financial liabilities). It clears its accounts using ECB reserves (the ECB debits its reserves and credits reserves of foreign banks that have claims against it). When it is short reserves needed for clearing, it must borrow them from other banks that have accounts at the ECB, or from the ECB itself.

As the Greek domestic private sector plus government sector purchase foreign goods, services, and assets, foreign central banks will accumulate claims on the Greek central bank. And as foreigners purchase Greek goods, services, and assets, the Greek central bank will accumulate claims on foreign central banks. If Greece runs a current account deficit (which it does now), there are net claims against Greece – net Greek debt that represents net financial assets held by foreigners. (Technically, a current account deficit is off-set by a capital account surplus – plus official transactions.) These consist of claims on the Greek private sector and on the Greek government. All of this can go on so long as foreigners are willing to accumulate claims on Greeks (private plus government debtors) and the ECB is willing to lend reserves to the Greek central bank. But Greece is subject to the "whims of the market" – the "market" might require a higher interest rate to induce it to continue to lend to Greece. That is exactly what happened – as Greek debt was downgraded to CC status (very risky "junk" rating).

5.7 The crisis of the Euro

With the global financial crisis that began in 2008, many "periphery" nations (especially Portugal, Ireland, Italy, Greece, and Spain – termed "PIIGS") experienced serious debt problems and downgrades. Markets pushed their interest rates higher, compounding the problems. The EMU was forced to intervene, taking the form of loans by the ECB (and even by the IMF). The US Fed even lent Dollars to many of the European central banks. Nations facing debt problems were forced to adopt austerity packages – cutting spending, laying off government employees and forcing wage cuts, and raising taxes and fees.

The nations like Germany (also Finland and the Netherlands) that largely escaped these problems pointed their fingers at "profligate" neighbors like Greece that purportedly ran irresponsible fiscal policy. Credit "spreads" (the difference in interest rates paid by the German government on its debt versus the rates paid by the weaker nations; a good indicator of expected default is the spread on "credit default swaps" that are a form of insurance against default) soared as markets effectively "bet" on default on their government debt by the weaker nations.

To put all this in context, it is important to understand that the Euro nations actually did not have outrageously high budget deficits or debt ratios, compared with those achieved historically by sovereign nations. (See Figures below.) Indeed, Japan's deficits and debt ratios at the time were very much higher, and the US ratios were similar to those of some Euro nations facing debt crises. Yet countries that issue their own floating rate currency do not face such a strong market reaction – their interest rates on government debt are not forced up (even when credit rating agencies occasionally downgrade their debt, as they did earlier in the case of Japan, and threatened to do against the United States). Debt ratios were actually small relative to those commonly achieved by sovereign currency-issuing governments:

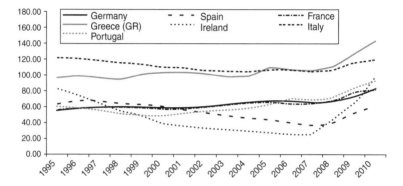

Figure 5.1 Government debt as a percentage of GDP, 1995–2010
Source: ECB.

Nor were deficits out of control, until the crisis:

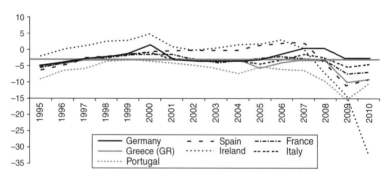

Figure 5.2 General government deficit, 1995–2010
Source: ECB.

So what is the difference between, say, Japan versus Greece? Why do markets treat Japan differently even though its debt ratio is higher than that of Greece?

As we've argued, the key is to understand that when Greece joined the EMU, it gave up its sovereign currency and adopted what is essentially a foreign currency. When Japan services its debts, it does so by making "keystroke" entries onto balance sheets, as discussed previously. It can never run out of the "keystrokes" – it can create as many Yen entries as necessary. It can never be forced into involuntary default. A sovereign government with its own currency can always "afford" to make all payments as they come due. To be sure, this requires cooperation between the treasury and the central bank to ensure the bank accounts get credited with interest, as well as a willingness of elected representatives to budget for the interest expenditures. But markets presume that the sovereign government will meet its obligations as they come due.

The situation is different for members of the EMU. First, the ECB has much greater independence from the member nations than the Fed has from the US government. The Fed is a "creature of Congress", subject to its mandates; the ECB is formally independent of any national government. The operational procedures adopted by the Fed ensure that it always cooperates with the US Treasury to allow government to make all payments approved by Congress (at least up to the Congressionally-imposed debt limit – see the Box on US debt limits). The Fed routinely purchases US government debt as necessary to provide reserves desired by member banks. The ECB apparently is prohibited from such cooperation with any member state (although the crisis in Euroland caused the ECB to bend the rules somewhat as it buys PIIGS government debt in secondary markets). While the ECB is prohibited from providing finance to member governments, it is allowed to buy debt in secondary markets to increase stability. Amazingly, the ECB's balance sheet by mid-January 2012 reached over $5 trillion – almost twice as big as the US Fed's, which does not have such strict constraints on its mandate to protect the financial system.

From the point of view of the EMU, this was not perceived to be a flaw in the arrangement but rather a design feature – the purpose of the separation was to ensure that no member state would be able to use the ECB to run up budget deficits financed by "keystrokes". The belief was that by forcing member states to go to the market to obtain funding, market discipline would keep budget deficits in line. A government that tried to borrow too much would face rising interest rates, forcing it to cut back spending and raise taxes. Hence, giving up currency sovereignty was supposed to rein in the more profligate spenders.

What finally "broke the camel's back"? Briefly, the combination of fixed exchange rates and sectoral balance identities, as well as a bit of data manipulation (Greece is reported to have hidden the true size of its government debt) and a global financial crisis created a monstrous government debt problem that spread around the edges of the EMU, threatening to bring down the whole union.

Since each nation had adopted the Euro, exchange rates were fixed among countries within the EMU. Some nations (Greece, Italy) were less successful at holding down inflation (especially wages) over the decade before the global financial crisis, and thus found they were increasingly less competitive within Europe. As a result, they ran chronic trade deficits, especially with Germany. As we know from our macro accounting, a current account deficit must be equal to a government budget deficit and/or a domestic private sector deficit. Thus, Germany could (rightfully) point to "profligate" spending by the government and private sector of Greece; and Greece could (rightfully) blame Germany for its "mercantilist" trade policy that relied on trade surpluses. Effectively, Germany was able to keep its budget deficits low, and its private sector savings high, by relying on its neighbors to keep the German economy growing through exports. But that meant, in turn, that its neighbors were building up debts – both public and private – and eventually markets reacted to that with credit downgrades.

The next figure shows the three financial balances for Euroland as a whole:

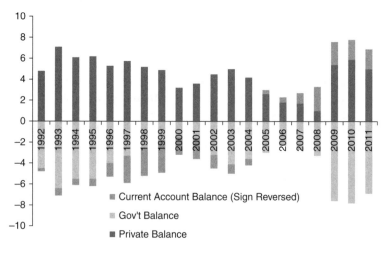

Figure 5.3   Sectoral balances as a percentage of GDP: Euro area

It is easy to see the cyclical swings, but it is also apparent that taken as a whole Euroland runs essentially balanced trade, so that its government deficits equal its private sector surpluses. But that varies tremendously among its member nations. Here is France:

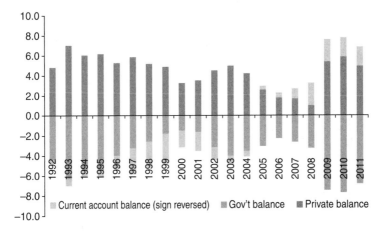

Figure 5.4 Sectoral balances as a percentage of GDP: France

France is running small current account deficits and since the crisis began big private sector surpluses; by identity this means it is running huge budget deficits. Here is Spain:

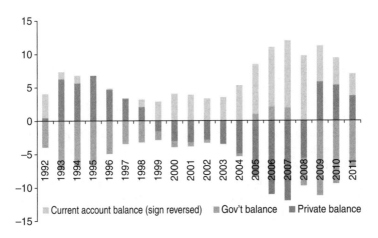

Figure 5.5 Sectoral balances as a percentage of GDP: Spain

Spain ran huge private sector deficits before the GFC – something like the United States during its Goldilocks Clinton years; that means it ran up big private deficits. Its government ran some surpluses, which meant that its current account balance was hugely in deficit. With the crisis, that all changed – the private sector began to run surpluses, the current account deficit fell, and the government's deficit exploded.

Finally, let us look at Italy, which is (in)famous for accumulating one of the largest outstanding government debts in the world (along with the United States and Japan):

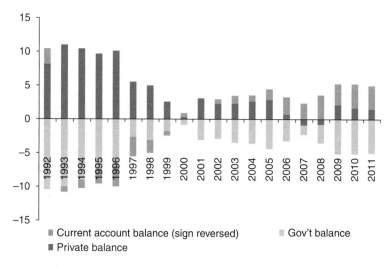

Figure 5.6   Sectoral balances as a percentage of GDP: Italy

Note that its swings are much smaller, and that actually the government deficits since unification (adoption of the Euro) were never very large – well under 5% of GDP until the crisis. Italy's private sector balances after unification were small but generally positive (except for 2007 and 2008) and it ran small current account deficits. And yet, when the Euro-area crisis began, Italy was singled out as one of the worst abusers – one of the members of the exclusive group called PIIGS, along with Spain which had been a paragon of fiscal prudence.

Unfortunately, some of these governments had engaged in creative accounting – concealing debt – and when that was discovered, the finger-pointing got worse. The global financial crisis also contributed to problems, as jittery markets ran to the safest debt (US government bonds, and within Europe to German and French debt). Bursting real estate bubbles hurt financial markets as well as indebted households. Bank problems within Europe also increased government debt through bailouts (Ireland's government debt problems were due to bailouts of troubled financial institutions). The economic slowdown also reduced government tax revenue and raised transfer spending.

To avert default, the ECB had to abandon its resolve, arranging for rescue packages. Officials began to recognize that a complete divorce between a nation and its currency (that is, separation of fiscal policy from a sovereign currency) is not a good idea. Even critics of Modern Money Theory – such as Paul Krugman – gradually came to realize that MMT had it right all along: while a government that issues its own sovereign currency cannot be forced to default on its IOUs, a government that adopts a foreign currency is subject to default risk.

While we won't go into details, most of the so-called PIIGS (Portugal, Ireland, Italy, Greece, and Spain) got into serious trouble only after the global financial crisis – both because tax revenue fell while fiscal demands increased but also because some of them tried to rescue their financial institutions. It was the crisis that exposed the dangerous levels of private sector debt. As financial institutions retrenched and savers tried to run to the safest assets, consumers got scared and cut back spending. Then, of course, firms downsized workforces as sales were sluggish. Tax revenues plummeted, and some government spending on social programs (such as unemployment compensation) grew. In other words, it is pretty much the same story that we saw in the United States – as the financial crisis led to an economic recession. All of that led to rapidly growing government debts, and then interest rate differentials (between troubled PIIGS and the stronger economies such as German, Dutch and French) exploded. The vicious interest rate dynamics set in – bigger debts entail more default risk so interest rates rise and increase spending on interest so that the debt rises more.

Had the European governments attempted to follow the restrictions of SGP (stability and growth pact that limits deficits to 3% and debts to 60% of GDP) – an attempt that would most certainly fail because of the endogenous nature of budget deficits – they would not have been able to support their economies in the global crisis, possibly leading to a global or at least a continental depression. Swings of the government budget balance need to be as large as swings of investment (or, more broadly, swings of the private sector balance) so that fiscal policy can be used to counteract the business cycle.

Instead of using the government budget as a tool to create a system that is relatively stable and supports high employment, the Europeans have made low deficits the policy goal without any regard for the consequences that will have for the economy. Yet even without the SGP, government spending is constrained by market perceptions of risk – precisely because these nations do not have a sovereign currency system like that of the United States, the United Kingdom, or Japan.

In other words, the arrangements of the EMU were not up to the task of dealing with the GFC. Now, the United States did not deal well with the GFC either – but that was almost entirely due to bad policy. In Euroland, even with the best possible policy the nations individually could not deal with the problems they faced. They needed something equivalent to a central Euro-wide treasury with the ability to spend on the necessary scale. Instead, they have bumbled through, relying on a combination of half-steps by the ECB plus austerity. And that is why Euroland is in much worse shape than the United States. Indeed, as I write this section, it looks like Europe is collapsing into another recession, and the financial sector is on the verge of another collapse. Only time will tell what the outcome will be. In the next section, let's look at possible solutions.

Box: Frequently asked questions

Q: But isn't it true that Germany behaved more responsibly, by keeping inflation in check – while the PIIGS deserve the blame for allowing inflation?

A: It is no secret that Germany held the line on wages while almost all other Euro-using nations allowed wages to rise – making labor in many nations noncompetitive with German workers. Where should we point the finger: at Germany or at Greece? Germany chose a race to the bottom strategy and if all others had followed that strategy, all wages would have been pushed competitively toward zero so that Euroland could "enjoy" falling living standards that at the extreme would fall to the lowest common denominator. Without "excessive" wage increases and spending beyond income in some of the PIIGS, Germany could not have enjoyed success as a net exporter. It took at least "two to tango". The relations within Euroland are dysfunctional, so we should not just point a finger at the debtor countries.

5.8 Endgame for the Euro?

In early fall of 2011, yet another rescue plan for the EMU was making its way through central Europe – raising the total funding available to the equivalent of $600 billion. It won't be enough. Another casualty (late fall 2011) was Dexia Group, a Belgian-French bank that specialized in sovereign debt. It had already been bailed out once, and needed yet another bailout. I expect that Dexia is just another domino – the other big European banks will likely face similar problems. This is not a Greek problem. It is not an Irish problem. It is not a Portuguese problem. It is not a Spanish problem. It is not an Italian problem. It is an EMU problem and Band-Aids will never suffice.

Even if the member states were not busy pointing fingers and squabbling over profligate spending by neighbors, the current arrangements prohibit any effective response to crisis. When markets decide to attack one member, it quickly finds itself in a vicious debt trap, with interest rates rising that blow a hole in the budget. At most, other members can put together a debt package – lending at slightly more generous terms. But what highly indebted members need is debt relief and economic growth, not more debt. With austerity demanded in order to get the proffered loans, growth turns negative, increasing budget deficits and leading to more desperate borrowing.

Either way, the indebted country gets into the debt trap: if it borrows from markets, interest rates rise; if it borrows from the EMU (or the IMF) the austerity is demanded in exchange, so its growth falls and tax revenue plummets.

One solution for a troubled country is to leave the EMU and return to a sovereign currency issued by the government – i.e., the Drachma for Greece, the Lira for Italy, and so on. The transition would be disruptive, with near-term costs. But the benefit would be to create domestic fiscal and policy space to deal with the crisis. Default on Euro-denominated debt would be necessary. Retaliation by the EU is possible. However, this is preferred to the "Teutonic versus Latin" two-currency scheme that some have recommended – splitting Euroland into two groups, a northern Teutonic group with its currency (say, Euro-T) and a southern Latin group with its currency (the Euro-L, presumably with a much lower exchange value). However, that would simply tie, say, Greece to another external currency. It would have no more fiscal or monetary policy space than it now has, albeit with a currency that would be devalued relative to the current Euro. To regain the biggest domestic policy space, it is best for each nation to adopt its own floating rate currency.

If dissolution is not chosen, then the only real solution is to reformulate the EMU. Many critics of the EMU have long blamed the ECB for sluggish growth, especially on the periphery. The argument is that it kept interest rates too high for full employment to be achieved. I have always thought that was wrong – not because lower interest rates are undesirable, but because even with the best-run central bank, the real problem in the set-up was fiscal policy constraints. Indeed, in a paper several years ago, Claudio Sardoni and I demonstrated that the ECB's policy was not significantly tighter than the Fed's – but US economic performance was consistently better (http://www.levyinstitute.org/pubs/wp_431.pdf).

The difference was fiscal policy – with Washington commanding a budget that is more than 20% of GDP, and usually running a budget deficit of several percent of GDP. By contrast, the EU Parliament's budget is less than 1% of GDP. While individual nations tried to fill the gap with deficits by their own governments, these created the problems we see in the Euro crisis.

The problem was that as deficits and debt rose, markets reacted by increasing interest rates – recognizing that unlike a sovereign country like the United States Japan, or the United Kingdom, the EMU members were users of an external currency. As I argued previously, they were more like a US state. On one hand, they could run much bigger deficits than the United States – in part due to the expectation that if things went bad, the ECB would probably help their state central banks. But on the other, US states have Washington to provide fiscal relief – something EMU members did not have. At best, they could borrow Euros – from European institutions or from the IMF. But borrowing would increase interest rates – bringing on the vicious debt trap. To some extent America avoids this as markets force balanced budgets on states and Washington eases the pain with fiscal transfers. As a result a larger percent of EMU national deficits went to interest payments than is the case with US states, which may not be the best stimulus as much leaks out to foreign holders of the debt.

Once the EMU weakness is understood, it is not hard to see the solutions. These range from ramping up fiscal policy space of the European Union Parliament – say, increasing its budget to 15% of GDP, with a capacity to issue debt. Whether the spending decisions should be centralized is a political matter – funds could simply be transferred to individual states on a per capita basis.

Virtually the same result can also be achieved by the ECB: change the rules so that the ECB can buy, say, an amount equal to a maximum of 6% of Euroland's GDP each year in the form of government debt issued by each EMU member. As buyer it can set the interest rate – it might be best to mandate that at the ECB's overnight interest rate target or some mark-up above the target. The allocation would then be based on each member's GDP; alternatively it could be distributed on a per capita basis across the members.

One can conceive of variations on this theme, such as creation of some EMU-wide funding authority backed by the ECB that issues debt to buy government debt from individual nations. What is essential, however, is that the backing comes from the center – the ECB or the EU stands behind the debt. That will keep interest rates low, removing "market discipline" and vicious debt cycles due to exploding interest rates. With lending spread across nations on some formula (e.g., per capita) every member should get the same interest rate.

All of these are technically simple and economically sound proposals. They are politically difficult. The longer the EU waits, the more difficult they become. Crises only increase the forces of disunion or dissolution, increasing the likelihood of eventual divorce and increasing hostility. That in turn forestalls a real solution, which makes the possibility of a Great Depression "2.0" – a combination of a downturn plus Fisher debt deflation dynamics – ever more probable.

Can Euroland be saved through reform?

At this point it is not possible to predict what path the EMU might take toward reform. There are two obvious solutions. The first would be to achieve a fiscal unification to match the monetary unification. That is, one solution is to make the European Union more like a United States, with a fiscally strong center. To maintain more independence of member nations, the funds could be directly provided to the individual governments, perhaps on a per capita basis.

Another alternative is to direct the ECB to purchase a designated amount of member government debt (again on a per capita basis). As the issuer of the Euro, the ECB can always "afford" to buy government debt – simply by crediting an entry on its balance sheet in favor of the member central banks.

Either of those solutions would achieve a "more perfect union", essentially reuniting the fiscal authority with its currency. The separation of a nation from its currency puts unnecessary constraint on fiscal policy that will almost certainly lead to a crisis. The only exception is the case of a nation that can run a sustained current account surplus – which is why Germany has not (yet) faced a crisis even though it also abandoned its currency for the Euro.

We return to the sectoral balances: with a private sector that desires to net save financial assets, then given a current account balance of zero, the government deficit must be equal to the private sector's surplus. For the EMU as a whole, the current account balance was not a problem. But for the individual members, some of which ran significant current account deficits, it meant unsustainable government budget deficits.

The final option is dissolution of the EMU. That could cause a lot of temporary chaos, but once each nation readopts its own currency, it regains domestic policy space to resolve its economic problems. We cannot rule out the end of the Euro – only time will tell.

Box: Frequently asked questions

Q: Can a fixed exchange rate ever be beneficial?
A: An advantage of a fixed rate is that uncertainty over exchange rate movement can be removed – so long as you really believe the peg can be maintained. Let us say you believe it. Then the disadvantage is that the nation gives up domestic policy space since it will have to ensure policy is consistent with maintaining the peg. That is a big trade-off. It could be possible that desired domestic policy is consistent with maintaining the peg. For example, let us

say that you want to run your country in a manner that maximizes net exports – so that your central bank accumulates foreign exchange. In that case, maintaining the peg is facilitated.

Now, exports are a cost while imports are a benefit – in real terms: you work hard to produce goods that will be consumed by foreigners (see Section 6.9). Again, it is possible that such a policy is consistent with domestic goals. Let us say you want to develop your productive capacity and want to ensure high quality products, so you need to perform to global standards. That is a big reason why China wanted to become an exporter. But the net exporter – China – must realize the drawbacks to such policy: workers produce goods and services they do not get to consume. I am not arguing that no country should ever adopt a peg – rather, countries should be aware of the relative costs of doing so. Finally, pegs invite speculators – who bet that you cannot maintain the peg. That is why it is foolish to peg unless you have an unassailable foreign currency reserve.

5.9 Currency regimes and policy space: conclusion

Let us quickly review the connection between choice of exchange rate regime and the degree of domestic policy independence accorded, from most to least independence:

- Floating rate, sovereign currency → most policy space; government can "afford" anything for sale in its own currency. No default risk in its own currency. Inflation and currency depreciation are possible outcomes if government spends too much.
- Managed float, sovereign currency → less policy space; government can "afford" anything for sale in its own currency, but must be wary of effects on its exchange rate since policy could generate pressure that would move the currency outside the desired exchange rate range.
- Pegged exchange rate, sovereign currency → least policy space of these options; government can "afford" anything for sale in its own currency, but must maintain sufficient foreign currency reserves to maintain its peg. Depending on the circumstances, this can severely constrain domestic policy space. Loss of reserves can lead to an outright default on its commitment to convert at the fixed exchange rate.

The details of government operations discussed in this primer apply in all three regimes: government spends by crediting bank accounts, taxes by debiting them, and sells bonds to offer an interest-earning alternative to reserves. However, the ability to use these operations to achieve domestic policy goals differs by exchange rate regime.

On a pegged currency, government *can* spend more so long as someone is willing to sell something for the domestic currency, but it might not be *willing* to do so because of feared exchange rate effects (for example, due to loss of foreign currency reserves through imports).

To be sure, even a country that adopts a floating rate might constrain domestic policy to avoid currency pressures. But the government operating with a pegged exchange rate can actually be forced to default on that commitment, while the government with a floating rate or a managed float cannot be forced to default.

The constraints are thus tighter on the pegged regime because anything that triggers concern about its ability to convert at the pegged rate automatically generates fear of default (they amount to the same thing). The fear can lead to credit downgrades, raising interest rates and making it more costly to service debt. All externally held government debt is effectively a claim on foreign currency reserves in the case of a convertible currency (where government promises to convert at a fixed exchange rate). If concern about ability to convert arises, then only 100% reserves against the debt guarantees there is no default risk. (Domestic claims on government might not have the same implication since government has some control over domestic residents – it could, for example, raise taxes and insist on payment only in the domestic currency.) It can also prohibit the domestic population from converting to the foreign currency. Recall that even when the United States was on a gold standard, it prohibited Americans from converting to gold.

6
Monetary and Fiscal Policy for Sovereign Currencies: What Should Government Do?

In this chapter we will turn to *what* government *ought to do*. This chapter will specifically treat only sovereign government – one that issues its own currency. From the chapters above, that will make it clear that we are addressing only a government that does not face an affordability constraint. In this chapter we will examine alternative views about the proper role for government – given that it can "afford" anything for sale in its own currency. We first look at five reasons why government spending ought to be constrained. We then compare and contrast a typical "conservative" versus "liberal" view about the scope of government. (These terms are used in the American sense, which is somewhat idiosyncratic. The liberal view in the United States is closer to the progressive, Social Democrat, "left" view in Europe; the conservative view is closer to what is called "liberal" or even "neoliberal" outside the United States.) In the next chapter we examine an example of a government program that is consistent with the MMT view of sovereign money – one that uses the principles we have established in previous chapters to resolve the problem of unemployment in a manner that is consistent with both the liberal and the conservative views.

6.1 Just because government can afford to spend does not mean government ought to spend

Understanding *how* government spends leads to the conclusion that *affordability* is not really the issue – government can always *afford* the "keystrokes" necessary to make expenditures as desired. But that does not mean it *should*. We can list several legitimate reasons for constraining government spending:

- too much spending can cause inflation
- too much spending could pressure the exchange rate
- too much spending by government might leave too few resources for private interests
- government should not do *everything* – impacts on incentives could be perverse
- budgeting provides a lever to manage and evaluate government projects

For example, suppose government decides to newly hire 1,000 rocket scientists for an expedition to Pluto. Our first consideration is whether there *are* 1,000 rocket scientists available for hire with the necessary skills. Even if government can *afford* its desired spending plan that does not mean it can accomplish its mission if the resources are not available. In other words, the government always faces a possible "real resource" constraint: do the resources exist, and are they for sale or hire? Related to this consideration, we need to determine whether the existing infrastructure, technology, and knowledge are up to the task of achieving program goals. That, of course, is an important question. Let us presume that these conditions are met.

The second consideration, then, concerns competition with alternative uses of the resources – what is called the "opportunity cost". If those 1,000 rocket scientists would otherwise be unemployed, then the opportunity cost of hiring them for the Pluto mission is low or zero. (We might find, for example, that if they were not employed they would take care of their children at home so the nonzero opportunity cost of employing them is the value of the forgone child-care services. You get the picture – it is not likely that opportunity costs *are* zero, but for unemployed labor they are probably very low relative to benefits of employment in appropriate jobs.)

More importantly, it is likely that many or most of them are already working, either in the private sector or on other government projects. Since sovereign government does not face an affordability constraint, it can win a bidding war against the private sector if it chooses to do so. In that case, it will push up the wages of rocket scientists so high that the private sector gives up and hires workers with other credentials, or shuts down private undertakings. The impacts on the private sector could be complex – likely leading to higher wages, higher product costs, and even less output in those sectors that use rocket scientists and other skilled workers who can substitute to some degree for rocket scientists (perhaps for some purposes, some types of engineers are almost as good, so firms bid up their wages, too). At the very least, the Pluto mission could lead to "bottlenecks" – relative shortages of key resources – and some (perhaps limited) price hikes. Public policy ought to consider the opportunity cost of hiring rocket scientists away from other employment.

In addition, other wages and prices might be increased through spill-over effects if a new government program is so big that it sets off a general bidding war for labor and other resources. For example, during a major war like WWII, government not only conscripts workers into the military but it also redirects resources to production for the war effort. Without rationing and wage and price controls, it is relatively easy for this to lead to a general price and wage inflation. Note that it does not take a major war for this to happen. If government spending pushes the economy to, and beyond, full employment it is likely that inflation will result even in the absence of a major war.

At the same time, high domestic employment and income can – under some circumstances – lead to a trade deficit (as domestic demand for imports rises relative to foreign demand for exports – discussed in the previous chapter). This might then pressure exchange rates (although the correlation between trade deficits and exchange rate depreciation is far from certain).

Hence, while government can afford to spend more, it must weigh the consequences in terms of withdrawing resources from other (perhaps more desirable) uses, as well as possible impacts on prices and exchange rates.

There are other reasons to constrain government spending. For example, conservatives often argue that spending on "welfare" affects incentives. A strong social safety net might send the signal that individuals do not really need to work because they can always live well enough on government handouts. Or, government bailouts of business might encourage management to take excessive risks on the belief that no matter what happens, government will cover the firm's losses. Further, a corrupt government might spend on programs that help friends, but refuse to do anything to assist more deserving groups – what is often called "crony capitalism". So there could be complex, and even unintended, consequences of government programs.

We also need to analyze effects on the private sector. The more resources we remove from private use to allocate to public use, the greater the likelihood that we could have a bloated government sector and a private sector that is too small. We need to leave an adequate supply of resources for the private sector to achieve the private purpose, even as we allocate sufficient resources to achieve the public purpose. Obviously, this is not merely an economic question (see the next section).

All of that must be considered when undertaking government spending programs, and negative consequences raise legitimate concerns about the size of government spending, not due to the (im) possibility of insolvency but rather to undesired (and even unknown unknowns, as Donald Rumsfeld might say) effects of government programs.

Finally, governments should, and do, use budgets, which are a form of self-imposed constraint. Typically, the elected representatives will allocate a sum to be spent on a particular project. Program managers are then held accountable for finishing the project within the budgeted amount. Overrunning the budget can be used as an indication of mismanagement. The budgeting process also helps to reduce the incentive for "mission creep", expanding the project to enhance the manager's power and prestige. In other words, budgeting by sovereign government provides a useful mechanism for project control and evaluation. Although government could always afford to spend more, budgeting offers a viable tool for accountability.

We conclude this section by observing that absence of an "affordability" constraint does not imply that government *ought* to spend without constraint. As we discuss in the next section, its spending ought to be aimed toward achieving the "public purpose".

6.2   The "free" market and the public purpose

The households and business firms in a modern capitalist economy make many of the important economic decisions that contribute to determination of the level of employment and output, the composition of that output, the distribution of income, and the prices at which output is sold.

Claims are sometimes made that a "free market" economy comprised of individuals seeking only their own self-interest can act "harmoniously", as if guided by an "invisible hand". While modern capitalist economies are often characterized as "market" economies, it must be admitted that much or even most economic activity takes place outside markets. For example, much activity takes place within the household or extended family and social groups. Parents (mostly) care for their children without monetary compensation and without inducement from "market forces". And as the economist Ronald Coase demonstrated long ago, the organization of production within a firm is, by design, an attempt to reduce the role played by "the market" to increase the firm's efficiency. Industrial structure – including vertical and horizontal integration – also takes place to subvert market forces. Labor unions and organization of management replace markets with collective bargaining.

Given such realities, it would be quite a stretch to conclude that capitalist economies approximate the "free market economies" of textbook economics, and it would require an even greater leap of faith to believe that government can be removed, to let the invisible hand guide our real world economies to equilibrium.

In fact, economists had rigorously demonstrated by the 1950s that the conditions under which even a highly stylized and simplified economy could reach such a result cannot be expected to exist in the real world. In other words, there is no scientific basis for the claim that "free markets" are best. (That doesn't "prove" it is impossible for the "invisible hand" to work – we simply do not know – but we should be highly skeptical of the possibility.) In any case, these claims that free markets are best – even if true for some hypothesized economy – are irrelevant for the modern capitalist economies that actually exist.

This is because all modern capitalist economies are "mixed", with huge corporations (including multinational firms), labor organizations, and big government. (The US federal government, for example, is said to be the biggest purchaser in the world.) Individuals and firms operate within socio-politico-cultural-economic structures that are constraining and also enabling. Sometimes the goals of individuals and firms coincide with what might be called the public purpose while often they do not. In this section we will discuss the public purpose and the role played by government in trying to align private interests with the public purpose.

What is the public purpose? It is not easy to define or to identify. One of the basic functions of any social organization is to provide the necessary food, clothing, shelter, education, health care, legal framework, and socialization for survival of the society. While the subject of this Primer is macroeconomics, there is no sharp distinction between the sphere of economics and the concerns of other social sciences that study social processes. We usually think of the economy as the main part of the social organization that is responsible for provision of the material means of survival: the food, clothing, shelter, and so on. However, the economy is always embedded in the social organization as a whole, affecting and affected by culture, politics, and social institutions. Even if we can agree that any successful economic organization should be able to produce adequate food for its population, that still leaves open many questions: What kind of food? How should it be produced? How should it be distributed? What does adequate mean?

Further, no society is comprised of harmonious individuals and groups. There are always conflicting claims and goals that must be moderated. There is no single, obvious public purpose to which all members of a society wish to strive. Even if we can identify a set of goals that the majority of society would like to work toward, that set will surely change over time as hopes and dreams evolve. The public purpose is an evolving concept. The national government must play an important role in society as it helps to identify the public purpose and to establish a social structure in which individuals and groups will work toward achieving the social (public and private) purpose. It has long been believed that a democratic government is better able to do this. But it is not even clear what form democracy should take.

We conclude with three important points. First, the public purpose is broad and evolving, and for these reasons it varies across time and place. The public purpose is inherently a progressive (liberal in the US sense) agenda that strives to continually improve the material, social, physical, and psychological well-being of all members of society. It is inherently "aspirational" in the sense that there is no endpoint as the frontiers of the public purpose will continually expand.

Second, the national government as well as international organizations must play important roles in shaping our vision regarding the types of societies to which we aspire. And beyond setting these goals, governments at all levels must take the lead in developing sets of institutions, rules of behavior, and sanctions for undesirable behavior in order to move toward reaching the goals set as the public purpose.

And that leads to the third point: all of this is highly contentious. Further, it is likely that some goals conflict with others, meaning that trying to ensure one might make it more difficult to ensure another. Domestic interest groups might fight hard against policy designed to meet the goals.

Clearly, all of this carries us far beyond economics and into the realm of politics, sociology, religion, ideology, and culture. Generally, conservatives tend to define the public purpose in narrow terms, desiring to constrain government. Liberals generally see a bigger role for the government to play in securing the public purpose. While economics can shed some light on this issue, it cannot provide a conclusive answer.

Below we will examine a conservative – Austrian economics – approach to MMT (see Section 7.6). We will see that MMT is perfectly consistent with a small government economy, one whose view of the "public purpose" is quite narrow. This is not a view embraced by this Primer, but it is one that is consistent with the MMT approach. That is an important recognition. MMT, by itself, is neither left nor right. On one level, it is a description. However, when we add MMT to the more liberal vision of the public purpose, or when we add to the public purpose considerations such as "full employment and price stability", or even just "economic stability", then MMT helps us to find a way to achieve that public purpose by quickly disposing of the notion that government cannot "afford" such policies.

6.3 Functional finance

In the 1940s Abba Lerner came up with what he called the functional finance approach to policy. He posed two principles:

First Principle: if domestic income is too low, government needs to spend more (relative to taxes). Unemployment is sufficient evidence of this condition, so if there is unemployment it means government spending is too low (or taxes are too high).

Second Principle: if the domestic interest rate is too high, it means government needs to provide more "money", mostly in the form of bank reserves, to lower the interest rate.

The idea is pretty simple. A government that issues its own currency has the fiscal and monetary policy space to spend enough to get the economy to full employment and to set its interest rate target where it wants. (We will address exchange rate regimes below; a fixed exchange rate system requires a modification to this claim.) For a sovereign nation, "affordability" is not an issue; it spends by crediting bank accounts with its own IOUs, something it can never run out of. If there is unemployed labor, government can always afford to hire it, and by definition unemployed labor is willing to work for money.

Lerner realized that this does not mean government should spend as if the "sky is the limit" – runaway spending would be inflationary (and, as discussed earlier, it does not presume that government spending won't affect the exchange rate). When Lerner first formulated the functional finance approach (in the early 1940s), inflation was not a major concern; the United States had recently lived through *deflation* in the Great Depression. However, over time, inflation became a serious concern, and Lerner proposed a form of wage and price controls to constrain inflation that he believed would result as the economy nears full employment. Whether or not that would be an effective and desired way of attenuating inflation pressures is not our concern here. The point is that Lerner was only arguing that government should use its spending power with a view to moving the economy toward full employment while recognizing that it might have to adopt measures to fight inflation.

Lerner rejected the notion of "sound finance" – that is, the belief that government ought to run its finances as if it were like a household or a firm. He could see no reason for the government to try to balance its budget annually, over the course of a business cycle, or ever. For Lerner, "sound" finance (budget balancing) is not "functional"; it does not help to achieve the public purpose (including, for example, full employment). If the budget were occasionally balanced, so be it; but if it never balanced, that would be fine too. He also rejected any attempt to keep a budget deficit below any specific ratio to GDP, as well as any arbitrary debt to GDP ratio. The "correct" deficit would be the one that achieves full employment.

Similarly the "correct" debt ratio would be the one consistent with achieving the desired interest rate target. (Contrast that with the conventional views of "sustainability" of deficit and debt ratios discussed earlier.) This follows from his second principle: if government issues too many bonds, it has by the same token issued too few bank reserves and cash. The solution is for the treasury and central bank to stop selling bonds, and, indeed, for the central bank to engage in open market purchases (buying treasuries by crediting the selling banks with reserves). That will allow the overnight rate to fall as banks obtain more reserves and the public gets more cash. Essentially, the second principle just says that government ought to let the banks, households, and firms achieve the portfolio balance between "money" (reserves and cash) and bonds desired. It follows that government bond sales are not really a "borrowing" operation required to let the government deficit spend. Rather, bond sales are really part of monetary policy, designed to help the central bank to hit its interest-rate target. All of that is consistent with the modern money view advanced in previous sections.

Box: Milton Friedman's version of functional finance: a proposal for integration of fiscal and monetary policy

In the context of today's conventional wisdom about the dangers of budget deficits, Lerner's views appear somewhat radical. What is surprising is that they were not all that radical at the time. As everyone knows, Milton Friedman was a conservative economist and a vocal critic of "big government" and of Keynesian economics. No one has more solid credentials on the topic of constraining both fiscal and monetary policy than Friedman. Yet in 1948 he made a proposal that was almost identical to Lerner's functional finance views. This demonstrates how far today's debate has moved away from a clear understanding of the policy space available to a sovereign government, but also that Lerner's ideas must have been "in the air", so to speak, widely shared by economists across the political spectrum. Below we will also visit Paul Samuelson's comment on this topic which provides a cogent explanation for today's confusion about fiscal and monetary policy. As Samuelson hints, the confusion was purposely created in order to mystify the subject.

Briefly, Milton Friedman's 1948 article, "A Monetary and Fiscal Framework for Economic Stability", put forward a proposal according to which the government would run a balanced budget only at full employment, with deficits in recession and surpluses in economic booms. There is little doubt that most economists in the early postwar period shared Friedman's views on that. But Friedman went further, almost all the way to Lerner's functional finance approach: all government spending would be paid for by issuing government money (currency and bank reserves); when taxes were paid, this money would be "destroyed" (just as you tear up your own IOU when it is returned to you). Thus, budget deficits lead to net money creation. Surpluses would lead to net reduction of money.

He thus proposed to combine monetary policy and fiscal policy, using the budget to control monetary emission in a counter-cyclical manner. (He also would have eliminated private money creation by banks through a 100 percent reserve requirement – an idea he had picked up from Irving Fisher and Herbert Simons in the early 1930s – hence, there would be no "net" money creation by private banks. They would expand the supply of bank money only as they accumulated reserves of government-issued money. We will not address this part of the proposal, but it ensures a one-to-one link between the fiscal deficit and money creation if it can be enforced.) This stands in stark contrast to later conventional views (such as those associated with the ISLM model taught in textbooks) that "dichotomized" monetary and fiscal policy. Friedman, too, later argued that the central bank ought to control the money supply, delinking in his later work the connection between fiscal policy and monetary policy. But at least in this 1948 paper he clearly tied the two in a manner consistent with Lerner's approach.

Friedman believed his proposal would result in strong counter-cyclical forces to help stabilize the economy as monetary and fiscal policy operate with combined force: deficits and net money creation when unemployment exists; surpluses and net money destruction when at full employment. Further, his plan for counter-cyclical stimulus is rules-based, not based on discretionary policy; it would operate automatically, quickly, and always at just the right level. As is well known, he later became famous for his distrust of discretionary policy, arguing for "rules" rather than "authorities". This 1948 paper provides a neat way of tying policy to rules that automatically stabilize output and employment at near full levels.

We see that Friedman's "proposal" is actually quite close to a description of the way things work in a sovereign nation. When government spends, it does so by creating "high powered money" (HPM) – that is, by crediting bank reserves. When it taxes, it destroys HPM, debiting bank reserves. A deficit necessarily leads to a net injection of reserves, to what Friedman called money creation.

Most have come to believe that government finances its spending through taxes, and that deficits force the government to borrow back its own money so that it can spend. However, any close analysis of the balance sheet effects of fiscal operations shows that Friedman (and Lerner) had it about right: government spends by "creating money" through keystroke entries to balance sheets.

But if that is so, why do we fail to maintain full employment? The problem is that the automatic stabilizers are not sufficiently strong to offset fluctuations of private demand. Note that Friedman would have had government deficits and, thus, net money emission so long as the economy operated below full employment. Again, that is quite close to Lerner's functional finance view, and as discussed above it was a common view of economists in the early postwar period. But almost no respectable economist or politician will today go along with that on the belief it would be inflationary and/or would bust the budget. Such is the sorry state of economics education today.

In Friedman's proposal, the size of government would be determined by what the population wanted government to provide. Tax rates would then be set in such a way so as to balance the budget only at full employment. Obviously that is consistent with Lerner's approach: if unemployment exists, government needs to spend more, without worrying about whether that generates a budget deficit. Essentially, Friedman's proposal is to have the budget move counter-cyclically so that it will operate as an automatic stabilizer. And, indeed, that is how modern government budgets do operate: deficits increase in recessions and shrink in expansions. In robust expansions, budgets even move to surpluses (this happened in the United States during the administration of President Clinton). Yet we usually observe that these swings to deficits are not sufficiently large to keep the economy at full employment.

6.4 Functional finance versus the government budget constraint

The functional finance approach of Lerner was mostly forgotten by the 1970s. Indeed, it was replaced in academia with something known as the "government budget constraint". The idea is simple: a government's spending is constrained by its tax revenue, its ability to borrow (sell bonds), and "printing money". In this view, government really spends its tax revenue and borrows money from markets in order to finance a shortfall of tax revenue. If all else fails, it can run the printing presses, but most economists abhor this activity because it is believed to be highly inflationary. Indeed, economists continually refer to hyperinflationary episodes – such as Germany's Weimar republic, Hungary's experience, or in modern times, Zimbabwe – as cautionary tales against "financing" spending through printing money. (We'll study higher inflation rates in the next chapter.)

Note that there are two related points that are being made. First, government is "constrained" much like a household. A household has income (wages, interest, profits) and when that is insufficient it can run a deficit through borrowing from a bank or other financial institution. While it is recognized that government can also print money, which is something households cannot do, this is seen as extraordinary behavior – sort of a last resort, and a bad idea to boot. There is no recognition that *all* spending by government is actually done by crediting bank accounts – keystrokes that are more akin to "printing money" than to "spending out of income". That is to say, the second point is that the conventional view does not recognize that as the issuer of the sovereign currency, government *cannot* really rely on taxpayers or financial markets to supply it with the "money" it needs. From inception, taxpayers and financial markets can only supply to the government the "money" they received *from* government. Taxpayers pay taxes using government's own IOUs; banks use government's own IOUs to buy bonds from government.

This confusion by economists then leads to the views propagated by the media and by policymakers: a government that continually spends more than its tax revenue is "living beyond its means", flirting with "insolvency" because eventually markets will "shut off credit". To be sure, many macroeconomists do not make these mistakes; they recognize that a sovereign government cannot really become insolvent in its own currency. They do recognize that government can make all promises as they come due, because it can "run the printing presses". Yet they shudder at the thought since that would expose the nation to the dangers of inflation or hyperinflation. The discussion by policymakers – at least in the United States – is far more confused. For example, President Obama frequently asserted throughout 2010 that the US government was "running out of money", like a household that had spent all the money it had saved in a cookie jar.

So how did we get to this point? How could we have forgotten what Lerner and Friedman clearly understood?

The United States (and many other nations) really did face inflationary pressures from the late 1960s until the 1990s (at least periodically). Those who believed the inflation resulted from too much government spending helped to fuel the creation of the balanced budget "religion" (see the Box on Paul Samuelson's view) to fight the inflation. The problem is that what started as something recognized by economists and policymakers to be a "myth" came to be believed as the truth. An incorrect understanding was developed.

Originally the myth might have been "functional" in the sense that it constrained a government that otherwise would spend too much, creating inflation. But like many useful myths, this one became a harmful myth – an example of what John Kenneth Galbraith called an "innocent fraud", an unwarranted belief that prevents proper behavior. Sovereign governments began to believe that they really could not "afford" to undertake desired policy, as they might become insolvent. Ironically, in the midst of the worst economic crisis since the Great Depression of the 1930s, President Obama repeatedly claimed that the US government had "run out of money" – that it could not afford to undertake policy that most believed to be desired. As unemployment rose to nearly 10 percent, the government was paralyzed; it could not adopt the policy that Lerner (and Friedman; see the previous discussion) advocated: spend enough to return the economy toward full employment.

However, throughout the crisis, the Fed (as well as some other central banks, including the Bank of England and the Bank of Japan) essentially followed Lerner's second principle: it provided more than enough bank reserves to keep the overnight interest rate on a target that was nearly zero. It purchased financial assets from banks (a policy known as "quantitative easing"), in record volumes ($1.75 trillion in the first phase of quantitative easing, with an additional $600 billion in the second phase). Chairman Bernanke was actually grilled about where he obtained all the "money" to buy those bonds. He (correctly) stated that the Fed simply created it by crediting bank reserves – through keystrokes (see the following Box). The Fed can never run out "money"; it can afford to buy any financial assets banks are willing to sell. And yet we have the President (as well as many members of the economics profession plus most politicians in Congress) believing government is "running out of money"! There are plenty of "keystrokes" to buy financial assets, but no "keystrokes" to pay wages!

That indicates just how dysfunctional the myth that government, like a household, must balance its budget has become.

Box: Paul Samuelson and Ben Bernanke on government finance

In a very interesting interview in a documentary produced by Mark Blaug on J. M. Keynes, Nobel winner Paul Samuelson explained:

> *"I think there is an element of truth in the view that the superstition that the budget must be balanced at all times [is necessary]. Once it is debunked [that] takes away one of the bulwarks that every society must have against expenditure out of control. There must be discipline in the allocation of resources or you will have anarchistic chaos and inefficiency. And one of the functions of old fashioned religion was to scare people by sometimes what might be regarded as myths into behaving in a way that the long-run civilized life requires. We have taken away a belief in the intrinsic necessity of balancing the budget if not in every year, [then] in every short period of time. If Prime Minister Gladstone came back to life he would say '"uh, oh what you have done"' and James Buchanan argues in those terms. I have to say that I see merit in that view."*

The belief that the government must balance its budget over some time frame is likened to a "religion", a "superstition" that is necessary to scare the population into behaving in a desired manner. Otherwise voters might demand that their elected officials spend too much, causing inflation. Thus the view that balanced budgets are desirable has nothing to do with "affordability" and the analogies between a household budget and a government budget are not correct. Rather, it is necessary to constrain government spending with the "myth" precisely because it does not really face a budget constraint.

More recently, Chairman Bernanke explicitly recognized that government can spend by crediting accounts. To be sure, he was talking about the Fed and not necessarily about the Treasury. Still, when he was grilled both on TV and in Congress by those asking where the Fed got all the money it was using in QE, he responded in a manner that should make anyone realize government cannot run out of "keystrokes".

On TV, when he was asked if it's tax money the Fed is spending, Bernanke said, "It's not tax money. The banks have accounts with the Fed, much the same way that you have an account in a commercial bank. So, to lend to a bank, we simply use the computer to mark up the size of the account that they have with the Fed. It's much more akin to printing money than it is to borrowing."

"You've been printing money?" (reporter) Pelley asked.

"Well, effectively," Bernanke said. "And we need to do that, because our economy is very weak and inflation is very low. When the economy begins to recover, that will be the time that we need to unwind those programs, raise interest rates, reduce the money supply, and make sure that we have a recovery that does not involve inflation" (http://www.cbsnews.com/2100-18560_162-4862191-2.html?pageNum=2&tag=contentMain;contentBody).

Before Congress, he had the following exchanges with elected officials:

"DUFFY: We had talked about the QE2 with Dr. Paul. When – when you buy assets, where does that money come from?
BERNANKE: We create reserves in the banking system which are just held with the Fed. It does not go out into the public.
DUFFY: Does it come from tax dollars, though, to buy those assets?
BERNANKE: It does not.
DUFFY: Are you basically printing money to buy those assets?
BERNANKE: We're not printing money. We're creating reserves in the banking system.
PAUL: I hate to interrupt, but my time is about up. I would like to suggest that you say it's not spending money. Well, it's money out of thin air. You put it into the market. You hold assets and

assets aren't – you know, they are diminishing in value when you buy up bad assets. But very quickly, if you could answer another question because I'm curious about this. You know, the price of gold today is $1,580. The dollar during these last three years was devalued almost 50 percent. When you wake up in the morning, do you care about the price of gold?

BERNANKE: Well, I pay attention to the price of gold, but I think it reflects a lot of things. It reflects global uncertainties. I think people are – the reason people hold gold is as a protection against what we call "tail risk" – really, really bad outcomes. And to the extent that the last few years have made people more worried about the potential of a major crisis, then they have gold as a protection.

PAUL: Do you think gold is money?

BERNANKE: No. It's not money."

Note when he says the Fed simply "marks up" the size of bank reserve deposits at the Fed he is essentially recognizing the Fed spends by "keystrokes". It is only self-imposed constraints that prevent the Fed from "marking up" the Treasury's deposit account at the Fed – but as we discuss in the Primer, the Fed and Treasury have developed operating procedures to get around that constraint. And, finally, note that in his reply to Ron Paul he summarily dismisses the view that "gold is money".

Even Chairman Greenspan had recognized long before this that the Fed cannot run out of keystrokes. The following comes from page 11 of the transcript of the FOMC's September 21, 2004 meeting (http://www.federalreserve.gov/monetarypolicy/files/FOMC20040921meeting.pdf):

"CHAIRMAN GREENSPAN: Should the Desk today and yesterday create sufficient reserves to keep the funds rate at 1.5 percent?

MR. KOHN: Yes.

MS. MINEHAN: Why not?

CHAIRMAN GREENSPAN: He's not doing it right.

MR. KOHN: Well, he's trying.

CHAIRMAN GREENSPAN: Now, wait a second. He has no limit on the amount of reserves he can create at will. You cannot tell me he is trying and failing; he's just not pushing the button hard enough."

That's right; if the operations desk at the NY Fed is failing to get the overnight rate down to its target, it is not "keystroking" enough reserves into existence! Punch those keys harder!

6.5 The debate about debt limits (US case)

This section looks at a "special case", and one that preoccupied Washington in mid-2011. As we know, governments spend by keystrokes that they can never run out of; a sovereign government that issues its own currency through keystrokes can never face a financial constraint. However, it can choose to "tie its hands behind its back" by imposing rules and procedures that limit its keystrokes. We should not be fooled by such self-imposed constraints. We should be able to see through them to understand that since they are imposed by government on itself, they can be removed. Unfortunately, virtually all economists and policymakers come to see such self-imposed constraints as "natural", something to never violate. Here we will look at the US "debt limit" that consumed policymakers in the United States in summer of 2011, and will likely be visited again and again.

In the United States, Congress establishes a federal government debt limit. When the outstanding quantity of federal government debt approaches that limit Congress must approve expansion of the limit. Note that this debt limit is established by policy, not by markets; that is, Congressional action is required by Congress's own rules, and not by market pressure. Hence it is not a question of whether the US government could sell more bonds, or even the interest rate it would pay on the debt it sells.

In the aftermath of the Global Financial Collapse of 2007, the US budget deficit increased (mostly due to loss of tax revenue, as discussed previously). Predictably, the amount of debt outstanding grew to the limit, and so each year Congress has had to increase the limit.

We now will look at current procedures to see if there is an alternative to increasing the limit, while allowing the Treasury to continue to spend. We examined most of the details of the operating procedures in the previous sections; here we extend that understanding to come up with an alternative procedure. We will use the distinction between High Powered Money (Federal Reserve notes and reserves, and Treasury Coins) and Treasury debt (bills and bonds); only Treasury debt is included in the debt limits, although we know that all of these are government IOUs.

So let us see how we can untie Uncle Sam's pursestrings while living with current debt limits. It is actually a relatively easy thing to do, requiring only a modest change of procedure.

First we need to review how things usually work. Congress (with the President's signature) approves a budget that authorizes spending. The US Constitution vests in Congress the power to create money which should mean that the Treasury creates the money used to finance Congressionally approved payments. But in practice the Treasury uses the US central bank – the Fed – to handle its payments. Current procedure is for the Treasury to hold deposits in its account at the Fed for the purposes of making payments. Hence, when it cuts a check or credits a private bank account, the Treasury's deposit at the Fed is debited.

The Treasury tries to maintain a deposit of $5 billion at the close of each day, as discussed at the end of Chapter 3. Taxes paid to the Treasury are first held in deposit accounts it has with special private banks. When it wants to replenish its deposit at the Fed, Treasury moves deposits from these banks. Obviously there are two complications: first, tax receipts bunch around tax due dates; and, second, the Treasury normally runs an annual budget deficit – more than a trillion Dollars in 2011. That means Treasury's account at the Fed is frequently short.

To obtain deposits, the Treasury sells bonds (of various maturities). The easiest thing to do would be to sell them directly to the Fed, which would credit the Treasury's demand deposit at the Fed, offset on the Fed's balance sheet by the Treasury's debt. Effectively, that is what any bank does: it makes a loan to you by holding your IOU while crediting your demand deposit so that you can spend.

But current procedures prohibit the Fed from buying Treasuries from the Treasury (with some small exceptions); instead it must buy Treasuries from anyone except the Treasury. That is a strange prohibition to put on a sovereign issuer of the currency, if you think about it, but it has a long history that we will not explore here. It is believed that this prevents the Fed from simply "printing money" to "finance" budget deficits so large as to cause high inflation – as if Congressional budget authority (and threatened Presidential veto) is not enough to constrain federal government spending sufficiently that it does not take the United States down the path toward hyperinflation.

So, instead, the Treasury sells the Treasuries (bills and bonds) to private banks, which create deposits for the Treasury that it can then move over to its deposit at the Fed. And then the Fed buys Treasuries from the private banks to replenish the reserves they lose when the

Treasury moves the deposits. Got that? (See Chapter 3 if you don't.) The Fed ends up with the Treasuries, and the Treasury ends up with the demand deposits in its account at the Fed, which is what it wanted all along but is prohibited from doing directly. The Treasury then cuts the checks and makes its payments. Deposits are credited to accounts at private banks, which simultaneously are credited with reserves by the Fed.

In normal times banks would find themselves with more reserves than desired so offer them in the overnight fed funds market. This tends to push the fed funds rate below the Fed's target, triggering an open market sale of Treasuries to drain the excess reserves. The Treasuries go back off the Fed's balance sheet and into the banking sector. (With the Global Financial Crisis, the Fed changed operating procedure somewhat: it began to pay interest on reserves, and adopted "Quantitative Easing" – see earlier discussion – that purposely leaves excess reserves in the banking system, then pays interest on them. Note that the operational significance of Treasury bonds is that they pay interest, so reserves that pay interest have exactly the same operational effect.)

And that is where the debt gridlock problem bites. Treasuries held by banks, households, firms, and foreigners are counted as government debt (and nongovernment wealth through accounting identities!) and thus are subject to the imposed debt ceiling. Bank reserves, by contrast, are not counted as government debt. One solution is to just stop the open market sales of Treasuries in order to leave the reserves in the banking system. That is essentially what Bernanke's Quantitative Easing 2 does: the Fed is buying hundreds of billions of Treasuries to inject reserves back into banks – the reserves that were drained by selling the Treasuries to banks in the first place. So we are getting Treasuries back onto the Fed's balance sheet, and yet gridlock over the debt limit occurs because there are still too many Treasuries outstanding. If Treasury just stopped selling them, the Fed could leave excess reserves in the banks. As bonds mature, they'd be replaced with reserves. And that would be the end of the "debt problem".

Other ways to eliminate the debt limit

There are two other ways to obviate the need to raise the debt limit: Treasury warrants and large denomination platinum coins. Let's examine each.

When Uncle Sam needs to spend and finds his deposit account at the Fed short, he can replenish it by issuing a nonmarketable "warrant" to be held by the Fed as an asset. With the full faith and credit of Uncle Sam standing behind it, the warrant is a risk-free asset to balance the Fed's accounts. The warrant is just an internal IOU – from one branch of government to another – really not anything more than internal record keeping. If desired, Congress can mandate a low, fixed interest rate to be earned by the Fed on its holdings of these warrants (to be deducted against the excess profits it normally turns over to the Treasury at the end of each year). In return, the Fed would credit the Treasury's deposit account to enable government to spend. When the Treasury spends, its account is debited, and the private bank that receives a deposit would have its reserves at the Fed credited.

From the Fed's perspective it ends up with the Treasury's warrant as an asset and bank reserves as its liability. The Treasury is able to spend as authorized by Congress, and its deficit is matched by warrants issued to the Fed. Congress would mandate that these warrants be excluded from debt limits since they are nothing but a record of one branch of government (the Fed) owning claims on another branch (the Treasury). The Fed's asset is matched by the Treasury's warrant – so they net out.

And Congress would not need to increase the debt limit when a crisis hits that results in growing budget deficits.

The second method is to return to Treasury creation of currency – on a massive scale, pun intended. Currently the US Treasury has the authority to issue platinum coins in any denomination, so it could, for example, make large payments for military weapons by stamping large denomination platinum coins. It would thereby skip the Fed and private banks. And since coins (and reserves and Federal Reserve notes) don't count as government debt for purposes of the debt limit this also allows the Treasury to avoid increasing debt as it spends platinum coins. The coins would be Treasury IOUs but would not be counted among the bills and bonds that total to the government debt. Like currency the coins would be "redeemed" in tax payment, hence demanded by those with taxes due. So that is another finesse to get around arbitrary limits or procedures put on Treasury spending

These proposals just show how silly it is to tie the Treasury's hands behind its back through imposing debt limits. We already require that a budget is approved before Treasury can spend. That constraint is necessary to impose accountability over the Treasury. But once a budget is approved, why on earth would we want to prevent the Treasury from keystroking the necessary balance sheet entries in accordance with Congress's approved spending?

The budgeting procedure should take into account projections of the evolution of macroeconomic variables like GDP, unemployment, and inflation. It should try to ensure that government keystroking will not be excessive, stoking inflation. It is certainly possibly that Congress might guess wrong, and might want to revise its spending plan in light of developments. Or it can build in automatic stabilizers to lower spending or raise taxes if inflation is fueled. But it makes no sense to approve a spending path and then to arbitrarily refuse to keystroke spending simply because an arbitrary debt limit is reached.

Before concluding, let us deal with common objections to such procedural changes.

Objection: We need to tie ourselves to budget limits to keep politicians from spending too much

Response: For better or worse we have a budgeting process through which Congress decides how much to allocate to programs, then submits the plan to the President. Once approved, this authorizes spending. That is the "democratic" process through which our elected representatives decide which programs are worthy of funding, and at what levels. Much of the spending is "open-ended" in the sense that it is contingent (unemployment benefits paid will depend on economic performance, for example). I do not see how adding a constraint beyond this is either necessary or consistent with democratic control and accountability. By its very nature a debt limit is arbitrary and inconsistent with the budgeting process. In the past, it never mattered; the budget trumped the limit and Congress routinely raised the limit. Now politics are subverting the budgeting process in an undemocratic manner.

Objection: We need the independent authority, the central bank, to constrain "money creation" to finance spending

Response: As discussed above, Congress and the President first work out a budget. That authorizes Treasury spending. We can come up with alternative procedures to allow Treasury to accomplish that task. A relatively primitive but effective one would be for it to simply print up Treasury notes and spend. Or it can directly keystroke entries into the deposit accounts of recipients, but that requires that Treasury can also keystroke reserves onto bank balance sheets. Since we divide the tasks between Treasury and Fed – having banks "bank at the Fed" – it must be the Fed that keystrokes the reserves. There is no fundamental reason for this; banks could have accounts at the Treasury used for clearing and then the Treasury would keystroke the reserves. But we don't do it that way.

So we could have the Fed act as the Treasury's bank, accepting a Treasury IOU and keystroking bank reserves. But we don't do that either; we say that although the Fed is the Treasury's bank, it is prohibited from directly accepting a Treasury IOU. And hence we created complex procedures that involve private banks, the Fed, and the Treasury to accomplish the same thing.

6.6   A budget stance for economic stability and growth

Lerner likened the role of government to the role played by the steering wheel of a car: government must take control and use its policy steering wheel whenever the economy threatens to veer off course. Because it takes time to recognize economic problems and to react to them, it is desirable to have "automatic stabilizers" in place. The national government's budget is an example of an automatic stabilizer: some kinds of spending automatically go up in a recession (social spending on unemployment compensation, for example) and taxes fall (as payrolls decline, income taxes as well as payroll taxes fall) so that a budget deficit increases. That is good – it helps to stabilize private sector income and provides safe net financial assets to satisfy demand.

To build in sufficient counter-cyclical swings to move the economy back to full employment requires two conditions. First, government spending and tax revenues must be strongly cyclical: spending needs to be counter-cyclical (increasing in a downturn), and taxes procyclical (falling in a downturn). One way to make spending automatically counter-cyclical is to have a generous social safety net so that transfer spending (on unemployment compensation and social assistance) increases sharply in a downturn. Alternatively, or additionally, tax revenues also need to be tied to economic performance – progressive income or sales taxes that move counter-cyclically.

Second, government needs to be relatively large. Hyman Minsky (1986) used to say that government needs to be about the same size as overall investment spending, or at least swings of the government's budget have to be as big as investment swings, moving in the opposite direction. (This is based on the belief that investment is the most volatile component of GDP. This includes residential real estate investment, which is an important driver of the business cycle in the United States. The idea is that government spending needs to swing sufficiently and in the opposite direction to investment in order to keep national income and output relatively stable; that, in turn, will keep consumption relatively stable.)

According to Minsky, government was far too small in the 1930s to stabilize the economy (in 1929 the federal government was about 3 percent of GDP); even during the height of the New Deal, it was just 10 percent of GDP. Today, all major OECD nations probably have a government that is big enough to stabilize their economies, although some developing countries might have a government that is too small by this measure. Based on current realities, it looks like the national government should range from the US low of about 20 percent of GDP to a high of 50 percent in France. The countries at the low end of the range need more automatic fluctuation built into the budget than those with a bigger government.

Moreover, from our sectoral balance identity we know that in the context of a private sector desire to run a budget surplus (to accumulate savings) plus a propensity to run current account deficits in the United States and some other developed nations, the government budget must be biased to run a deficit *even at full employment*. A country with a current account balance at zero *could* achieve a government budget balance, but that means the domestic private sector's surplus (or saving) is zero. So, normally, we should expect a government budget deficit even at full employment except for nations that run current account surpluses (see the Box on Twin Deficits below).

The other thing to be recognized is that a budget surplus (like the one President Clinton presided over) is not something to be celebrated as an accomplishment – it falls out of an identity, and is indicative of a private sector deficit (again, except in the case of a country that runs a current account surplus). Unlike the sovereign issuer of the currency, the private sector is a user of the currency. It really does face a budget constraint. And as we now know, the decade of deficit spending by the US private sector (from 1996 to 2006) left it with a mountain of debt that it could not service. That is part of the explanation for the global financial crisis that began in the United States.

To be sure, the causal relations are complex. We should not conclude that the *cause* of the private deficit was the Clinton budget surplus; and we should not conclude that the global crisis can be attributed solely to US household deficit spending. But we can be sure that accounting identities do hold: with a current account balance of zero, a private domestic deficit equals a government surplus. And if the current account balance is in deficit, then the private sector can run a surplus ("save") only if the budget deficit of the government is larger than the current account deficit.

The conclusion we should reach from our understanding of currency sovereignty is that a government deficit is more sustainable than a private sector deficit: the government is the issuer, while the household or the firm is the user of the currency. Unless a nation can run a continuous current account surplus, the government's budget will need to be biased to run deficits on a sustained basis to promote long-term growth. That would be the "normal", proper budget stance for sustainable growth in such circumstances.

Further, we want to be clear: the appropriate budget stance depends on the balance of the other two sectors. A nation that tends to run a current account surplus can run tighter fiscal policy; it might even be able to run a sustained government budget surplus (this is the case in Singapore, which pegs its exchange rate, and runs a budget surplus because it runs a current account surplus while it accumulates foreign exchange). A government budget surplus is also appropriate when the domestic private sector runs a deficit (given a current account balance of zero, this must be true by identity). However, for the reasons discussed above, that is not ultimately sustainable because the private sector is a user, not an issuer, of the currency.

Finally, we must note that it is not possible for all nations to run simultaneous current account surpluses: Asian net exporters, for example, rely heavily on sales to the United States, which runs a current account deficit to provide the Dollar assets the exporters want to accumulate. We conclude that at least some governments will have to run persistent deficits to provide the net financial assets desired by the world's savers. It makes sense for the government of the nation that provides the international reserve currency to fill that role. For the time being, that is the US government.

6.7 Functional finance and exchange rate regimes

It is clear that Lerner was analysing the case of a country with a sovereign currency (or what many call "fiat" currency). Only the sovereign government can choose to spend more whenever unemployment exists, and only the sovereign government can increase bank reserves and lower (short-term) interest rates to the target level. It is important to note that Lerner was writing as the Bretton Woods system was being created – a system of fixed exchange rates based on the dollar. Thus it would appear that he meant for his functional finance approach to apply to the case of a sovereign currency regardless of exchange rate regime chosen.

Still it must be remembered that all countries in Lerner's time adopted strict capital controls. In terms of the "trilemma", they had a fixed exchange rate and domestic policy independence, but did not allow free capital flows. We have seen that domestic policy space is greatest in the case of a floating currency, but that adopting capital controls in combination with a managed or fixed exchange rate can still preserve substantial domestic policy space. That is probably what Lerner had in mind at the time. Most countries with fixed exchange rates and free capital mobility would not be able to pursue Lerner's two principles of functional finance because their foreign currency reserves would be threatened (only a handful of nations have amassed so many reserves that their position is unassailable). Managed or fixed exchange rates, with some degree of constraint on capital flows, can provide the required domestic policy space to pursue a full employment goal, although matters are simpler for a nation that allows its currency to float.

We conclude: the two principles of functional finance apply most directly to a sovereign nation operating with a floating currency. If the currency is pegged, then the policy space is more constrained and the nation might have to adopt capital controls to protect its international reserves in order to maintain confidence in its peg.

Box: The US twin deficits debate: the functional finance approach

Deficit hawks claim that US government budget deficits impose a burden on America's grandkids, who will have to pay interest in perpetuity to the Chinese who are accumulating US Treasuries as well as power over the fate of the Dollar. This often leads to the claim that the US Dollar is in danger of losing its status as international reserve currency.

In this Box we will address the connection among budget deficits, trade deficits, and foreign accumulation of Treasuries and the interest burden supposedly imposed on America's children.

There is a positive relation between budget deficits and the current account deficit that goes behind the identity. All else equal, a government budget deficit raises aggregate demand so that US imports exceed US exports (American consumers are able to buy more imports because the US fiscal stance generates household income used to buy foreign output that exceeds foreign purchases of US output.) There are other possible avenues that can generate a relation between a government deficit and a current account deficit (some point to effects on interest rates and exchange rates), but they are at best of secondary importance. To sum up: a US government deficit can prop up demand for output, some of which is produced outside the United States – so that US imports rise more than exports, especially when a budget deficit stimulates the American economy to grow faster than the economies of our trading partners.

When foreign nations run trade surpluses (and the United States runs a trade deficit), they are able to accumulate Dollar-denominated assets. A foreign firm that receives Dollars usually exchanges them for domestic currency at its central bank. For this reason, a large proportion of the Dollar claims on the United States end up at foreign central banks. Since international payments are made through banks, rather than by actually delivering US Federal Reserve paper notes, the Dollars accumulated in foreign central banks are in the form of reserves held at the Fed, nothing but electronic entries on the Fed's balance sheet. These reserves held by foreigners (mostly central banks) do not earn interest. Since the central banks would prefer to earn interest, they convert them to US Treasuries – which are really just another electronic entry on the Fed's balance sheet, albeit one that periodically gets credited with interest. This conversion from reserves to Treasuries is akin to shifting funds from your checking account to a certificate of deposit (CD) at your bank, with the interest paid through a simple keystroke that increases the size of your deposit. Likewise, Treasuries are CDs that get credited interest through Fed keystrokes.

In sum, a US current account deficit will be reflected in foreign accumulation of US Treasuries, held mostly by foreign central banks. While this is usually presented as foreign "lending" to "finance" the US budget deficit, one could just as well see the US current account deficit as the source of foreign current account surpluses that can be accumulated as Treasuries. In a sense, it is the proclivity of the US to simultaneously run trade and government budget deficits that provide the wherewithal to "finance" foreign accumulation of US Treasuries. Obviously there must be a willingness on all sides for this to occur – we could say that it takes (at least) two to tango – and most public discussion ignores the fact that the Chinese desire to run a trade surplus with the United States is linked to its desire to accumulate Dollar assets. At the same time the US budget deficit helps to generate domestic income that allows our private sector to consume – some of which fuels imports, providing the income foreigners use to accumulate Dollar saving, even as it generates Treasuries accumulated by foreigners.

In other words, the decisions cannot be independent. It makes no sense to talk of Chinese "lending" to the United States without also taking account of Chinese desires to net export. Indeed, all of the following are linked (possibly in complex ways): the willingness of Chinese to produce for export; the willingness of China to accumulate US Dollar-denominated assets; the shortfall of Chinese domestic demand that allows China to run a trade surplus; the willingness of Americans to buy foreign products; the (relatively) high level of US aggregate demand that results in a trade deficit; and the factors that result in a US government budget deficit. And of course it is even more complicated than this because we must bring in other nations as well as global demand taken as a whole.

While it is often claimed that the Chinese might suddenly decide they do not want US Treasuries any longer, at least one but more likely many of these other relationships would also need to change. For example it is feared that China might decide it would rather accumulate Euros. However, there is no equivalent to the

US Treasury in Euroland. China could accumulate the Euro-denominated debt of individual governments – say, Greece! – but these have different risk ratings and the sheer volume issued by any individual nation is likely too small to satisfy China's desire to accumulate foreign currency reserves. Further, Euroland taken as a whole (and this is especially true of its strongest member, Germany) attempts to constrain domestic demand to avoid trade deficits, meaning it is hard for the rest of the world to accumulate Euro claims because the EMU does not generally run trade deficits. If the United States is a primary market for China's excess output but Euro assets are preferred over Dollar assets, then exchange rate adjustment between the (relatively plentiful) Dollar and (relatively scarce) Euro could destroy China's market for its exports.

This should not be interpreted as an argument that the current situation will go on forever, although it could persist much longer than most commentators presume. But changes are complex and there are strong incentives against the sort of simple, abrupt, and dramatic shifts often posited as likely scenarios. The complexity as well as the linkages among balance sheets ensure that transitions will be moderate and slow – there will be no sudden dumping of US Treasuries that would destroy the value of the financial wealth held by the Chinese, as well as the export market they currently rely upon.

Before concluding, let us do a thought experiment to drive home a key point. The greatest fear that many have over foreign ownership of US Treasuries is the burden on America's grandkids, who, it is believed, will have to pay interest to foreigners. Unlike domestically held Treasuries, this is said to be a transfer from some American taxpayer to a foreign bond holder (when bonds are held by Americans, the transfer is from an American taxpayer to an American bond holder, believed to be less problematic). So, it is argued, government debt really does burden future generations because a portion is held by foreigners. Now, in reality, interest is paid by keystrokes – but our grandkids might decide to raise taxes on themselves to match interest paid to Chinese bond holders and thereby impose the burden feared by deficit hawks. So let us continue with our hypothetical case.

What if the United States managed to eliminate its trade deficit so that it ran a perpetually balanced current account? In that case, the US government budget deficit would exactly equal the US private sector surplus. Since foreigners would not be accumulating Dollars in their trade with the United States, they could not accumulate US Treasuries (yes, they could trade foreign currencies for the Dollar but this would cause the Dollar to appreciate in a manner that would make balanced trade difficult to maintain). In that case, no matter how large the budget deficit, the United States would not "need" to "borrow" from the Chinese to finance it.

This makes it clear that foreign "finance" of the US budget deficit is contingent on the current account balance; foreigners need to export to the United States so that they can "lend" to its government. And if the US current account is in balance then no matter how big the government budget deficit, the United States will not "need" foreign savings to "finance" it, because its domestic private sector surplus will be exactly equal to its government deficit. Indeed, one could quite reasonably say that it is the budget deficit that "finances" domestic private sector saving.

In conclusion, while there are links between the "twin deficits", they are not the links usually imagined. US trade and budget deficits are linked, but they do not put the United States in an unsustainable position vis-à-vis the Chinese. If the Chinese and other net exporters (such as Japan) decide they prefer fewer Dollar assets, this will be linked to a desire to sell fewer products to America. This is a particularly likely scenario for the Chinese, who are rapidly developing their economy and creating a nation of consumers. But the transition will not be abrupt. The US current account deficit with China will shrink, just as its sales of US government bonds to Chinese (to offer an interest-paying substitute to reserves at the Fed) decline. This will not result in a crisis. The US government does not, indeed cannot, borrow Dollars from the Chinese to finance deficit spending. Rather, US current account deficits provide the Dollars used by the Chinese to buy the safest Dollar asset in the world – US Treasuries.

To be clear: the US Dollar probably will not remain the world's reserve currency. From the US perspective, that might be a disappointment. In the long view of history, it is inconsequential. There is little doubt that China will become the world's biggest economy. Its currency is a likely candidate for international currency reserve, but that is not a foregone conclusion, nor something to be feared.

6.8   Functional finance and developing nations

Most of the developing nations have a sovereign currency, which means they can "afford" to buy whatever is for sale in the domestic currency, including unemployed labor. As Lerner would put it, unemployment is evidence that there is an unmet demand for domestic currency that can be filled by additional government spending. At the same time, many developing nations have fixed or managed exchange rates that reduce domestic policy space to some degree. They can increase policy space either through policies that generate foreign currency reserves (including development that increases exports), or they can protect foreign currency reserves through capital controls.

In addition, they can favor policy that generates employment and development without increasing imports (import substitution policies, for example). They can create jobs programs that are labor intensive (so that foreign-made capital equipment is not needed) or programs that provide the output that the newly employed workers need (so that they do not spend their new incomes on imports).

Government can favor domestic producers over foreign producers. It can limit its purchases of foreign goods and services to export earnings. It can try to avoid borrowing in foreign currency in order to limit its need to devote foreign currency earnings to interest payments.

As discussed previously, ability to impose and collect taxes can be impaired in a developing nation. This will limit government's ability to directly command domestic output. And even if it finds plenty of unemployed labor willing to work for its currency, those workers might find it difficult to purchase output with that currency at stable prices. More diligent tax collection will help to increase demand for the currency (since taxes are paid in the domestic currency). In addition, government needs to focus job creation in those areas that will lead to increased production of the kinds of goods and services the new workers will want to purchase. That can relieve inflationary pressures resulting from rising employment.

For the long run, avoiding foreign currency indebtedness and moving toward floating exchange rates would be conducive to expansion of domestic policy space. Full utilization of domestic resources (most importantly, labor) will allow developing nations to maximize output while reducing inflation caused by insufficient supply. Full employment of labor also provides many other well-known benefits that will not be detailed here.

A sovereign currency provides more policy space to government: it spends by crediting bank accounts and thus is not subject to the budget constraint that applies to a currency user. A floating exchange rate (or a managed rate with capital controls) expands the policy space further, because the government does not need to accumulate sufficient reserves to maintain a peg. Well-planned use of this policy space will allow the government to move toward full employment without setting off currency depreciation or domestic price inflation. To that end, the employer of last resort or job guarantee model is particularly useful, a topic pursued in the next chapter (Mitchell and Wray 2005; Wray and Forstater 2004).

6.9 Exports are a cost, imports are a benefit: a functional finance approach

In real terms, exports are a cost and imports are a benefit from the perspective of a nation as a whole. The explanation is simple. When resources, including labor, are used to produce output that is shipped to foreigners, the domestic population does not get to consume that output, or use it for further production (in the case of investment goods). The nation bears the cost of producing the output, but does not get the benefit. On the other hand, the importing nation gets the output but did not have to produce it. For this reason, in real terms net exports mean net costs, and net imports mean net benefits.

Now there are several caveats. First, from the perspective of the producer of output, it does not matter who buys the produced goods or services; the firm is equally happy selling domestically or to foreign buyers. What the firm wants is to sell for domestic currency in order to cover costs and reap profits. If the output is sold domestically, the bank accounts of purchasers are debited, and the accounts of the producing firm are credited. Everyone is happy. If the output is sold to foreigners, the receipts will need to go through a currency exchange so that the producer can receive domestic currency while the ultimate purchasers are using their own currency. We will not concern ourselves with the details, but usually a domestic bank or the central bank will end up holding reserves of the foreign currency (this will normally be a credit to a reserve account at the foreign central bank). The fact remains, however, that in terms of real resources, the "fruit of the labor" is enjoyed by foreigners when the output is exported, even though in financial terms the producing firm receives a net credit to a bank account and the nation receives a net financial asset in terms of foreign currency.

Second, net exports add to aggregate demand and increase measured GDP and national income. Jobs are created to produce goods and services for export. Hence, a nation that would otherwise operate below full employment can put resources to work in the export sector. Wages and profits are generated, families receive incomes they would not have received so that they are able to purchase consumption goods, and firms stay in business that otherwise might have gone bankrupt. This is probably the main reason why governments encourage growth of exports. In the midst of the economic downturn, President Obama announced that his goal for the US economy was to double its exports. This is a common strategy for nations that want to grow. However, note that for every export there must be an import; for every trade surplus there must be a trade deficit. Obviously it is not possible for all countries to simultaneously grow in this manner; it is fundamentally a "beggar thy neighbor" strategy.

To the extent that resources are mobilized to produce for foreigners, the domestic population does not receive any net real benefit. So in real terms an export strategy is a "beggar thyself" strategy. True, labor and other resources that would have been left idle are now employed; workers who would not have received a wage now get income; owners of firms who would not have sold output now receive profits. Yet, if the produced output is sent abroad, there is no extra output for domestic residents to purchase. What happens is that existing output gets redistributed to these additional claimants, who now have wage and profit income. Thus, if we have only put unemployed resources to work in order to produce exports, there is no net benefit: the domestic population is working "harder" but not consuming more in the aggregate because the "pie" available for the domestic population has not increased.

The redistribution process itself will probably require inflation as those who now have jobs compete for a piece of the pie, bidding up prices. To be sure, this could be a desirable social outcome – output gets redistributed from the "haves" to the "have-nots", and putting unemployed people to work has numerous benefits for families and society as a whole (in terms of crime, family breakups, and social cohesion). Further, there can be a "multiplier": the new workers spend wages and producers sell more, generating jobs in the private sector as the economic "pie" grows.

Still, a nation does not need to export to enjoy the multiplier effects. Higher government spending also increases employment and sales. More of the benefits of growth remain in the domestic economy as compared with export-led growth.

But note that these examples rely on the presumption that the nation has excess capacity to begin with. If it is operating at full capacity of labor, plant, and equipment, then it could only increase exports by reducing domestic consumption, investment, or government use of resources. Labor and other resources would be shifted from producing for domestic use toward satisfying foreign demand for output. Clearly it would usually be preferable to achieve full employment by producing for domestic use rather than for export. The additional employment would provide both income as well as more output. The "pie" available for domestic use would be larger, so that rather than redistributing from "haves" to "have-nots", the newly employed would get pieces of the larger pie made available by not sending it abroad.

Another obvious caveat is that producing output for foreigners can be in a nation's economic and political interests for a variety of reasons. A nation might produce goods and services that are sent abroad for humanitarian reasons – to aid in disaster relief, for example. It might produce military supplies to aid allies. Foreign direct investment could aid a developing country that might become a strategic partner. And there is certainly no reason for a nation to balance its current account on an annual basis – something that would be nearly impossible in a highly globalized economy with international links in production processes. Hence we would not want to ignore various strategic reasons for exporting output and running trade surpluses.

We conclude that we should also take a "functional" approach to international trade: it makes no more sense for a sovereign government that issues its own floating currency to pursue a trade surplus than it does for that government to seek a budget surplus. Maximization of a current account surplus imposes net real costs (given the caveats discussed above). Instead, it is best to pursue full employment at home, and let the current account and budget balances adjust. That is far better than the usual strategy, which is to pursue a trade surplus in order to get to full employment.

In the next chapter we will turn to a detailed analysis of a program that would promote full employment and price stability. In an important sense, it follows directly from recognition that "taxes drive money" and hence unemployment results from improper management of the monetary system by government.

7
Policy for Full Employment and Price Stability

In this chapter we will examine policy that will promote full employment with price stability. Most economists believe that full employment and price stability are inconsistent. Indeed, unemployment is seen as a "tool" to be used to promote price stability. In this chapter we first examine an approach to full employment that is consistent with MMT, that is, with the operation of a sovereign currency. We will argue that it is possible to pursue full employment in a manner that actually enhances price stability. We will conclude the chapter with an examination of high inflation and hyperinflation. Many critiques of MMT argue that if the principles of MMT were followed (in particular those that follow from the functional finance approach of Lerner) the result would be runaway inflation. We will dispel those fears.

7.1 Functional finance and full employment

A government that issues its own currency can always afford to hire unemployed labor. However, achieving full employment might affect inflation rates and the exchange rate. Further, there may be different ways to achieve full employment, from "pump-priming" (government spending to boost overall demand) to direct hiring by government.

In recent years, a number of economists have returned to the idea of a government program to operate an "employer of last resort" (ELR) program, also called the "job guarantee" (JG). This was proposed during the 1930s as a counterpart to the central bank's operations

221

as "lender of last resort". Just as the central bank's monetary policy would include provision of loans of reserves to any bank that could not otherwise obtain them, the treasury's fiscal policy would include provision of jobs to workers unable to find them. In this section we will examine one version of the JG/ELR proposal. This version is consistent with the functional finance approach of Lerner but it also helps to address the potential inflation problem that he worried about.

Indeed, we will see that a JG/ELR program actually acts as a powerful macroeconomic stabilizer, achieving full employment (as defined), while enhancing price stability. The key is that the JG provides a price anchor even as it provides jobs for anyone wanting work at the program wage and benefits package. We must be brief, but will provide a list of readings that provide more detail. It would be easy to write a whole book on the program, but we can devote only a few pages here. Proponents of a universal jobs program funded by the federal government argue that no other means exist to ensure that everyone who wants to work will be able to obtain a job. (Keynesian "pump-priming" demand stimulus programs might achieve full employment temporarily, but cannot ensure continuous full employment because they destabilize the economy, generating inflation pressures plus unsustainable bubbles.)

Program design

A JG or ELR guarantee program is one in which government promises to make a job available to any qualifying individual who is ready and willing to work. The national government provides funding for a universal program that would offer a uniform hourly wage with a package of benefits (Wray 1998; Burgess and Mitchell 1998). The program could provide for part-time and seasonal work, as well as for other flexible working conditions as desired. The package of benefits would be subject to Congressional approval, but could include health care, child care, old-age retirement or Social Security, and the usual vacations and sick leave. The wage would be set by government and fixed until government approved a rate increase, much as the minimum wage is usually legislated. The advantage of the uniform basic wage is that it would limit competition with other employers as workers could be attracted out of the JG/ELR program by paying a wage slightly above the program's wage.

Program advantages

Benefits include poverty reduction, amelioration of many social ills associated with chronic unemployment (health problems, spousal abuse and family break-up, drug abuse, crime), and enhanced skills due to training on the job. Forstater (1999) has emphasized how such a program can be used to increase economic flexibility and to enhance the environment. The program would improve working conditions in the private sector as employees would have the option of moving into the program. Hence, private sector employers would have to offer a wage and benefit package and working conditions at least as good as those offered by the program. The informal sector would shrink as workers were integrated into formal employment, gaining access to protection provided by labor laws. There would be some reduction of racial or gender discrimination because unfairly treated workers would have the JG/ELR option; however, the program by itself cannot end discrimination. Still, it has long been recognized that full employment is an important tool in the fight for equality (Darity 1999).

Finally, some supporters emphasize that a program with a uniform basic wage also helps to promote economic and price stability. The JG/ELR program will act as an automatic stabilizer as employment in the program grows in recession and shrinks in economic expansion, counteracting private sector employment fluctuations. The federal government budget will become more counter-cyclical because its spending on the ELR program will likewise grow in recession and fall in expansion. Furthermore, the uniform basic wage will reduce both inflationary pressure in a boom and deflationary pressure in a bust. In a boom, private employers can recruit from the program's pool of workers, paying a markup over the program wage. The pool acts like a "reserve army" of the employed, dampening wage pressures as private employment grows. In recession, workers downsized by private employers can work at the JG/ELR wage, which puts a floor on how low wages and income can fall. We explore some details in the following subsections.

Macroeconomic stability issues

As discussed, the program would set a fixed (but periodically adjusted) basic compensation package. This will ensure that the JG/ELR wage will not pressure private wages in a competitive spiral.

Such a wage would only set a floor below which private sector wages could not fall; thus, it operates like an agricultural commodity price floor, which does not cause prices to rise but only prevents them from falling. Indeed, an JG/ELR program designed along these lines can be analyzed as a buffer stock program that operates much like Australia's wool price stabilization program used to operate (an Australian advocate of the JG, William Mitchell, actually developed his proposal after recognizing that it could operate in a manner similar to his government's wool program). The government purchases wool when the market price falls below the price support level, and sells wool when the market price rises above that level. By design, the program stabilizes wool prices in order to stabilize farm income and thus consumption spending by those who raise sheep.

In the JG/ELR program, government offers a floor price for labor, paying the program wage to participants. Government "sells" labor at any price above the JG/ELR wage to firms (and non-JG/ELR government employers). Just as in the case of a floor price for wool, a floor price for labor cannot directly generate inflationary pressures on the market wage. Indeed, so long as the buffer stock pool of labor is large enough, it will help to restrain market pressures on wages in general as government "sells" labor in a boom. Further, because labor is an input to all production, to the degree that wages are stabilized by the program, production costs will be more stable. Above we noted that income and thus consumption by wool suppliers is stabilized by a wool buffer stock; JG/ELR will directly stabilize income and consumption of program workers, and if other wages and incomes become more stable because of the program, that will further enhance macroeconomic stability.

Critics fear that existence of the program will embolden workers, leading to rising wage demands and inflation. However, there are two reasons to doubt that this effect will be large. First, an effective labor buffer stock will tend to dampen wage demands because employers always have the option of hiring out of the pool if the wage demands of non-JG/ELR workers are too high. The price demands of wool suppliers are attenuated by the government's buffer stock of wool; stubborn wool suppliers cannot raise wool prices much above the government's sell price. The second reason to doubt that obstinate workers will adopt accelerating wage demands is because the further their wages rise above the JG/ELR wage, the greater the costs to them of losing their higher-paying jobs. If the JG/ELR wage is $10 per hour, it may well be true that nonprogram workers earning $10.50 per hour will be emboldened to demand $10.75, but they are not likely to continue to demand ever-higher wages in subsequent years simply because they can fall back on a $10 per hour JG/ELR job. The cost of losing a $15 per hour job is not the same as the cost of losing a $10.50 per hour job.

What about exchange rate effects?

A related argument concerns the exchange rate: if jobs are created that provide income to the poor, consumption will rise, including purchases of imports. This will worsen the trade deficit, depreciate the currency, and possibly lead to accelerating inflation through an exchange rate "pass through" effect (import prices rise as the currency depreciates, adding to inflation of the price level of the domestic consumer basket). In other words, unemployment and poverty are viewed as the cost of maintaining not only low inflation, but also the value of the currency. (This is related to the "Phillips Curve" argument: we need lots of unemployed people to keep wages and inflation in check.)

Two kinds of responses can be provided. The first is ethical. Should a nation attempt to maintain macroeconomic stability by keeping a portion of its population sufficiently poor that it cannot afford to consume imports? More generally, is unemployment and poverty an acceptable policy tool to be used to maintain currency stability? Are there other tools available to achieve these ends? If not, should policymakers accept some currency depreciation in order to eliminate unemployment and poverty? There are strong ethical arguments against using poverty and unemployment as the primary policy tools to achieve price and exchange rate stability.

However, we can challenge the notion that the program actually threatens price and currency stability. To be clear, we should not argue that the program would have no effects on a particular index of prices (such as the Consumer Price Index; see the discussion later in this chapter) or on the exchange rate. Instead we argue that the JG/ELR program provides an anchor for the domestic and foreign value of the currency, hence actually increases macroeconomic stability. As argued above, JG/ELR will not cause domestic inflation, although it can lead to a one-time wage and price increase, depending on where the wage (and benefit package) is initially set.

Similarly, if JG/ELR does increase income when implemented, this can lead to a one-off increase of imports. Even if the exchange rate does decline in response (and even if there is some pass-through inflation), the stable wage will prevent a wage–price spiral. If a nation is not prepared to allow its trade deficit to rise with rising employment and income in the JG/ELR program, it still has available all policy tools with the lone exception of forcing the poor and unemployed to bear the entire burden. In other words, it can still use trade policy, import substitution, luxury taxes, capital controls, interest rate policy, turnover taxes, and so on, if desired to minimize pressure on exchange rates should they rise. (Personally, I would not support such efforts in a wealthy, developed economy. Recall that exports are a cost and imports are a benefit; once unemployment is removed as a problem, then the main argument against imports is removed.)

Affordability issues

As we have seen, a sovereign nation operating with its own currency in a floating exchange rate regime can always financially afford an JG/ELR program. So long as there are workers who are ready and willing to work at the program wage, the government can "afford" to hire them. It pays wages by crediting bank accounts. In no sense is the government spending on JG/ELR constrained either by tax revenues or the demand for its bonds.

Nor will spending on the JG/ELR program grow without limit. As discussed above, the size of the pool of workers will fluctuate with the cycle, automatically shrinking when the private sector grows. In recession, workers shed by the private sector find JG/ELR jobs, increasing government spending and thereby stimulating the private sector so that it will begin to hire out of the pool. Estimates by Harvey (1989) and Wray (1998) put net spending by the government on a universal ELR program at well under 1 percent of GDP for the United States; Argentina's *Jefes* program (a limited JG/ELR program; see below) peaked with gross spending at 1 percent of GDP (this figure undoubtedly overstates net spending because in the absence of the *Jefes* program government would have had to provide more spending on other anti-poverty programs).

Employment swings

I have previously calculated that the typical swing of employment in a US JG/ELR pool would be about 4 million workers – say from a low of 8 million workers in the program during an economic boom and 12 million in a slump. This is necessarily a rough estimate, based on data for the number of unemployed plus those who are out of the labor force but who might be expected to accept a job offer. We also must make a guess about the normal swing of employment outside the program over the course of a business cycle. (The loss of jobs in the aftermath of the Global Financial Crisis was of course much bigger – perhaps three times "normal" – but that was because there was no buffer stock program in place to stop the downturn.) The point is that the swing is manageable; even in a boom there would be a substantial number of workers in the pool so that most projects could continue, and in a slump the new workers could be absorbed into existing projects and some other projects could be resumed or created. Some types of projects would need to be continued even as the pool shrinks, say, "meals on wheels" projects that deliver hot lunches to elderly people. Other types of projects – public infrastructure restoration, or "Habitat for Humanity" home construction for the poor – could be cut back in an economic boom.

7.2 The JG/ELR for a developing nation

A small developing nation presents several challenges. First, it may produce a small range of commodities and import a large number of types of goods that it does not produce (although many of these may not directly enter the consumption basket of much of the population). Further, its exports might be limited to an even smaller range of commodities. Growth of monetary income could immediately pressure the exchange rate. Second, the formal sector could be small, with most production and employment in the informal sector, and with a large disparity between wages paid in the formal versus the informal labor markets. Third, the administrative capacity of the national government might be quite limited. Domestic infrastructure might be inadequate to allow significant expansion of productive capacity. And, finally, its exchange rate is likely to be pegged.

If a universal JG/ELR program is implemented nationally with a wage equal to the minimum wage in the formal sector, there would be a flood of workers from the informal sector. Monetary incomes would rise and the demand for consumption goods – including, most significantly, the "luxury" imports that had been beyond reach for most of the population – would increase. The trade balance could deteriorate and the government would quickly lose the international reserves necessary to maintain the peg. Domestic prices would rise (although direct pressures on prices of domestically produced goods would be limited if these were what economists call inferior goods, mostly purchased by poor families), but more importantly, import prices would rise as the currency depreciates. An exchange rate crisis would be likely to trigger an economic crisis. Is there any way to avoid these consequences?

First, let us see how this nation can reduce impacts on prices, the exchange rate, and the trade balance. It will need to limit the program's impact on *monetary* demand, which can be done by keeping the program's *monetary* wage close to the average wage earned in the informal sector. Thus, rather than setting the wage at the minimum wage in the formal sector, it is set at the wage of the informal sector. However, poverty can be reduced if the JG/ELR total compensation package includes extra-market provision of necessities. This could include domestically produced food, clothing, shelter, and basic services (health care, child care, elder care, education, transportation). Because these would be provided "in kind", the program's workers would be less able to use monetary income to substitute imports for domestic production. Further, production by the workers could provide many or most of these goods and services, minimizing impacts on the government's budget, as well as impacts on the trade balance.

If the program directly provides basic necessities as well as monetary income equal to that previously earned in the informal markets, there will be some net impact on monetary demand. Further, production by JG/ELR workers might require imports of tools or other inputs to the production process. Careful planning by government can help to minimize undesired impacts. For example, imports of required tools and materials can be linked to export earnings or to international aid. Because production techniques used in a JG/ELR program are flexible (production does not have to meet usual market profitability requirements – see Forstater 1999), government can gradually increase "capital ratios" in line with its ability to finance imports of machinery. Further, JG/ELR projects can be designed to enhance the nation's ability to increase production for export. The most obvious example is the provision of public infrastructure to reduce business costs and attract private investment.

A phased implementation of the program will help to attenuate undesired impacts on formal and informal markets, while also limiting the impact on the government's budget. Further, starting small will help the government to obtain the necessary competence to manage a larger program. For example, Argentina limited its program by allowing participation by only one head of household from each poor family. The program can start even smaller than that, allowing each family to register a head of household, but allocating jobs by lottery so that the program grows at a planned pace. The best projects proposed by individual community organizations (for example, at the village level) can be selected to employ a given number of heads of households from the community (again, with selection of workers by lottery). Decentralization of project development, supervision, and administration can reduce the administrative burden on the central government while also ensuring that local needs are met.

As another example, India is implementing a JG only for rural workers, who now have the right to demand 100 days of work (see below). Limiting the program to rural workers helps reduce the migration of population to cities in search of jobs, and limiting the program to 100 days of work per year reduces the number of projects created (and also reduces disruption in the local agricultural sector that typically needs labor for only part of the year; the program employs workers when they are not employed in agriculture).

To be clear, we would prefer implementation of a universal JG/ELR program that pays a living wage. But for practical reasons it might be necessary to start with something less and work toward that goal. In formulating a program, country-specific conditions must be taken into account, including political realities.

International aid agencies can provide some financing for the program, as they did in the case of Argentina's program. Of course, a sovereign government can always pay wages in the domestic currency, so international aid is not needed in order to pay the wages. However, if imports increase because of poverty reduction, the international aid can provide needed international currency. Further, the program might need some tools or equipment that must be imported. For these reasons, international aid in the form of foreign currency could be welcome in some cases. However, international borrowing should be avoided unless the JG/ELR program will directly increase exports to service international debt.

Some of the output of the JG/ELR program can be sold in domestic and perhaps in international markets to generate revenue. For example, *Jefes* workers in Argentina produce clothing and furniture that is sold in formal markets. Further, some of the output of the program can substitute for government purchases; for example, *Jefes* workers produce uniforms for the government. Generally, however, JG/ELR production should not compete with the private sector.

Government should avoid building up foreign currency indebtedness that would be difficult to service. Finally, government can use the traditional methods of protecting its trade balance and exchange rate peg: tariffs, import controls, and capital controls. To the extent that JG/ELR raises monetary wages and monetary consumption, its impact on the trade balance and exchange rates is similar to the impact of domestic growth more generally. The arguments for and against "intervention" in the area of international trade and capital flows are well known and need no further discussion here. While there has been a strong bias against such intervention, the consensus has shifted somewhat in recent years toward the view that protection is acceptable on a case-by-case basis.

7.3 Program manageability

Some critics have argued that the program could become so large that it would be unmanageable. The central government would have difficulty keeping track of all the program participants and ensuring that they are kept busy working on useful projects. Worse, corruption could become a problem, with project managers embezzling funds. We will briefly look at some methods that can be used to enhance manageability.

First, it is not necessary for the national government to formulate and run the program. It can be highly decentralized – to local government, local not-for-profit community service organizations, parks and recreation agencies, school districts, and worker cooperatives. Local communities could propose projects, with local agencies or governments running them. National government involvement might be limited to providing funding and – perhaps – project approval. That is the way that Argentina's program and the new program in India, to some extent, is run.

In order to reduce the likelihood that funds are embezzled, the national government could pay wages directly to program participants. This can be facilitated by using something like a Social Security number, and paying directly into a bank account much as Social Security programs pay retirement pensions. If project managers never get their hands on government funds, it will be difficult to embezzle them. To be sure, there will be some cases of fraud, such as paying to a Social Security number of someone who is not working, or who is dead. Transparency is one way to fight corruption – public recording of all participants and all payments, through use of the Internet, for example, with rewards for whistle-blowers. (Privacy is a concern. However, note that even in the United States the wages of public sector employees are commonly made available. As JG workers would have wages paid by the public sector, there already is a precedent for transparency for public programs.)

To cover management and materials costs, the national government might provide some nonwage funding to projects. In direct job creation programs, an amount equal to 25 percent of the wage bill has been common. The greater the payment, the greater the adverse incentive for project managers, who might create projects simply to get this funding. For this reason, nonwage funding should be kept small, and the national government should require matching funds from projects to cover nonwage expenses.

While it is tempting to include private for-profit employers in such a program, adverse incentives are even greater where production is for profit. A private employer might replace employees with JG/ELR employees to reduce the wage bill. Worker cooperatives might work better. A group of workers could propose a project designed to produce output for sale in markets. The JG/ELR program could pay a portion of their wages for a specific period of time (say, for one year) after which time the cooperative would have to become self-supporting. If it could not stand on its own, the workers would have to move into regular JG/ELR projects. (Argentina's *Jefes* program experimented with worker's co-ops.)

Obviously, there are many more management issues that must be explored. There are many real world examples of direct job creation programs funded by government. Programs must be adapted to the specific conditions of each nation. There will be many trial-and-error experiments. Some projects will not be successful, in terms of providing useful jobs that produce socially useful output. But what must always be kept in mind is that the alternative – unemployment – is more socially wasteful.

Box: Keynes on unemployment

John Maynard Keynes was arguably the greatest economist of the twentieth century, and is commonly called the father of modern macroeconomics. Economic policy adopted after World War II was modeled on what policymakers believed to be his main message: government ought to raise aggregate demand to promote growth and employment. The "Age of Keynes" did see higher growth and lower unemployment rates for several decades after World War II. However, as discussed in Chapter 6, the commitment to high employment was dropped by most countries as economists and policymakers came to believe that full employment is not consistent with price stability. Maintaining a large pool of unemployed people was believed to be necessary to keep wages in check (this is the famous Phillips Curve idea). Keynes, however, had already rejected this idea as "crazily improbable". While Keynes did not put forward a JG/ELR program, he did argue for direct job creation by government. He also appeared to favor directed spending rather than pump-priming. However, I won't go into all that here. Instead, I will present my two favorite quotes from Keynes: the first on unemployment and the second on "doing things", that is, tackling problems.

"The Conservative belief that there is some law of nature which prevents men from being employed, that it is '"rash"' to employ men, and that it is financially 'sound' to maintain a tenth of the population in idleness for an indefinite period, is crazily improbable – the sort of thing which no man could believe who had not had his head fuddled with nonsense for years and years.... Our main task, therefore, will be to confirm the reader's instinct that what *seems* sensible *is* sensible, and what *seems* nonsense *is* nonsense. We shall try to show him that the conclusion, that if new forms of employment are offered more men will be employed, is as obvious as it sounds and contains no hidden snags; that to set unemployed men to work on useful tasks does what it appears to do, namely, increases the national wealth; and that the notion, that we shall, for intricate reasons, ruin ourselves financially if we use this means to increase our well-being, is what it looks like – a bogy" (John Maynard Keynes 1972, 90–2).

"As soon as we have a new atmosphere of *doing things*, instead of one of smothering negation, everybody's brains will get busy, and there will be masses of claimants for attention, the precise character of which it would be impossible to specify beforehand" (Keynes [1929] 1972, 99). (For an excellent discussion of New Deal jobs programs, see the piece by John Henry here: http://neweconomicperspectives.blogspot.com/2012/01/federally-funded-jobs-program-lessons.html#more).

7.4 The JG/ELR and real world experience

There have been many job creation programs implemented around the world, some of which were narrowly targeted while others were broad-based. The American New Deal included several moderately inclusive programs such as the Civilian Conservation Corps and the Works Progress Administration. Sweden developed broad-based employment programs that virtually guaranteed access to jobs (Ginsburg 1983). From World War II until the 1970s a number of countries, including Australia, maintained a close approximation to full employment (measured unemployment below 2 percent) through a combination of high aggregate demand plus loosely coordinated direct job creation. (Often there would be an informal "employer of last resort", such as the national railroads, that would hire just about anyone.) As Mitchell and Muysken (2008) argued, a national commitment to full employment spurred government to implement policies that created jobs, even if it did not explicitly embrace a national and universal JG/ELR program.

During the Great Depression of the 1930s, like many other nations the United States adopted several jobs programs. Again, these were not part of a universal JG/ELR program, but the New Deal programs were huge, and had lasting effects, in the form of public buildings, dams, roads, national parks, and trails that still serve America. For example, workers in the WPA (Works Progress Administration):

> shouldered the tasks that began to transform the physical face of America. They built roads and schools and bridges and dams. The Cow Palace in San Francisco, LaGuardia Airport in New York City, and National (now Reagan) Airport in Washington, DC, the Timberline Lodge in Oregon, the Outer Drive Bridge on Chicago's Lake Shore Drive, the River Walk in San Antonio. ... Its workers sewed clothes and stuffed mattresses and repaired toys; served hot lunches to schoolchildren; ministered to the sick; delivered library books to remote hamlets by horseback; rescued flood victims; painted giant murals on the walls of hospitals, high schools, courthouses, and city halls; performed plays and played music before eager audiences; and wrote guides to the forty-eight states that even today remain models for what such books should be. And when the clouds of an oncoming world war loomed over the United States, it was the WPA's workers who modernized the army and air bases and trained in vast numbers to supply the nation's military needs. (Taylor 2008)

The New Deal jobs programs employed 13 million people; the WPA was the biggest program, employing 8.5 million, lasting eight years and spending about $10.5 billion. (Taylor 2008, 3) It took a broken country and in many important respects helped to not only revive it, but to bring it into the twentieth century. The WPA built 650,000 miles of roads, 78,000 bridges, 125,000 civilian and military buildings, 700 miles of airport runways; it fed 900 million hot lunches to kids, operated 1,500 nursery schools, gave concerts before audiences of 150 million, and created 475,000 works of art. It transformed and modernized America (Taylor 2008, 523–4).

Dimitri Papadimitriou summarizes a number of real world experiences with direct job creation by government, several of them in developing countries:

> direct public-service job creation programs by governments have a history of long-term positive results. Throughout the last century, the United States, Sweden, India, South Africa, Argentina, Ethiopia, South Korea, Peru, Bangladesh, Ghana, Cambodia and

Chile, among others, have intermittently adopted policies that made them "employers of last resort" – a term coined by economist Hyman Minsky in the 1960s – when private sector demand wasn't sufficient. South Korea, for example, during the meltdown of 1997–'98, implemented a Master Plan for Tackling Unemployment that accounted for 10% of government expenditure. It employed workers on public projects that included cultivating forests, building small public facilities, repairing public utilities, environmental cleanup work, staffing community and welfare centers, and information/technology-related projects targeted at the young and computer-literate. The overall economy expanded and thrived in the aftermath. (http://www.latimes.com/news/opinion/la-oe-papadimitriou-job-creation-20120105,0,607208.story?track=rss&mid=56)

For more recent examples, we will turn to Argentina and India.

In the aftermath of its economic crisis that came with the collapse of its currency board, Argentina created *Plan Jefes y Jefas* that guaranteed a job for poor heads of households (Tcherneva and Wray 2005). The program successfully created 2 million new jobs that not only provided employment and income for poor families, but also provided needed services and free goods to poor neighborhoods. More recently, India passed the National Rural Employment Guarantee Act (2005) that commits the government to providing employment in a public works project to any adult living in a rural area. The job must be available within 15 days of registration, and must provide employment for a minimum of 100 days per year (Hirway 2006). These programs represent a relatively explicit recognition that government can and should act as employer of last resort. Indeed, India's program is seen as part of a commitment to a human right: the right to paid employment.

These experiences allow us to move from the realm of theory to the reality of practice. Many of the fears of the critics of direct job creation programs have been shown to be fallacious. Job creation, even on a massive scale and under difficult circumstances, can be successful. Participants welcomed the chance to work, viewing participation as empowering. As the *Jefes* experience shows, the program can be democratically implemented, increasing participation in the political process, and with relatively few instances of corruption and bureaucratic waste. Useful projects can be undertaken. Even with a huge program that employed 5 percent of the population, communities were able to find useful work for participants. *Jefes* reduced social unrest, and provided demand for private sector production.

Could a program like *Jefes* work elsewhere? At the very least, we can learn from the program's successes and failures. As one of the Argentinean organizers put it to me, "The people that actually have the answers are the ones with the needs, those that suffer from starvation. If you target your policies to these people you cannot go wrong. This government did a good job; they addressed the root of the problem. ... They didn't look to the top; they went straight to the bottom." (See Tcherneva and Wray 2005.)

In a sense, the JG/ELR program really is targeted "to the bottom" since it "hires off the bottom", offering a job to those left behind. Its wage and benefit package is the lowest, setting the minimum standard that private employers can offer. It does not try to outbid the private sector for workers, but rather takes those who cannot find a job. Further, by decentralizing the program, it allows the local communities to create the projects and organize the program. The local community probably has a better idea of the community's needs, both in terms of jobs and in terms of projects. Hence it is a "bottom up" alternative to the more typical "trickle down" approach to job creation.

7.5   Conclusions on full employment policy

Lerner proposed to use monetary and fiscal policy to achieve full employment. He argued that unemployment is evidence that government spending is too low, and thus that "functional finance" dictates it is government's responsibility to increase spending to eliminate unemployment. Note also that there is nothing that is inherently inconsistent in believing that market forces are equilibrating and at the same time promoting a functional finance approach to the government budget. All economists recognize that there is some role for the government to play, including provision of a police force and army. Even if that is all government does, we can still argue that government should pay for police and military service by crediting banks accounts, and tax by debiting them, with a budget that moves toward deficit when tax revenue falls and toward a surplus when tax revenue rises. This would not subvert market forces but would enhance stability in exactly the manner that Friedman advocated (see Box in the previous chapter).

In this chapter we devoted considerable space to examination of policy to achieve full employment. To be sure, functional finance is more than a justification for focusing policy on achieving full employment. The basic conclusion of functional finance is that government can afford whatever is for sale in its own currency. That includes unemployed labor. The reason we are so concerned with unemployment is because it is one of the most serious failings of economies around the world. Not only do the unemployed suffer, but their unemployment imposes huge costs on society, both in terms of forgone production but also in terms of the social costs of dealing with the consequences.

One of the reasons why governments do not pursue full employment is because they believe they cannot afford to hire all the unemployed. Clearly, there are also other reasons, but at least we can dispense with that one if we understand the principles of functional finance. Other objections to pursuit of full employment include potential inflation and exchange rate effects. But it can be argued that those effects are minimized through proper design of a full employment program.

In terms of domestic policy options, the sovereign floating rate currency regime makes it possible to pursue full employment policy, for example through a direct job creation program. Even in the case of the developing country, however, a sovereign currency allows government to buy anything for sale in the domestic currency, including all unemployed labor. The program can be designed so as to minimize inflation pressure, but we do admit that excessive government spending can be inflationary. This is quite a different issue from affordability; sovereign government can afford to hire all the unemployed, but it must design such a program to reduce inflation pressure.

The other issue is the exchange rate, and a possible outcome of full employment is that imports might rise and put pressure on the exchange rate. And, again, we conclude that some combination of floating exchange rate and/or capital controls usually will be required to resolve the "trilemma" problem: if government wants policy space for domestic programs, it needs to float the currency and/or to control capital flows. In addition, as discussed, government can design the program to minimize imports and to encourage exports. While moving to a floating exchange rate is often a desired policy, in the meantime it is possible to implement a job creation program even with a fixed exchange rate.

Before closing this topic and moving on to an examination of price instability, let us pose a question: can one who prefers small government adopt MMT?

7.6 MMT for Austrians: can a Libertarian support the JG?

MMT is not just for advocates of big government. Among the most vehement critics of Modern Money Theory (MMT) are the libertarians and Austrians who are certain that MMTers are united in their effort to ramp up government until it consumes the entire economy. This section will attempt to put those fears to rest.

First, on one level MMT is a description of the way a sovereign currency works. Love it or hate it, our sovereign government spends by crediting bank accounts. A few critics of MMT understand this, but they fear that if we tell policymakers and the general public how things work, democratic processes will inevitably blow up the government's budget as everyone demands more from government. This reminds one of Paul Samuelson's argument that we need "old time religion", without which off we go to Zimbabwe-land, with hyperinflation that destroys the currency (see the next sections).

Yet, MMTers fear inflation, too. Indeed, "price stability" has always been one of the two key missions of UMKC's Center for Full Employment and Price Stability (http://www.cfeps.org/). To be sure, many libertarians and Austrians believe that the only foolproof method for avoiding inflation is to go back to gold. Earlier we dispelled some of the myths about the operation of "commodity money" systems. In any case, even if a gold standard were desirable, it is not politically feasible (much less feasible than a JG in my opinion!). Anyway, we (also) do not want black helicopters flying around dropping bags of cash; and we (also) oppose government "pump-priming" demand stimulus (the libertarians and Austrians and even Milton Friedman are correct in their argument that beyond some point this would generate inflation).

It is true that there is a second level to MMT: we use our understanding of the way money works to bring rational analysis to government policymaking. Since involuntary default is, literally, impossible for a sovereign government, we quickly move beyond fears about government deficits and debt ratios and all the other nonsense that currently grips policymakers in Washington and elsewhere. Can we "afford" full employment? Yes. Can we "afford" Social Security? Yes. Can we "afford" to put wine in all the drinking fountains? Yes. The problem *is not, cannot be* about affordability. It is about resources.

Unemployment is easy: by definition, the unemployed are available to hire so government can put them to work. Social Security is a little more difficult: can we move enough resources to the aged (plus their dependents, and people with disabilities) so that they can enjoy a comfortable life? For rich, developed nations, on all reasonable projections of demographics and ability to produce, the answer is yes. The projections could turn out to be wrong. But if they do, affordability still will not be the problem; it will be a resource problem. Finally, wine in drinking fountains? There probably is not enough fine wine, but we could probably fill all the drinking fountains with cheap wine. Again, it is a resource problem and if we convert the American and Canadian prairies to wine production we could probably even resolve that one.

Perhaps the most important policy pushed by most MMTers is the Job Guarantee/Employer of Last Resort proposal. Our libertarian/ Austrian fellow travelers seem to hate this program. I suspect that they have misinterpreted it as a Big Government/Big Brother program. The criticism is simultaneously that it "forces" everyone to work, and that it also pays everyone for "not working". Actually, it is a purely voluntary program, only for those who want to work. Those who will not work cannot participate. Libertarians and Austrians ought to love it. It is not Big Brother. It is not even Big Government. The jobs do not have to be provided by government at all. No one has to take a job. It is consistent with, I think, the most cherished norms of freedom-loving libertarians and Austrians.

So to sum up:

1. MMT is consistent with any size of government. It can be a small libertarian government if desired. But it issues a sovereign floating

currency. It supports the currency by imposing a tax payable in that currency.

2. A Job Guarantee/Employer of Last Resort is also consistent with any size of government. If you want a big private sector and small government sector, keep taxes and government spending low. That frees up resources to be used by the big private sector. But you will still need the JG/ELR to take up the labor resources the private sector cannot fully employ. If Austrians are right about the efficacy of private markets, the JG/ELR will always be small.

3. The JG/ELR program can be as decentralized as desired. I think there are massive incentive problems if you have federal government pay wages of for-profit firms. So I would have federal government pay the wages in the program but have the jobs actually created and managed by: not-for-profits, local government, maybe state government, and maybe only as a final last resort, the federal government. Argentina experimented with cooperatives and they looked to me to be highly successful. And why not let our Austrian/libertarian groups organize their own JG/ELR projects, hiring workers for not-for-profit activities dear to the right-wing heart?

4. The problem with a monetary economy (you can call it capitalism) is that from inception imposition of taxes creates unemployment (those looking for money to pay taxes). If we scale this up to our modern, almost fully monetized economy (you need money just to eat, watch TV, play on cell phones, etc.), we get everyone looking for money (and not just to pay taxes). It is sheer folly to then force the private sector to solve the unemployment problem created by the government's tax. The private sector alone will never provide (never has provided) full employment on a continuous basis. JG/ELR is a logical and empirical necessity to support the private sector. It is a complement not a substitute for private sector employment.

How can the belief that all ought to work (to the best of their ability), and contribute to society, rather than lay about and collect welfare be called socialism?

Let us now turn to several sections that examine inflation and hyperinflation in some detail. Much of the Austrian fear of "fiat money" and fiscal policy derives from their interpretation of supposed inflationary consequences.

Box: Frequently asked question

Q: Does MMT rely on the assumption that government is benevolent, having the interests of the population in mind?

A: Emphatically "NO". MMT "works" no matter how depraved or democratic the government is. That is an entirely separate question. MMT is for Austrians, too, who want a small and weak government.

7.7 Inflation and the Consumer Price Index

The most commonly used measure of inflation is the CPI (Consumer Price Index). In the United States the CPI has increased by a factor of 7 since 1966. Many inflation hawks believe that is due to errant fiscal and monetary policy, and more specifically to abandonment of a "hard currency" with gold backing. Let us look at the issue of inflation and its measurement in this section.

We can quibble about the use of the CPI as a measure of inflation; it has well-known problems we pursue in a moment. But certainly prices have risen, generally, in virtually all countries of the world since the mid 1960s, indeed on trend since World War II. And this is a problem of some concern. As Keynes argued, you need some "stickiness" of wages and prices in the money of account, or you might abandon money. That is what can happen in a hyperinflation; with money's value falling quickly (see the next section), people try to find something else that can hold value.

But clearly except for a few goldbugs, inflation in the United States and in most countries of the world since 1966 has been sufficiently low that the domestic currency remained a useful money of account, and the domestic currency has been voluntarily held in spite of inflation. In truth, economists are hard pressed to find significant negative economic effects from inflation at rates under 40 percent per year. But clearly people do not like inflation when it gets to double digits, and policymakers usually react to double-digit inflation by adopting austerity programs in an effort to reduce aggregate demand.

The question is whether austerity is the right policy. If an economy is operating beyond full employment, then by Lerner's first principle of functional finance, government needs to dampen demand by reducing spending or raising taxes. There are instances in a variety of countries over the past half-century in which demand probably did get excessive, raising production beyond the full employment level. Big wars are the typical trigger for inflation. But in most developed countries, demand has not usually been sufficient to move the economy beyond full employment since World War II. Instead, inflation has mostly occurred in positions of substantial unemployment. Indeed, economists came up with the word "stagflation" to describe this typical position: inflation and unemployment. They even came up with a "misery index" that adds inflation and unemployment together, an index that is really adding apples and oranges but it resonated with voters in the United States in the late 1970s.

In the previous sections we have argued that we can ameliorate the unemployment problem without worsening the inflation problem by creating a JG/ELR program. We won't rehash the arguments here, but such a program would most likely even enhance price stability. But it would be too much to claim that the JG/ELR program would *eliminate* inflation. Let us try to understand why measured inflation is likely to persist in the modern capitalist economy. We need to know a little about the construction of a price index. To be sure, the following discussion is quite general. Every nation has its own experience, its own structure, and its own institutions that affect wage and price setting behavior. To really understand inflation in any particular case, we would need to undertake a detailed study of the particular conditions driving prices (and wages) in each institutional context.

Let's first look at the CPI as a measure of the purchasing value of a currency before proceeding since it is always a concern when we talk about money. To measure price changes, we must compare prices in one year – a base year – with prices in later (and earlier) years. This is much harder than it sounds, because not only do prices change, but products and services change, too. We must adjust the CPI or other measures of price for quality improvements. How much would a modern laptop have cost in 1966? Millions of dollars? Billions? As Warren Mosler always jokes, your iPhone has more electronic wizardry than NASA was able to muster for the trips to the moon. The CPI is more of an art than a science since we have to put prices on things that did not exist, and make hard to quantify quality adjustments. So, yes, the price of a new car today is more than ten times higher than it was in 1974, but it is also much more sophisticated, safer, and more comfortable.

Further, there is something called the Baumol disease. A symphony orchestra back in Mozart's time was as large as one today, give or take a few performers. And it took about the same time to perform a piece, depending on the conductor. There has been virtually no productivity improvement (same number of "workers" working the same number of hours). Yet workers in other fields are infinitely more productive than they were in Mozart's day. There is a similar problem in many other areas, mostly services where you really cannot improve productivity much (think barbers, teachers, doctors).

The relative price of these things should have become insanely expensive over the past 200 years relative to, say, manufacturing output with tremendous productivity gains. It still takes one barber to keep 100 heads of hair looking good. By contrast, a single farmer feeds as many hungry consumers as 100 farmers used to feed. And if we rewarded workers only for productivity gains, our musicians would still be working for Mozart-era wages. But the musician and barber still earn about the same living (give or take a bit) as our farmers and factory workers. Rather than vastly underpaying the farmer and factory worker, we choose to overpay the barber.

At the same time the Baumol disease thesis is that an ever-growing portion of our nation's output is in those sectors that suffer the disease (developed countries are "service economies" in the sense that most workers are in the service sector, where Baumol's disease is more common). So we overpay ever more workers in those sectors. The trend for wages (and thus prices) is up.

Nominal wages grow faster than productivity because we have those low productivity sectors that get the same wage increases. And to carry the analysis a bit further, the thesis is that over time government tends to take over more of these "diseased" sectors, so government tends to grow as a percent of GDP as the private sector sheds the low productivity areas. This is not meant to be a criticism, and of course there are countervailing tendencies. But think of the US health care system and the projected tens of trillions of Dollars of US government budget deficits and you've got the picture.

Blame the concert violinist for erosion of the value of the Dollar! In a sense, a part of inflation is to even these things out, otherwise all our musicians and artists would live like paupers relative to our factory workers. Think of it this way: inflation is the cost of pre-serving culture. Occasionally we like fine art, too. And we like our kindergarten teachers to maintain a class size of 15 students. To keep pace with productivity growth in manufacturing, each kindergarten teacher today would have to have hundreds of five-year-olds crowded into every classroom. It didn't happen. (Well, with state and local government budget cuts, it still might!) To preserve "inefficiency" in the kindergarten classroom we need inflation.

Now, the alternative would have been to hold the line on nomi-nal wages in those areas experiencing productivity increases. Today's factory workers would still be earning, say, $10 per week (along with concert violinists) and prices of output would have fallen on trend, so that a new Honda would cost $200, because of productivity improve-ments. Of course, that did not happen either. And a big part of the reason is that it is hard to be profitable in a "monetary production economy" (analyzed in Chapter 8) if nominal prices are falling.

Indeed, some inflation is probably good. Keynes argued it helps to encourage investment, by increasing nominal returns and making it easier to service debt. When I graduated from college with mountains of student loan debt, I really appreciated the Carter years' inflation (late 1970s) since my loan payments were fixed in nominal terms but my nominal wage rose more or less with inflation! The alternative would be rapidly declining prices in every sector that does not suffer from the Baumol disease, but deflation itself is a dangerous disease. This would be like fighting the common cold with a good dose of terminal cancer.

Let's return to the argument of our goldbugs who are pushing eve-ryone to buy gold as protection against inflation. We might ask: why would anyone hold "fiat money" that is continually declining in "real value"? Why don't we all store our wealth in gold?

Keynes said that no one would hold money as a store of value in the absence of uncertainty. Holding wealth in a highly liquid form like money makes sense only if you are uncertain, and even scared, about the future. In a financial crisis, everyone runs to cash. It gives a very low return, but that is better than a huge loss! If you wanted a good store of wealth, and you were making a decision back in 1966 as to the portfolio you would hold until 2011, it is unlikely that you would have held much cash for the next 45 years. There would have been many assets that would be better stores of value, such as US

Treasuries. However, if we are talking about a desirable portfolio to be held over the next few months, you probably would hold some cash. There is a trade-off between liquidity and return.

I know the goldbugs like gold, but those who bought it in 1980 were kicking themselves for the next 30 years, and still have not recouped their losses in spite of the huge run-up of gold prices since the Global Financial Crisis. In general, commodity prices fall over time in real terms – they are terrible inflation hedges – plus they have storage costs. Indeed, if you take a basket of the globally traded commodities, the inflation-adjusted price trend has been steadily down, with prices falling on average about 1 percent per year for the past 100 years. The reason is productivity increases in extraction, plus discoveries of new reserves. To be sure, we cannot predict commodities prices over the next century; prices could trend up. Further, over the past decade commodities markets have come to be dominated by speculative traders, leading to the biggest speculative bubble in human history. And that, itself, could help to fuel inflation since commodities go into production processes. Still, it would probably be a bad bet to buy and store commodities as an inflation hedge since what goes up in price can go down.

In sum, prices have trended upward for a variety of reasons. Some price rises have to do with measurement issues; some with Baumol disease. Some have to do with market power – unions and oligopolies – which is not necessarily a bad thing. Deflations are worse than inflations. While aggregate demand is most likely not the cause of trend price increases, it is true that lack of depressions in the postwar period is a cause. This is because our "big government" economies with government intervening to prevent return of a 1930s-style Great Depression do not usually experience deflation. If we compare the twentieth century with the nineteenth we find that in the earlier period prices rose in good times and fell in bad times so that the overall price level was just about the same in 1900 as in 1800. But without significant deflation after World War II, there is only one way for prices to go: up. And I repeat: there isn't much evidence that low but persistent inflation actually harms economic performance, although people do not like it.

Let us turn to much higher inflation rates, which do harm economies. We will see that extremely high inflation is unusual. Further, there appears to be no reason to believe that the sort of "creeping" inflation that is common will gradually rise to hyperinflationary rates.

7.8   Alternative explanations of hyperinflation

Many fear that if a government operates along MMT lines, then we are on the path to ruinous hyperinflation. Indeed, MMTers are commonly accused of promoting policy that would recreate the experiences of Zimbabwe or Weimar Republic hyperinflations. These were supposedly caused by governments that resorted to "money printing" to finance burgeoning deficits, increasing the money supply at such a rapid pace that inflation accelerated to truly monumental rates.

It is very easy to titillate audiences with stories about the hyperinflations of the Weimar Republic's paper money, or with Zimbabwe's – which shares the all-time record for number of zeroes on a currency. To be sure, no one wants to defend high inflation, much less hyperinflation. In his classic 1956 paper Phillip Cagan defined hyperinflation as an inflation rate of 50 percent or more per month. Clearly the zeroes would add up quickly, and economic life would be significantly disrupted.

The most popular explanation of hyperinflation is the Monetarist quantity theory of money: government prints up too much, causing prices to rise. However, as prices rise, the velocity of circulation increases; no one wants to hold on to money very long as its price falls rapidly. Wages are demanded daily, so as to spend income each day because tomorrow it will purchase less. What that means is that even though the money supply grows as rapidly as government can print notes, it never keeps up with rising prices. And the faster prices rise, the higher velocity climbs; eventually you demand hourly payment and run to the stores at lunchtime because by dinner prices will be even higher.

Essentially this was Cagan's explanation for the fact that a simple version of the quantity theory did not fit the data: if prices rise so much faster than the money supply, how can we conclude that the hyperinflation is caused by "too much money chasing too few goods"? To fit the facts of experience, the quantity theory was revised to say that in a high inflation environment, the old quantity theory presumption that velocity is stable (which is necessary to maintain a link between money and prices) no longer holds.

So armed with the revised quantity theory, we can still claim that high and even hyperinflationary inflation result from too much money even though velocity is not stable (it rises as money growth lags behind inflation). And as Monetarists claim that government controls the money supply, hyperinflation must be due to government policy. Add to that the observation that in hyperinflation periods, the supply of government currency (paper notes) rises rapidly (with extra zeroes added). Finally, government runs deficits as it finds its tax revenue cannot keep up with its spending, so is said to frantically print money to make up the difference and that adds to the "too much money chasing too few goods".

Critics argue most of the blame for hyperinflation falls to government printing money to finance deficits. The reader can see the parallels to the United States, the United Kingdom, and Japanese situation today: large budget deficits (plus quantitative easing) that stuff banks full of reserves that they can supposedly use to pump up the money supply and prices. Solution? Tie the hands of government. In the old days, gold could serve as the anchor (and of course some goldbugs want to return to those good old days). Today what we need is discipline, in the form of balanced budget amendments, debt limits, or, for deficit doves like Paul Krugman, a commitment to "eventually" slash deficit spending once recovery gets underway.

Let's take a look at an MMT response to these explanations of hyperinflation. I want to make three points:

1. When MMT says that government spends by "keystrokes", this is a description, not a prescription. If critics were correct that government spending by "printing money" necessarily leads to high inflation or hyperinflation, then most developed nations would have at least high inflation, if not hyperinflation all the time because they all spend by keystrokes. Logically, all governments that issue their own currency have to spend it before they can collect it in taxes (or bond sales) – no one else can create it – so there is no alternative way for these governments to spend. Yet they rarely experience hyperinflation. That we have to look to cases like Weimar or Zimbabwe (or way back in time to American Continentals) tells us a lot about the connection between "printing money" and hyperinflation. The causation cannot be found there.

2. Hyperinflations are caused by quite specific circumstances, although there are some shared characteristics of countries and monetary regimes that experience hyperinflation. I will not claim to fully understand the causes of hyperinflation, but the Monetarist explanation sheds almost no light on the experience. There is a sensible alternative. We'll look at three well-known cases from the alternative point of view.
3. There is nothing in the current or prospective condition of the United States (or the United Kingdom or Japan – all high deficit nations at the end of 2011) that would lead one to expect high inflation, let alone hyperinflation.

Most critics of MMT and of so-called fiat money in general imagine a past in which money was closely tied to a commodity like gold, which constrained the ability of both government and banks to create money "out of thin air". The best example was the precious metal coin that supposedly gave a "real" value to government money, and forced government to actually get gold in order to spend. A strict gold standard with 100 percent gold backing against paper notes (issued by government or banks) accomplished the same task.

The reality was always quite different, however, as argued in Chapter 4. Obviously I cannot present a history of money here; please see the discussion above on "commodity money". Put it this way: gold and silver coins were the sovereign's IOUs that happened to be recorded on metal (rather than on paper or electronic balance sheets). In truth, coins usually circulated far above metallic value, at a nominal value proclaimed by the sovereign (this is termed "nominalism"; the Sovereign set the nominal value through proclamation, just like today's pennies that are worth a cent). And their value was not necessarily stable: governments devalued them by "crying down the coin" (announcing they'd be accepted at half the former value in payments to government). They also "debased" them by reducing metallic content, which did not necessarily change their nominal value at all. To be sure, there are cases of relatively stable coinage and prices for long periods of time, but these are associated with strong and stable governments that adopted strong "nominalism" rather than "metalism" (the principle that a coin would be accepted at a value determined by its metallic content).

Indeed, the most unstable periods for coins coincided with weak kings who resorted to weighing coins to catch clippers (those who would clip coins to obtain bullion), while rejecting light coins. As discussed, this created "Gresham's Law" dynamics, forcing everyone to weigh coins, accepting heavy coins in payment but trying to make payments in light coins. A real monetary mess. This was finally resolved by going all the way to nominalism, coining only base metal and destroying the coin clipper's business model.

Further, the gold standard did not operate in the manner imagined by today's goldbugs. First, countries went on and off gold. When a crisis hit, they'd abandon gold. With recovery they would go back on, until the gold constraints imposed forced them to go off when the economy crashed again. Rather than contributing to monetary stability, the gold standard destabilized the economy.

Second, no one really played by the rules. The temptation was always too great to leverage gold: to issue more IOUs than one could ever convert. (Even Milton Friedman admitted this, which is why he argued that while a gold standard might be ideal in theory, it doesn't work in practice.)

Third, the periods of relative stability – Bretton Woods post–World War II, or Pax Britannica pre–World War I – were really dollar and sterling standards, respectively. In each case, the dominant nation agreed to peg the price of gold, and other nations pegged to the dominant currency. It really amounted to a buffer stock program for gold (price ceilings and floors for gold), with international trade actually taking place in Pounds and then later in Dollars (with the Bretton Wood's gold safely impounded at Fort Knox). Conditions required for stability were difficult to maintain, which is why neither system lasted long. After World War I the sterling system could not be restored, and indeed set up the conditions for both Weimar (discussed below) and finally Adolf Hitler. The Bretton Woods system collapsed in the early 1970s, having lasted barely one generation. In both cases, collapse of these fixed exchange rate systems led to international turmoil.

And that is generally the eventual conclusion of most attempts to tie a domestic currency to some sort of fixed exchange rate standard (whether gold or foreign currency): it works until it inevitably collapses.

The goldbug and currency board aficionados are correct that a country that is experiencing high inflation can fairly quickly bring it down by adopting a strict external standard. Argentina did that with its currency board. But that then creates two problems: most countries cannot earn sufficient foreign currency to provide the fiscal policy space needed to keep the economy growing. Second, there is no easy way off the currency board once it is recognized that fiscal policy space has evaporated, making it impossible to deal with a burgeoning problem of no domestic growth and rising unemployment. Argentina experienced a speculative attack on its dollar reserves (even though fiscal policy was quite tight and unemployment was high) and it took a crisis to get off the dollar. Once it did so, it fairly quickly restored economic growth with the fiscal space provided by return to its own Peso currency. The point is that tying to gold or a foreign currency might successfully reduce inflation but it constrains growth. And it is hard to get off the fixed exchange rate standard when stimulus is needed, except through a crisis.

That brings us back to "how governments really spend". Any government that issues its own currency spends by "keystrokes" – crediting the account of the recipient and simultaneously crediting reserves to the recipient's bank. (It could print currency and make payments that way, but the effect will be the same because recipients would make deposits in banks, which would receive credits to their reserves.) I repeat, this is not a proposal. It is reality. There's no other way. You cannot print up Dollars in your basement; government has to keystroke them into existence before you can pay your taxes or buy treasuries.

On a floating exchange rate that is the end of the story. Banks can use their reserves to buy Treasuries, and depositors can demand cash (in which case the central bank ships it to the banks while debiting the banks' reserves). But no one can return government IOUs to demand gold or foreign currency at a fixed exchange rate. There is no affordability constraint; there is no foreign currency or gold constraint. Government can meet all demands to convert to cash and can pay all interest as it comes due through additional keystrokes.

However, on a fixed exchange rate, or gold standard, or currency board, central bank and Treasury IOUs have to be converted to foreign currency (or gold). And for that reason a prudent government must limit its keystrokes. It can run out of foreign currency or gold.

It can be forced to default on its promise to convert. That of course counts as a default on debt. Its "affordability" is called into question by markets when they doubt government's ability to do the conversions at the promised exchange rate. Imprudence is deadly, but history is of course filled with imprudent governments – those that issue too many IOUs relative to the reserves promised for conversion on demand.

The floating rate provides policy space that can be used by prudent governments to pursue domestic policy goals with a greater degree of freedom. History is of course filled with imprudent governments there, too. There is no substitute for good governance. Still, it is curious that except for the losers of World War I (plus Poland and Russia, which were on the winning side but lost the war – so to speak – anyway as they left the capitalist world), there are no cases of nominally democratic Western capitalist countries that have experienced hyperinflation in the past century. And if we limit our data set to those with floating currencies, there aren't any with exchange rate crises either.

Quite curious, isn't it? Only countries with fixed exchange rates or other promises to deliver foreign currency or gold (such as debts in foreign currencies) seem to have hyperinflations and currency crises. And that always seems to come down to imprudent expansion of these IOUs relative to ability to actually deliver the foreign currency or gold.

While it appears that the fixed exchange rate guarantees prudence, that seems to be a foolish notion. The fixed exchange rate introduces exchange rate crises plus involuntary default as possibilities, in the pious hope that government will be prudent. Unfortunately, governments on fixed exchange standards more often adopt the prayer of Saint Augustine: "Lord, please make me prudent, but not just yet."

Far from ensuring prudence and protection from high inflation, when a sovereign government promises to deliver foreign currency it actually exposes the nation to Weimar Republic hyperinflationary risks. It is not true that fixed exchange rates eliminate risks of exchange rate crises and hyperinflations, because sovereign governments are not necessarily prudent. And even if they are, their banks are not necessarily prudent. (Think of Ireland! While the government was the paragon of fiscal prudence, its banks lent in foreign currency until the cows came home. When borrowers defaulted, the Irish government took on all the foreign currency debt – quite imprudent!)

Further, it is not true that floating rate standards invariably lead to hyperinflations. If that were true, we'd have hyperinflation all the time. And it is not true that the ability to "print money" through keystrokes necessarily leads to hyperinflations. All sovereign governments that issue their own currency spend by keystrokes. Even if they promise to convert at a fixed exchange rate, they still spend by keystrokes. If keystrokes invariably cause hyperinflation, we'd have hyperinflation all the time.

We don't. Hyperinflations are unusual outcomes.

7.9   Real-world hyperinflations

High inflation and hyperinflation are rare events. In this section we look at historical examples of hyperinflation periods. Hyperinflations are caused by quite specific circumstances, although there are some shared characteristics of countries and monetary regimes that experience hyperinflation. The simple "printing money" to finance "excessive budget deficits" explanation sheds almost no light on the experience.

First, however, it is important to examine the relation between budget deficits and high or hyperinflation. When Luiz Carlos Bresser-Pereira was finance minister for Brazil during a high inflation period (in 1990 the CPI inflation rate reached 3,000 percent) he provided an insightful analysis of the alternative view. In an important sense, tax revenues are "backward-looking", based on past economic performance. Income taxes, for example, are calculated and collected with a rather long lag. Even sales taxes are collected with a lag. When inflation is running at 2 percent per year, the lag does not matter much, but if it is running 10 percent or 50 percent per month, even a short lag makes a big difference. Government spending is more contemporaneous: as prices rise, government pays more. With high inflation, tax revenue will tend to fall behind government spending, producing a deficit.

Of course, this effect will depend on indexing: how often are the wages, prices, and transfer payments increased as prices rise. In countries like Brazil, with high inflation, the reset period for indexing tends to fall, so that government spending rises nearly as fast as inflation. With tax revenues growing more slowly, a budget deficit is created. Indexing also tends to build in inertial inflation (a wage–price spiral is created as rising prices trigger wage increases that induce firms to raise prices to cover costs). Sure enough, after a temporary dip in 1991, Brazil's inflation rate climbed above 1,000 percent in 1992 and 2,000 percent in 1993. The government budget deficit, which was under 10 percent of GDP in 1992, exploded to over 50 percent by 1993 as tax revenues lagged spending that was largely indexed.

Bresser realized that the way to reduce growth of the deficit and to cut inflation was to check indexing. While it is painful, if government can postpone the increases to wages, welfare payments, and prices paid by government, it can reduce inflation pressures and at the same time reduce the budget deficit.

The important point, however, is that budget deficits are at least to some degree an effect, not a cause, of inflation. Still, it is generally true that if government reduces its deficit (by eliminating indexing, for example) it will reduce inflation pressures. To be sure, it can achieve the same result through draconian tax hikes. Note also that this policy recommendation is not inconsistent with the conventional view that fiscal austerity can reduce high inflation. Indeed, MMTers have always agreed that one way to fight high inflation is to cut government spending or to raise taxes. What they reject is the Monetarist belief that the cause of high inflation is a simple matter of "too much money".

Stopping the inflation (for example by eliminating indexation of government spending) will probably reduce the growth of deficits and the growth of HPM and treasuries outstanding. (That will also reduce interest payments by government, slowing growth of nongovernment incomes and depressing demand.) Alternatively, accelerating tax collection would achieve the same goal. Lowering the interest rate target could also help.

Let us turn to historical episodes with hyperinflation. America has had two such well-known experiences: the "Continentals", and the Confederate currency (Americans still have the phrase, "not worth a Continental"). In the pre-revolutionary period, the American colonies actually experimented fairly successfully with paper "fiat" currencies. To some extent, this was emergency behavior – they were prohibited by the English Crown from coining currency. Some commentators at the time – including Adam Smith – noted that even though these Colonial notes were not redeemable for precious metal, they maintained their value so long as the issue was not too excessive relative to total taxes (see Wray 1998).

As MMTers say, "taxes drive money" – so long as paper IOUs of government are accepted in tax payment, they will be accepted in payment. Still, their value will be determined by "how hard" they are to obtain. If money "grew on trees" (as our mothers used to say), it would be worth only the effort required to pick it. Smith warned that if colonial governments spent too much into existence so that it was easy to obtain paper notes to pay taxes, then they would circulate at lower value.

Both the Continentals and the Confederate currency shared common defects. First, the requirements of wars (Britain versus the Colonies, North versus South) made the currencies overly abundant. Certainly there is nothing new about that – wars generally do generate inflation as government spending ramps up demand, causes shortages, and chases prices up. However, that was also true of the currency issued in the Union (North), which suffered from very high inflation, but not nearly so bad as that experienced in the South. The difference was taxes; essentially there were no taxes backing either Continentals or the Confederate currency.

In the first case, the loose confederation of the Colonies did not have sufficient authority to impose and enforce taxes; in the second, the representatives of the Confederate states believed that the population was already suffering too much from prosecuting the war of rebellion, so legislators did not want to add the burden of taxation. By contrast, even though the North ran large deficits, it retained a tax system to drive the currency and thus avoided hyperinflation. While it might be thought that the South's much worse experience can be attributed to pessimism over its prospects of winning, that does not seem to be the case. Even near the end of the war, when prospects were bleakest, the Confederacy was still able to float bonds at relatively low interest. (For those who are interested in these cases, see my book, *Understanding Modern Money* for more discussion.) It seems that the difference really was due to inability to enforce taxes in both the Revolutionary War and in the Southern Seccession.

Today, the best known cases of hyperinflation occurred during the Weimar Republic and more recently in Zimbabwe. (Less well known but more spectacular was the Hungarian hyperinflation.) The best analyses of these are by William Mitchell (at billyblog: http://bilbo. economicoutlook.net/blog/?p=10554; http://bilbo.economicoutlook. net/blog/?p=13035); Rob Parenteau: http://www.nakedcapitalism. com/2010/03/parenteau-the-hyperinflation-hyperventalists.html; Cullen Roche: http://pragcap.com/hyperinflation-its-more-than-just-a-monetary-phenomenon; and at http://rabble.ca/print/blogs/ bloggers/progressive-economics-forum/2011/08/mythologies-money-and-hyperinflation.

Roche actually looked at ten modern (post-1900) hyperinflations and found several common themes. First, most of the ten occurred during civil wars, with regime changes. A majority also occurred with large debt denominated in foreign currency (this included Austria, Hungary, Weimar Germany, Argentina, and Zimbabwe). I am not going to reproduce these excellent analyses, but let me just very quickly summarize key points about the Weimar and Zimbabwe hyperinflations to assure readers these were not simple cases of too much "money printing" to finance government that was "running amuck".

The typical story about Weimar Germany is that the government began to freely print a fiat money with no gold standing behind it, without regard for the hyperinflationary consequences. The reality is more complex. First, we must understand that even in the early twentieth century, most governments spent by issuing IOUs – albeit many were convertible on demand to UK Sterling or gold. Germany had lost World War I and suffered under the burden of impossibly large reparations payments that had to be made in gold. To make matters worse, much of its productive capacity had been destroyed or captured, and it had little gold reserves left. It was supposed to export to earn the gold needed to make the payments demanded by the victors. (Keynes's first globally famous book, *The Economic Consequences of the Peace*, argued that Germany could not possibly pay the debts. Note these were external debts denominated essentially in gold.)

The nation's productive capacity was not even sufficient to satisfy domestic demand, much less to export to pay reparations. The government believed that it was politically impossible to impose taxes at a sufficient level to move resources to the public sector for exports to make the reparations payments. So instead it relied on spending. This meant government competed with domestic demand for a limited supply of output – driving prices up. At the same time, Germany's domestic producers had to borrow abroad (in foreign currency) to buy needed imports. Rising prices plus foreign borrowing caused depreciation of the domestic currency, which increased necessitous borrowing (since foreign imports cost more in terms of domestic currency) and at the same time increased the cost of the reparations in terms of domestic currency.

While it is often claimed that the Weimar central bank contributed to the inflation by purchasing debt from the treasury, actually it operated much like the Fed: it bought government debt from banks, offering them a higher earning asset in exchange for reserves. For the reasons discussed above, budget deficits grew rapidly from the high and then hyper inflation as tax revenue could not keep pace with rising prices.

Finally in 1924 Germany adopted a new currency, and while it was not legal tender, it was designated acceptable for tax payment. The hyperinflation ended. To say that Weimar's hyperinflation simply came down to a matter of government "printing money" is obviously far too simple.

Let us turn to Zimbabwe. Here is a country that was going through tremendous social and political upheaval, with unemployment reaching 80 percent of the workforce and a GDP that had fallen by 40 percent. This followed controversial land reform that subdivided farms and led to collapse of food production. Government had to rely on food imports and IMF lending – another case of external debts. With food scarcity and government and the private sector competing for a much reduced supply, prices were pushed up.

This was also another case in which government could not have raised taxes, for both political and economic reasons. Again, to label this a simple Monetarist case of government "printing money" really sheds no light on Zimbabwe's problems, which were caused mostly by social unrest, collapse of agriculture, and heavy external debt.

7.10 Conclusions on hyperinflation

My point is not to argue that greater constraints on government spending (or greater capacity to increase taxes) might not have successfully prevented inflation in these cases. However, as one studies specific cases of hyperinflation one recognizes that it is not a simple story of government adopting a fiat money and suddenly finding itself printing so much that it causes hyperinflation. There are probably many paths to hyperinflation, but there are common problems: social and political upheaval; civil war; collapse of productive capacity (that could be due to war); weak government; and foreign debt denominated in external currency or gold. Yes, we do observe rising budget deficits and (by identity) growing outstanding government IOUs. But we also find banks creating money to finance private spending that competes with government to drive up prices.

And, yes, tighter fiscal policy would have helped to reduce inflationary pressures. This probably would not have reduced overall suffering, since a common cause of hyperinflation is some kind of supply constraint on output. But the solution to the problems does not require adoption of a gold standard. Rather, to tackle a problem of high inflation policymakers should try to reduce indexing, stabilize production, reduce demand relative to supply, and quell social unrest. When high inflation has persisted for some time, it also helps to adopt a new currency and to default on external debts.

In conclusion, there is a link among high (or hyper) inflation, budget deficits, and "money supply", although it is not a simple Monetarist dynamic. As discussed, government always spends by "keystrokes" that credit accounts, and taxes (or sells bonds) by reverse keystrokes that debit accounts. Deficits mean government credited more to accounts than it debited, so that government IOUs have been net created in the form of "high powered money" (HPM or reserves plus cash) and treasuries (bonds and bills). As discussed above, in high or hyper inflation periods, taxes (debits to accounts) grow more slowly than government spending (credits to accounts) so we expect deficits to result, which means government IOUs outstanding (HPM plus Treasuries) grow.

This is not the simple Monetarist story in which government "prints too much money" that causes high inflation, but rather a more complicated causal sequence in which high inflation helps to create deficits, that by identity equal net credits to balance sheets. Matters are made worse if a high interest rate policy is pursued by the central bank. This is because government typically sells a lot of treasuries as its deficit rises (sometimes this is actually required by operating procedures adopted, or it is due to a policy of setting the overnight interest rate target above the support rate – in the United States this would be a case where the Fed's fed funds target was above the rate it pays on excess reserves), and interest payments on treasuries add to government spending. If the central bank reacts to growing deficits by raising interest rate targets, it helps to fuel growth of the deficit and also adds demand stimulus to the economy in the form of interest payments by government.

7.11 Conclusion: MMT and policy

On one level, the MMT approach is descriptive: it explains how a sovereign currency works. When we talk about government spending by keystrokes and argue that the issuer of a sovereign currency cannot run out of them, that is descriptive. When we say that sovereign governments do not borrow their own currency, that is descriptive. Our classification of bond sales as part of monetary policy, to help the central bank hit its interest rate target, is also descriptive. And, finally, when we argue that a floating exchange rate provides the most domestic policy space, that is also descriptive.

Functional finance then provides a framework for prescriptive policy. It says that sovereign government ought to operate fiscal and monetary policy to achieve full employment. In Lerner's view this is done by setting the government's budget at the right level – spending more and taxing less when there is unemployment – and setting the interest rate at the right level. That isn't very radical; it was adopted by postwar Keynesians, and also as we saw even by Milton Friedman (who had his own version of functional finance).

However, Lerner's initial proposal was formulated in an economic environment of low inflation, indeed, when the greater worry was over a return to deflation such as that suffered in the 1930s. Later, after inflation reared its ugly head during the 1960s, Lerner became quite concerned about price stability. He developed a policy proposal to push a particular type of wage and price controls. We did not examine that in this Primer, but a somewhat different form of wage and price controls actually was tried by President Nixon in the United States in the early 1970s. Whether or not they worked is controversial, but they were dropped in favor of austerity under President Carter to deal with double-digit inflation. And ever since the late 1970s the major countries have always relied on fiscal and monetary policy austerity to fight inflation.

The problem is that governments had to abandon any pretense that they were pursuing full employment. Indeed, unemployment became a tool for achieving price stability. It got even worse than that, with conventional wisdom arguing that central banks ought to pursue *only* price stability, and with use of fiscal policy downgraded altogether. Lerner's "steering wheel" approach to policy was abandoned. The result has been typically high unemployment and substandard economic growth. In the United States poverty and inequality have risen. Globally, growing unemployment has been a problem even during economic expansions.

In this chapter we examined an alternative strategy to create jobs without sparking inflation: the JG/ELR approach. We have explained that because it "hires off the bottom" by operating a buffer stock and wage floor it does not suffer from the inflationary bottlenecks that "pump-priming" demand stimulus is likely to experience. Using general tax cuts or spending increases tends to favor the already relatively well-off in the hope that jobs will "trickle down" to the unemployed and poor. The JG/ELR program directly targets the unemployed to lift them out of poverty.

There has been a debate about the inclusion of the JG/ELR proposal in the MMT approach. Some argue that MMT ought to remain purely descriptive, stripped of any policy recommendations. Others have argued that the JG/ELR program has been part of MMT from the very beginning.

Indeed, that is factually correct, since those of us who began to develop the MMT approach two decades ago all incorporated the jobs program into it from the earliest days. Further, we believe that a sovereign currency needs an "anchor", and by setting the basic wage in a JG/ELR program, the program itself becomes the anchor. On the margin, the currency is worth the amount of labor it can hire. If, for example, the wage in the JG/ELR program is set at ten dollars an hour, we know that ten dollars can purchase an hour of labor. As long as the program wage is held steady, and so long as there are employees in the program, an employer can recruit a new worker out of the program at a wage that is set a few cents higher than the program's ten dollars per hour.

We believe this is a much more effective monetary anchor than an ounce of gold "backing" the currency. I will not go into all the technical arguments surrounding this, but a labor buffer stock is more effective at stabilizing the economy than is a gold buffer stock because labor goes into the production of all goods and services.

Further, the income of the worker is the most important source of the demand for final output of consumer goods. So operating the economy at full employment and with a relatively stable wage in our buffer stock jobs program will help to stabilize not only consumption spending and household income, but it also helps to stabilize wages and therefore prices.

My colleague Stephanie Kelton has used this analogy. Milton Friedman is famous for pushing his version of the "quantity theory of money", known as Monetarism. We won't go into this in detail as it is presented in every economics textbook. The basic idea is that increases to the money supply cause income and spending to rise; and if the money supply grows too quickly that causes inflation. He is famous for saying "inflation is always and everywhere a monetary phenomenon". On one level Monetarism is descriptive: it claims to find a correlation between money growth and inflation. On another level it is prescriptive: the central bank should control growth of the money supply to fight inflation. One cannot imagine Monetarism without both the descriptive and prescriptive elements; it is impossible to strip the Monetarist policy recommendation from the Monetarist claim that money causes inflation.

Stephanie argues that the policy prescription of MMT is that government *should* pursue full employment without causing inflation. And no one has come up with a better program to do that than the JG/ELR. Hence we cannot separate that policy proposal from the description. I happen to agree with her. Indeed, I believe that MMT is much more than a description and prescription. I think it provides a coherent approach to understanding our economy as a whole; it provides a "world view" that begins with an understanding of the "nature" of money. We will come back to that in the last chapter of the Primer.

However, I also believe that most of the tenets of MMT can be adopted by anyone. It does not bother me if some simply want to use the descriptive part of MMT without agreeing with the policy prescriptions. The description provides a framework for policymaking. But there is room for disagreement over *what government should do.* Once we understand that affordability is not an issue for a sovereign currency-issuing government, then questions about what government *should* do become paramount. And we can disagree on those.

8
What Is Money? Conclusions on the Nature of Money

In an important sense our task throughout this monograph has been to develop a theory of the *nature* of money. When asked "What is money?", most people respond – quite reasonably – that money is used to buy something. This gets at money's use as a *medium of exchange*, which is of course the most familiar use. If pressed further, most would also say that money is something one can hold as *a store of value*. Indeed, economists recognize money as the safest and most *liquid* store of value available, at least outside situations with high inflation, when money's value falls rapidly. Some people will also mention the use of money to pay down debt, with money used as a *means of payment*, or *means of final settlement of contractual obligations*. Finally, if we ask people "How much is that worth?" – pointing to just about anything – a common response would be to evaluate worth in terms of money, this time acting as the *unit of account* used to measure wealth, debt, prices, economic value.

These answers take us quite far in understanding *what money is*, each focusing on a different but widely recognized *function* or use of money, identifying money with what money does. But we might try to dig deeper, and ask what is the nature of that "thing" that serves these functions? When we go to the store, we might use cash or a bank check or a plastic credit card as our medium of exchange. When we file our tax return with the treasury, we might simply make an electronic payment. We can buy books or collectible Barbies over the Internet using PayPal. But we can assess the value of a used car in terms of a purely representational unit of account, much as we can

261

guess the weight of our neighbor in pounds, kilograms, or stones, units we cannot touch.

8.1　Is money a physical thing?

As discussed in Chapter 1 and elsewhere, many people rather instinctively believe that money must have some real physical existence, or at least it must be "backed up" by hoards of precious metals kept safely in government vaults. Some who know that is not true fear that the money we use today is somehow illegitimate, a "false" money precisely because it is "worthless" pieces of paper or electronic entries down at the bank. That is a typical response by Austrian-leaning "goldbugs", often followers of Ron Paul (a sometime US presidential candidate and thorn in the side of the Fed).

What we have tried to do in this monograph is to present a careful and coherent exposition on the nature of money. We have consistently distinguished between the *money of account* (Dollar, Pound, Yen) and *money things* denominated in that money of account. We have argued that all those money things, in turn, are liabilities, obligations, IOUs, of their issuer. At the same time, they are assets of the holder. The nature of the obligation of the issuer is this: one must always accept one's IOU in payment to oneself. The bank that issues demand deposits as its liabilities must accept its demand deposits in payments on the loans it holds as assets. The government that issues currency as IOUs in its payments must accept its currency in payment to itself (for fees, fines, and taxes).

So there really is something standing behind the money things: the promise of the issuer to take them back. Issuers commonly add another promise to increase acceptability: to convert their IOUs to the IOUs issued by some entity whose liabilities are even more acceptable. That led us to the notion of a debt pyramid. Liabilities of households and firms are converted to demand deposits of banks (one promises to deliver bank liabilities in redemption against one's debts), and bank IOUs are convertible to government currency (cash and reserves – HPM).

It is certainly possible for an issuer to promise to convert its liabilities to gold. This does not turn gold into money, or even into a money thing, through some sort of alchemy. But in some conditions one might be more willing to accept an IOU if it can be converted to something that has recognized value – something like gold, that is itself not a monetary IOU.

Note, however, that for gold-backing to work, gold would have to have already obtained social status to give it widely recognized value. This could happen more or less spontaneously (if gold had socially useful properties that gave it high demand), or it could be given its value by authorities. Really that is what the gold standard did: authorities gave gold certain value by promising to peg its value relative to the money of account (i.e. the US government set the value of an ounce of gold at 35 Dollars per ounce). The "goldbugs" have mostly got it backwards: it was not gold that gave money its value but rather gold had money value because its price was pegged in terms of money by the government authorities. This was done by promising to redeem gold for currency at a fixed exchange rate. (That is not to deny that gold has uncertain nominal value even without government backing it up!)

Ironically, that is mostly (and wrongly) interpreted today as a case of gold giving currency its value. But that cannot be true on a gold standard which has a fixed exchange rate maintained by the authorities that pegs the price of gold in terms of the currency. If instead the currency were to float against gold (as it now does in most developed nations), then a promise to convert the currency against gold at the reigning exchange rate would give to money the nominal value of gold. If the price of gold rises to 900 US Dollars per ounce, then $900 can get an ounce of gold from a government that promises to convert at that market value, and if gold crashes to $9 an ounce then government would promise to buy at that price.

But if a government promises to peg the price of gold at $900 an ounce, then it makes no sense to argue that the value of gold determines the value of the currency! At most, such a promise merely increases the acceptability of the currency to those who otherwise would not want to hold it. (Note that a wool buffer stock program is essentially a "gold standard" for sheep's wool: it pegs wool's price, but money doesn't derive its value from wool.)

We have seen that there is no automatic reason to fear use of money things that are not backed by precious metals (or foreign currencies). This does not mean that a monetary system will necessarily be handled well. But it does mean that with proper understanding of the operation of the monetary system, it is possible to implement good fiscal and monetary policy that will simultaneously maintain money's value while also allowing the economy to operate close to capacity. In spite of all the praise one hears about the supposed operation of the gold standard, the two centuries (more or less) that Western society operated on a gold standard do not stand out as particularly great. They were periods of periodic inflations and deep depressions, with major financial panics and crises every couple of decades (at least in the United States). Economic growth and unemployment experienced wide swings over the period, and entire populations had to emigrate to try to find a way to survive (remember the Irish potato famine).

In any case, this monograph has tried to analyze the economy we've got, with the monetary system we actually have. And that is one that is based on a money of account chosen by government, and almost everywhere subject to the "one country, one currency" rule. The currency is issued by a sovereign government when it spends, and received by government in payment of taxes and other payments to the government. Even if the gold standard existed at one time, and even if it operated smoothly in the manner fantasized by the goldbugs, it no longer matters in any significant way.

8.2   Propositions on the nature of money

Let us try to go a bit further into the nature of money in this section. The exposition here will be somewhat more difficult – and will rely more on Keynes's theory – than the analysis up to this point. I will focus the discussion around three fundamental propositions regarding money:

1. As Clower (1965) famously put it, money buys goods and goods buy money, but goods do not buy goods.
2. Money is always debt; it cannot be a commodity from the first proposition because if it were that would mean that a particular good is buying goods.
3. Default on debt is possible, which means that creditworthiness matters. Not all money things are created equal.

These three propositions will provide sufficient structure to dig a bit deeper into our theory of money. The following discussion will be at a theoretical, mostly logical level. This will require some reference to alternative theories and stories about money. For that reason, it will require more familiarity with the typical exposition of textbooks. Readers with less exposure to economics can safely skip the following subsections. Others can brush up a bit on their Samuelson textbook. We examine the first two propositions here – including some implications – and the third proposition is analyzed in the next section.

Goods don't buy goods

The typical textbook story of money's origins is by now too well known to require much reflection: because of the inefficiencies of barter, traders choose one particular commodity to serve as the money commodity (Innes 1913; Wray 1998; Ingham 2000). Exchange is then facilitated by using that money commodity rather than bartering directly one good for another. A hypothetical evolutionary process runs through the discovery of a money multiplier (notes issued on the basis of reserves of the money commodity, such as gold) to government monopolization of the commodity reserve and finally to the substitution of commodity money by a fiat money that is not backed by a commodity.

As we promised at the beginning of this Primer, we are not detailing a history of money, so what is important for our purposes about the conventional story is not the historical accuracy of this hypothetical transformation but rather the view of the story's role for money. Since the market and commodity production analytically precede money in this account, money is not essential, although it plays a lubricating role. This is why it is tempting to do "real analysis" and to presume that in the long run money must be neutral (something that determines only prices, the usual assumption in conventional treatments).

However, if we begin with the proposition that goods cannot buy goods then we must look elsewhere for the nature of money since there could never have been a commodity money. And we cannot presume that markets come before money for the simple reason that until money exists there cannot be "exchanges" (sales). Further, money is not something that is produced, it is not a commodity that is produced by labor (otherwise it would be a "good buying a good"), nor is it something sought to directly satisfy the kinds of individual needs or desires that motivate production of commodities. At most, we can say that we seek money because it provides access to the commodities that satisfy those desires.

It is important that money is not directly produced by labor. Imagine that we could "grow money on trees" or in the ground like corn, something your mother understood to be impossible. Workers who lost their jobs could go harvest money from trees or from cornstalks, as self-employed money producers. Those who have read Keynes's *General Theory* will recall his argument that money "cannot be readily produced" so that "labour cannot be turned on at will by entrepreneurs to produce money" (1964, 230), and as well his argument that "Unemployment develops, that is to say, because people want the moon – men cannot be employed when the object of desire (i.e. money) is something which cannot be produced and the demand for which cannot be readily choked off" (1964, 235). While it might be nice if we could grow money in window pots, our economic world would look quite different than it does now if we could do so.

Keynes also noticed that "the characteristic which has traditionally supposed to render gold especially suitable for use as the standard of value, namely, its inelasticity of supply, turns out to be precisely the characteristic which is at the bottom of the trouble" (1964, 235–6). In other words, even if we could imagine that gold could become money, we would still suffer from unemployment because the distribution of gold reserves makes it unlikely that all the unemployed could become miners of gold. And if we *could* grow money on trees, just how could it maintain its value? Money leaves would be harvested from trees until the amount of effort required to produce money directly equaled the amount of money one could get indirectly from other production processes (in the form of wages and profits). Leaf collection would set a low standard, indeed. Maintaining relative scarcity of money keeps it valuable, but that at the same time means that it should not be something produced by labor.

But there is a more important point to be made. Elsewhere – especially in the drafts to the *General Theory* – Keynes explicitly presumed that the *purpose* of production in a monetary economy is to accumulate money (Wray 1990, 1998). It is this desire to accumulate money but at the same time the inability to use labor to produce it that prevents labor from being diverted to its production. Hence,

Clower's argument that "goods do not buy goods", that money is not a commodity produced by labor, must underlie Keynes's view. And that is why unemployment develops when people want the "moon" (money), but cannot produce it with labor.

The claim that a capitalist economy is a "monetary production economy" was also adopted by Karl Marx and Thorstein Veblen and their followers (Dillard 1980). To put it simply, the purpose of production is to accumulate money, not to barter the produced commodities for other commodities. As Heilbroner (1985) argues, this provides a "logic" to production that makes it possible to do economic analysis. Indeed, our previous analysis of sectoral balances and stock-flow consistency, and even GDP accounting itself, all rely on this "logic". On one level, this is obvious. We need a unit for accounting purposes to aggregate heterogeneous items: wages, profits, rents; investment, consumption, government spending; apples, oranges, and widgets. As Keynes (1964, Chapter 4) argued, there are only two obvious units of account at hand: labor hours or the money wage unit. The Classical tradition (that followed Marx) focused on the first while most of Keynes's followers focused exclusively on the second, although some, like Dillard, followed Keynes's lead by using both.

But the Marx-Veblen-Keynes monetary theory of production means to say something more than that we need a handy universal money unit for accounting purposes. Money is the *object* of production, it is not merely the way we measure the value of output. It is because money does not take any particular commodity form that it can be the purpose of production of all particular commodities. It is the general representation of value; it buys all commodities and all commodities buy (or, at least attempt to buy) money. Actually, if a commodity cannot buy money, it really is not a commodity; it has no market value. Commodities obtain their value – they *become* commodities – by exchanging for the universal representation of social value, money. By the same token, obtaining money allows us access to all commodities that are trying to buy money.

This presents the possibility of disappointment: the fruits of production enter the market but fail to buy money. There are consequences following on the failure to sell produced commodities, including a decision to cease production. Labor power itself is a produced commodity (separate from the free laborer, of course, who cannot be bought or sold) that seeks to exchange for money but may find unemployment instead. However, not only is the purpose of production to obtain money, but the production process itself is one of "production of commodities by means of commodities" as Sraffa (1960) put it. That is to say, one needs commodities in order to produce: one must buy raw materials, equipment, and labor power in order to produce output.

And those commodities (including labor power as well as other produced means of production) can only be purchased with money things (IOUs denominated in the money of account). In other words, the production process itself "begins with money" on the expectation of ending up with "more money" (M-C-C'-M', as Marx put it: begin with money to purchase commodities as inputs, produce a different commodity, and then sell it for more money). Not only is production required to result in sales for money (things), but it must begin with money (things). Production is thoroughly monetary, from beginning to end. It cannot begin with commodities, because the commodities must have been produced for sale for money (things). Analysis must also therefore begin with money.

Indeed it is the necessity of producing commodities and then selling them for money that underlies capitalism. If money can just be produced directly from flowerpots, we would not need to market output, and most of the features of a capitalist economy would be unnecessary.

We cannot begin with the barter paradigm. We cannot remove money from the analysis as if it were some veil hiding the true nature of production. We cannot imagine that in some hypothetical long run money will somehow become a neutral force, just as it supposedly was back in the days when Robinson Crusoe bartered with Friday. Beginning with barter sheds no light on production in a monetary production economy.

Indeed, if you think about it, if you exchange one commodity for another there is no need for money, even as a measuring unit. I've got coconuts and you've got fish; I'd rather have the fish and you want the coconuts, so we trade. We need to higgle and haggle to reach agreement on the exchange ratio: how many fish per coconut. That gives us a "relative price" measured in real things. We have no need for a unit of account. No doubt such exchanges occur all the time: I'll wash the dishes if you cook the dinner; I'll swap two Barry Bonds baseball cards for one Mickey Mantle. Or two Mickeys if you'll clean the house. We don't need money.

The story told in many textbooks is that economies began with such barter, found it inconvenient, and so chose one among dozens or hundreds or millions of commodities to serve as the universal unit of account. That was supposed to be gold (see the earlier argument for objections to this account). Now, think about that. Even if we only had dozens of commodities exchanged, the mental gymnastics involved in coming up with an equilibrium vector of relative price ratios – every other commodity's value measured in terms of gold – would be extremely difficult, since somehow all the traders in the society would need to converge on the equilibrium prices. Indeed, even George Selgin (an advocate of this approach to money) has admitted that you might need a powerful modern computer to come up with the list of equilibrium relative prices! Yet our relatively primitive ancestors supposedly ran their economies this way!

Note that there is no historical or anthropological evidence to support the story. But let us say that it is historically accurate. Does it shed any light at all on modern society? Do you exchange your coconuts for gold? Do you calculate relative exchange rates across the full range of everything that is traded (if there are 1,000 commodities, do you keep track in your mind – or even on a computer – all the relative exchange rates as you wander the aisles of your supermarket)? Or do you calculate nominal values in terms of the state money of account (Dollar in the United States, RMB in China, and so on)? Does a firm begin with coconuts it trades for labor hours, or does it begin with a short-term commercial loan denominated in Dollars from its bank? And does the firm want to end up with more coconuts than it began the production process with, or is it interested in ending with its bank account credited with more Dollars than it started with? In other words, which is the more relevant story for today's economy?

Let us begin with a money of account in which we "price" the goods and services we buy and sell. And we use something that is denominated in that money of account, receiving it when we sell and surrendering it when we buy. So, what is that "thing"? Is it a commodity, like gold denominated in Dollars? No.

8.3 Money is debt

Throughout this monograph, we have argued that money is not a commodity, rather it is a unit of account. A unit of measurement is not something that can ever be obtained through a sale. No one can touch or hold a centimeter of length or a centigrade of temperature. We might say that we buy money by selling commodities, but it is clear that if money is just a unit of account – the Dollar, the Euro, the Yen – that is impossible.

We can get somewhat closer if we recall our earlier analogy to the electronic scoreboard at a football game. As the game progresses, point totals are adjusted for each team. The points have no real physical presence other than as hyperactive electrons; they simply reflect a record of the performance of each team according to the rules of the game. Similarly, in the game we call the "economy", sales of commodities for money lead to "points" credited to the "score" that is (mostly) kept by financial institutions. While the game of life is a bit more complicated than the football game, the idea that record keeping in terms of money is a lot like record keeping in terms of points can help us to remember that money is not a "thing", but rather is a unit of account in which we keep track of all the debits and credits – or "points".

Recall that we said the "scores" on a bank's balance sheet are liabilities; its IOUs are the points credited to players. We will have much more to say about the role played by financial institutions in the next section. Here we only want to focus on the "dual" debt nature of the money "scores".

First, as discussed above, production must begin with money, and that money is a "score" that represents an IOU. Typically, it is a demand deposit liability of a bank. It is matched on the other side of the bank's balance sheet by a loan, which represents the debt of the borrower in whose name the bank's IOU is issued. In other words, one who wants to undertake production of commodities (by means of purchasing commodities) must issue an IOU to the bank (a "loan" held as the bank's asset) and obtain in return a bank deposit (the bank's liability). The commodities to be used as means of production are then purchased by transferring the deposit (the bank debits the producer's deposit and credits the deposits of the sellers of means of production). When the producer finishes the production process and sells the produced commodities, her deposit account is credited and the purchasers of the sold commodities have their deposit accounts debited. At this point, if the producer desires, she can use her deposit account to "repay" the loan (the bank simultaneously debits the demand deposit and the loan). All of this can be done electronically and is rather like our scorekeeper who takes points off the scoreboard.

However, if we end up back where we started – with the deposit and the loan wiped clean – the producer seems to have engaged in an entirely purposeless endeavor, borrowing to produce commodities sold to repay the loan. The money created in the first step is simply retired in the last. That of course is not the monetary production economy of Marx, Keynes, and Veblen which must aim to end up with more money (profits) than it starts with. Further, the bank's engagement in this process would also be senseless; it accepted an IOU and created one, and finally ends up with all "scores" back at zero. Hence we have to account for profits of producers and interest (hence, profits) earned by banks. Let us ignore that for now and conclude that the debt of the producer is retired by selling the produced commodities ("realizing" the monetary value) and retiring the loan by surrendering its deposits accumulated through the sales. The bank cancels its debt (demand deposit) at the same time that it cancels the producer's IOU (loan). We'll return to a discussion of profits in the Box at the end of this section.

The second sense in which the producer is indebted is Schumpeterian (after the famous economist Josef Schumpeter): the producer commands some of society's means of production at the beginning of the production process before actually contributing to society. The producer's IOU (held by the bank) represents a social promise that she will temporarily remove commodities on the condition that she will later supply commodities to society. We can view all commodity production as social, beginning with commodities that were already socially produced, in order to combine them in some manner to produce a (usually) different set of commodities. When those newly produced commodities find a market (buying money), the entrepreneur's social debt is redeemed.

Schumpeter (1934) argued that when the entrepreneur removes means of production from the sphere of circulation this can lead to temporary inflation. However, if the production process actually results in commodities of greater total value, the redemption of the debt to society more than makes up for the temporary inflation, imparting a long-term deflationary tendency.

For Schumpeter, this is expected when the entrepreneur innovates – a new production process that increases capacity to produce commodities. Hence, Schumpeter focused on the role played by banks in financing innovation: providing credit to allow the entrepreneur to claim social productive resources for a new production process that will increase social production. While he recognized that all production begins and ends with money, he did not view money as very important when it comes to normal production and circulation of commodities. A given quantity of money can circulate a given amount of production, something like Keynes's (1973, 208) "revolving fund of finance" renewed at the end of every production cycle to allow new production to go forward. (The idea is that a firm borrows to finance the production process and can repay the loan at the end, after output is produced and sold. But the loan is then renewed to begin again the production process.) But new credit allows the innovative entrepreneur to break free from the circular flow, creating new purchasing power that shifts resources from some existing use toward the innovative practice. If successful, the debt is repaid, in both senses: the producer can retire her debt to the bank and to society as a whole. (See the Box for discussion of the source of profits.)

Money is debt (again!)

We conclude: money is debt. It need not have any physical existence other than as some form of record, mostly an electrical entry on a computer. Money always involves at least two entries: debt of the issuer and asset of the creditor. Delivering an IOU back to the debtor results in its extinction: the debt is stricken, and so is the asset of the creditor. In practice, creation of money usually requires four entries: a prospective producer issues an IOU to a bank and receives a demand deposit as an offsetting asset; the bank holds the producer's IOU as its asset and issues the demand deposit as its liability. By convention we say that the producer is a "borrower" and the bank is a "lender"; we call the bank's acceptance of the borrower's IOU a "loan", and the bank's IOU "money". However, that is rather arbitrary because both have borrowed and both have lent in the sense that both are debtors and both are creditors.

If money is debt, then as Minsky (1986, 228) said, anyone can create money by issuing an IOU denominated in the social unit of account. The problem is to get it accepted, that is, to get someone to hold one's IOU. To become a debtor requires finding a creditor willing to hold the debt. But there are two sides to the equation: each must be willing to "create money" (issue an IOU) and each must be willing to "hold money" (hold the other's IOU). And that raises many issues, of which we can only touch on a few. In the next section we address two issues related to willingness to hold money IOUs: liquidity and default.

Box: Where do profits come from?

Schumpeter's "vision" did not really allow him to see how profits (and interest) are generated at the aggregate level because he did not have an adequate theory of effective demand. However, many economists including Marx, Keynes, Kalecki (1971 [1936]), Kaldor (1955–1956), and Kenneth Boulding (see Boulding 1985) recognized the social creation of a "surplus" from which profits and interest are derived. There are many ways to approach this, but the most straightforward is through the Kalecki equation: aggregate profit equals the sum of investment plus the government deficit plus the trade surplus plus capitalist consumption (or, consumption out of profits) and less worker saving (saving out of wages). This can be derived from the GDP identity:

GDP = consumption + investment + net exports + government spending = Gross National Income = Wages + Profits + Taxes

Note that wages and profits are net of taxes. Now divide consumption into two categories: consumption out of wages (Cw) and out of profits (Cp); also subtract taxes from government spending to get the government's deficit (Def); and use the usual abbreviations: C = consumption, I = investment, NX = net exports, P = profits. Finally, note that $W = Cw + Sw$ where Sw is saving out of wages. Substituting and rearranging we obtain:

$I + NX + Def + Cp + Cw = Cw + Sw + P$;
Rearranging we get $P = I + NX + Def - Sw + Cp$

Which is known as the Kalecki profits equation. It has a passing resemblance to our sectoral balance approach, which is not surprising. NX is the counterpart to the current account balance; Def is counterpart to the government balance, and $P - I + Sw - Cp$ is the counterpart to the private balance since it tells us that the income of capitalist-firms (profits) less consumption out of profits and investment (spending by capitalists, in other words) plus the saving by households out of wages gives us the private sector's balance.

There is no need to go through this in more detail. The basic idea is that because the wages received by workers who produce consumption goods represent only a part of the receipts from the sales of consumption goods (in other words, workers in the investment, foreign trade, and government sectors also buy consumer goods), the capitalists producing consumption goods receive gross profits (equal to total sales receipts less costs of producing the goods, which can be simplified to equal the wage bill in the consumption goods sector). A great number of extensions can be made: workers can save and receive profits; capitalists can consume; we can analyze distributional effects as well as equilibrium growth paths; and so on. But that is not necessary for our purposes.

We can also return to our initiating bank loan and analyze a complete monetary circuit to repayment of the loan, as discussed above (see Graziani 1990; Lavoie 1985; Parguez 2002; Parguez and Seccareccia 2000). It can be shown that if we have two sectors (investment and consumption), profits can be realized in the form of bank deposits by one sector (consumption) equal to the wage bill in the other (investment) sector. These profits can then be used to purchase the output of the second sector (i.e. investment goods; the production of the investment goods generates the profits needed to finance their purchase). However, it is more difficult to show how the second sector gets profits, and how interest on loans can be paid.

A variety of solutions has been offered: banks pay interest on deposits so firms can pay equivalent interest on loans (which begs the question of bank profitability, sometimes resolved by having banks serve as a third sector that buys commodities). Or everything can be put in terms of rates of growth: the profits "deux ex machina" can be found in heterogeneous and overlapping production periods and circuits (only a portion of outstanding loans are retired), or by having ever-growing bank balance sheets (with interest essentially lent). Again, these complications do not concern us.

8.4   Liquidity and default risks on money IOUs

Goodhart (2008) argues that the reason that conventional economics cannot find an important role for money or for financial institutions in its rigorous ("general equilibrium") models is because default is ruled out by assumption. All IOUs are presumed to be equally safe because all promises are always kept as all debts are always paid. (This is the so-called "transversality condition". Indeed, many such models employ a representative agent who is both debtor and creditor and who quite rationally would never default on herself in a schizophrenic manner!)

This means that all can borrow at the risk-free interest rate and that any seller would accept a buyer's IOU; there is no need for cash and never any liquidity constraint. Nor would we need any specialists, such as banks, to assess creditworthiness, nor deposit insurance, nor a central bank to act as lender of last resort.

Obviously, almost all interesting questions about money, financial institutions, and monetary policy are left out if we ignore liquidity and default risk.

Let us return to the most fundamental question about debt, examined in detail earlier: just what is owed when an IOU is issued? All IOUs share one common requirement: the issuer must accept back her own IOU when it is presented. (Innes 1913; Wray 2004) As we discussed above, the bank takes back its own IOU (demand deposit) when a debtor presents it to pay off a loan. Government takes back its own IOU in tax payments. If you issue an IOU to your neighbor for a cup of sugar, the neighbor can present it to you to obtain sugar. Refusing your own debt when submitted for payment is a default.

Another promise that many *monetary* IOUs carry is convertibility on demand (or on some specified condition such as a waiting period) to *another* monetary IOU or even to a commodity. For example, on a gold standard the government might promise to convert its currency (an IOU stamped on coin or paper) to so many ounces of precious metal. Or a country on a fixed exchange rate might promise to convert its currency to so many units of a foreign currency. Banks promise to convert their demand deposit IOUs to domestic high powered money (currency or reserves at the central bank).

It is important to remember that a promise to convert is not fundamental to issue of an IOU; it is in a sense voluntary. For example, modern "fiat" currencies on floating exchange rates are accepted with no promise to convert. Many attribute this to legal tender laws, where sovereign governments have enacted legislation requiring their currencies to be accepted in payments. On the other hand, the Euro paper currency as well as the Queen of England's notes make no such promises. Further, throughout history there are many examples of governments that passed legal tender laws, but still could not create a demand for their currencies (see the discussion above in Chapter 2 and in Wray 1998 and Knapp 1973 [1924]). Hence, there are currencies that readily circulate without any legal tender laws as well as currencies that were shunned even with legal tender laws.

If currency cannot be exchanged for precious metal in many countries, and if legal tender laws are neither necessary nor sufficient to ensure acceptance of a currency, and if the government's "promise to pay" really amounts to nothing (except exchanging its currency for its currency), then why would anyone accept a government's currency? As we have emphasized, it is because the sovereign government has the authority to levy and collect taxes (and other payments made to government, including fees and fines). Tax obligations are levied in the national money of account: dollars in the United States, Canada, and Australia.

Further, the sovereign government also determines what can be delivered to satisfy the tax obligation. In all modern nations, it is the government's own currency that is accepted in payment of taxes. While taxpayers mostly write checks drawn on private banks to make tax payments, actually when government receives these checks it debits the *reserves* of the private banks, reserves that are the central bank's IOU. Effectively, private banks *intermediate* between taxpayers and government, making payment in currency and reserves on behalf of the taxpayers. Once the banks have made these payments, the taxpayer has fulfilled her obligation, so the tax liability is eliminated.

We conclude that government's "fiat" currency is accepted because it is the main thing (and usually the only thing) accepted by government in payment of taxes. It is true, of course, that government currency can be used for other purposes: currency can be used to make purchases, to settle debts, or to save in "piggy banks". However, these other uses of currency are *subsidiary*, deriving from government's willingness to accept its currency in tax payments. Ultimately, it is because anyone with tax obligations can use currency to eliminate these liabilities that government currency is in demand, and thus can be used in purchases or in payment of private obligations.

For this reason, neither reserves of precious metals (or foreign currencies) nor legal tender laws are necessary to ensure acceptance of the government's currency. We can conclude that *taxes drive money.* The government first creates a money of account (the Dollar, the Pound, the Euro), and then imposes tax obligations in that national money of account. In all modern nations this is sufficient to ensure that many (indeed, most) debts, assets, and prices will also be denominated in the national money of account. The government is then able to issue a currency that is also denominated in the same money of account, so long as it accepts its currency in tax payment.

This gets us partway to an explanation of why money IOUs are almost without exception denominated in some state's money of account. The sovereign power chooses the money of account when it imposes a tax liability in that unit. Keynes also recognized the state's role in choosing the money of account when he argued that the state "comes in first of all as the authority of law which enforces the payment of the thing which corresponds to the name or description in the contracts. But it comes in doubly when, in addition, it claims the right to determine and declare what thing corresponds to the name, and to vary its declaration from time to time – when, that is to say, it claims the right to re-edit the dictionary. This right is claimed by all modern states and has been so claimed for some four thousand years at least" (Keynes 1930, vol. 1, 4). Enforceability of monetary contracts in court is part of the reason nongovernment money IOUs are written in the state's money of account.

In addition, money IOUs are often made convertible to the state's IOUs – high powered money. This can make them more acceptable. Here's the problem, however: merely agreeing to accept your own IOU in payment is a relatively easy promise to keep. But promising to convert your IOU to another entity's IOU (especially on demand and at a fixed exchange rate, which is necessary for par clearing in a money of account) is more difficult. It requires that one either maintain a reserve of the other entity's IOUs, or that it have easy access to those IOUs when required to do the conversion. Failure to meet the promise of conversion is a default. Hence, there is additional default risk that arises from a promise to convert, to be weighed against the enhancement to an IOU's general acceptability.

This gives rise to the concept of liquidity: how quickly can an asset be converted with little loss of value? Generally, the most liquid asset is the state's own IOUs (the state promises to convert its IOUs to its own IOUs, and to accept those in all payments due to the state), so the conversion of other liabilities is often to HPM. Banks hold some HPM so that they can meet demands for conversion, but it is access to deposit insurance as well as to the central bank that makes the bank's promise to convert secure. Deposit insurance means the government itself will convert the bank liabilities to HPM at par; access to the central bank means that a bank can always borrow HPM as necessary to cover conversions.

We introduced the concept of a pyramid of liabilities: IOUs issued by other institutions and households are convertible to bank liabilities (Bell 2000; Foley 1989). These other entities then work out arrangements that make it more likely that they can meet demands for conversion, such as overdraft facilities. Everything is then pyramided on the state's IOUs; we can think of that as a leveraging of HPM.

All promises are not equally valid, however; risk of default varies on the IOUs. There is another fundamental principle of debts: one cannot pay one's debt using one's own IOUs. But the sovereign state is special. As discussed, when the sovereign is presented with its own IOU, it promises to exchange that IOU for another of its IOUs or it allows the presenter to "redeem" it in payment of taxes. The state makes its own payments – including redeeming its debts – using its own IOUs. To be sure, the state can retire its liabilities – by running a budget surplus – but it does not have to pay them down by using another's IOU. So the sovereign state really is special. All other entities must provide a second party or third party IOU to retire debt. For most purposes, it will be the liability of a bank that is used to make payments on one's debt.

Default risk on a bank's IOUs is small (and nonexistent in the case of government-guaranteed deposits), hence bank liabilities are widely accepted. Banks specialize in underwriting (assessing creditworthiness of) "borrowers" – those whose IOUs they hold. Not only do banks intermediate between government and its taxpayers, they also intermediate by accepting borrowers' IOUs and issuing their own bank IOUs, such as deposits. The IOUs they hold generally have higher default risk (except in the case of government debt) and are less liquid than the IOUs they issue. For this service, they earn profits, in large part determined by their ability to charge a higher interest rate on the IOUs they hold than the rate they must pay on their own. Again, the image of a debt pyramid is useful: those lower in the pyramid use the IOUs issued by entities higher in the pyramid to make payments and to retire debt.

This leads us to the interest rate, which as Keynes said is a reward for parting with liquidity. Since government-issued currency (cash) is the most liquid asset, it does not have to pay interest; bank demand deposits can be just as liquid and for many purposes are even more convenient than cash, so they do not necessarily need to pay interest (in some cases banks charge fees for checking accounts; in others they do pay positive interest – this has to do with regulation and competition, issues we will not address). Other IOUs that are less liquid must pay interest to induce wealth-owners to hold them. In addition, interest compensates for default risk; this is in addition to the compensation for illiquidity of the asset. "Money", the most liquid asset, sets the standard (all other assets must earn a higher return) because it best satisfies the preference for liquidity. Keynes goes on to explain how the desire for liquidity constrains effective demand and results in unemployment, topics beyond our scope (Keynes 1964 [1936]; Davidson 1978).

8.5   Why are banks special?

We return to Goodhart's (2008) argument that conventional economics has no room for money because there is no default risk in rigorous models. For Keynes, conventional economics lacks a plausible theory of money holding precisely because there is no fundamental uncertainty in the models, which is necessary to explain why liquidity has value. The two arguments are related, and explain why financial institutions are important: they issue liquid IOUs with little (or no) default risk. This is the reason why their IOUs are frequently classified as "money" while the money IOUs of others are not. Hence, as Minsky (1986, 228) claimed, "everyone can create money"; but he goes on: "the problem is to get it accepted" (ibid.).

Banks are special in another way: almost all the assets they hold are purchased by issuing IOUs. Typically, a bank has 5 to 8 percent equity against its assets, meaning that its liabilities are equal to 92 to 95 percent of the value of its assets. This is an extremely high leverage ratio (the bank's asset to capital ratio is from 12.5 to 20). As

Minsky (1986) put it, banks finance their positions in assets by issuing debt. Without guarantees of access to the central bank (to make their liabilities more liquid) and to government insurance (to reduce default risk on their liabilities), banks could not operate with such high leverage ratios.

(Note also that banks are strange firms: they do not produce commodities and mostly do not utilize commodities in their "production" – they are not a case of Sraffa's "production of commodities by means of commodities"; other than a bit of labor, a computer, and a building, bank "production" does not require many input commodities. They are true "intermediaries", making profits not out of commodity production but rather by providing the liquid "money" needed for commodity production – creating their IOUs to purchase the IOUs of others, and reaping profits from the interest rate differential. It is this "alchemy" that leads to so much suspicion about the legitimacy of banks that seem to create "money" out of "thin air". To be sure, it is also the potential source of financial crisis, another topic beyond our scope but one whose importance was highlighted with the financial crisis that began in 2007!)

Finally, IOUs are not just held or presented for payment (of one's own liability). They are also to varying degrees transferable. For example, your neighbor might transfer your sugar IOU – perhaps in payment of some sugar debt – to another neighbor, who could present it to you with a demand for sugar. Transferability of your IOU is limited to those who know you well and who trust that you are good for the sugar.

Since "money" is commonly associated with transferability of a debt among third parties, it is not surprising that government currency as well as bank liabilities are most often included in empirical definitions of money. The liabilities of nonfinancial corporations or households are not usually called money because they do not circulate readily among third parties. (Securitization of home mortgage loans – as well as various kinds of insurance plus certified credit ratings – made them transferable to some degree.) What the lay person identifies as money is usually even narrower, something that can be used in a market as a medium of exchange to buy a commodity. And that, of course, must be a monetary IOU that is highly acceptable: a government IOU, a bank IOU, or an IOU closely backed by a bank (such as your credit card debt).

This brings us back to Clower's dictum: money buys goods and goods buy money, but goods do not buy goods. That surprisingly insightful statement has led us on a long path through theory, institutions, and even a bit of monetary history and law. To be sure, we just barely scraped the surface of many of the issues of what turns out to be a complex and contentious topic. Indeed, "money" is arguably the most difficult and controversial subject in macroeconomics: what is money, what role does it play, and what policy should do about it are the questions that have busied most macroeconomists from the very beginning. The three basic propositions examined in this chapter have allowed us to construct the beginnings of answers to these questions.

Conclusions

In this Primer we have explored the macro identities as well as the stock-flow implications that are necessary to formulate policy for any sovereign nation, including developing nations. We carefully examined operational realities for a nation that adopts a sovereign currency. We have also explored the constraints imposed by different currency regimes on domestic policy formation. We concluded that floating a currency, even if it is a managed float, opens up more domestic policy space. Still, even in the context of a developing nation operating with a pegged currency, the space available to the issuer of the currency (the sovereign government) is almost certainly greater than what is generally recognized. Understanding how a currency issuer spends and taxes, and why a currency issuer sells bonds, helps to expand policy options under all exchange rate regimes. That led us to the functional finance approach that argues that government should use its budget to achieve what it perceives to be in the public purpose. Importantly, government should promote full employment with price stability. We analyzed one possible program that could be used to achieve that goal: the job guarantee or employer of last resort program. Finally, we examined the "nature" of money.

All of this serves as a Primer – a prerequisite to understanding how "modern money" really works – and what policy options are open to a government that issues its own sovereign currency.

Notes

2 Spending by Issuer of Domestic Currency

1. Thanks to Eric Tymoigne for providing the mathematical exposition.

3 The Domestic Monetary System: Banking and Central Banking

1. All of this is described in Scott Fullwiler's paper in much greater detail (probably way too much detail for the casual reader) here: http://papers.ssrn.com/sol3/papers.cfm?abstract_id=1874795.
2. The following discussion is adapted from *Treasury Debt Operations – An Analysis Integrating Social Fabric Matrix and Social Accounting Matrix Methodologies*, by Scott T. Fullwiler, September 2010 (edited April 2011), http://papers.ssrn.com/sol3/papers.cfm?abstract_id=1874795.

5 Modern Money Theory and Alternative Exchange Rate Regimes

1. *Payback: Debt and the Shadow Side of Wealth*, by Margaret Atwood (Toronto: House of Anansi Press, 2008).
2. *Coins, Bodies, Games, and Gold*, by Leslie Kurke (Princeton, NJ: Princeton University Press, 1999), xxi, 385.
3. I thank Chris Desan, David Fox, and other participants of a recent seminar at Cambridge University for the discussion I draw upon here. People might find this of interest: http://www.boston.com/bostonglobe/ideas/articles/2011/08/21/which_came_first_money_or_debt/

Bibliography

Aspromourgos, T. 2000. "Is an Employer-of-Last-Resort Policy Sustainable? A Review Article." *Review of Political Economy* 12, no. 2: 141–155.

Atwood, Margaret. 2008. *Payback: Debt and the Shadow Side of Wealth*, Anansi.

Bell, Stephanie. 2000. Do Taxes and Bonds Finance Government Spending? *Journal of Economic Issues*. 34: September.603–620.

——. 2001. "The Role of the State and the Hierarchy of Money". *Cambridge Journal of Economics*, 25(2), March, 149–163.

Bell, Stephanie and L.R. Wray. "Fiscal Effects on Reserves and the Independence of the Fed", *Journal of Post Keynesian Economics*, Winter 2002–2003, Vol 25, No 2: 263–271.

——. 2004. "The War on Poverty after 40 Years: A Minskyan Assessment", *Public Policy Brief*, The Levy Economics Institute of Bard College, no. 78.

Boulding, Kenneth E. 1985. "Puzzles Over Distribution," *Challenge* 28, no. 5: 4–10.

Burgess, J. and Mitchell, W.F. 1998. 'Unemployment Human Rights and Full Employment Policy in Australia,' in M. Jones and P. Kreisler (eds), *Globalization, Human Rights and Civil Society*, Sydney, Australia: Prospect Press.

Clower, Robert. 1965. "The Keynesian Counter-Revolution: A Theoretical Appraisal", in F.H. Hahn and F.P.R. Brechling, (eds), *The Theory of Interest Rates*, 103–125, London: Macmillan.

Commons, John R. 1955 [1924]. *Legal Foundations of Capitalism*. New Brunswick, N.J.: Transaction Publishers.

Cramp, A.B. 1962. Two views on money. *Lloyds Bank Review*, July, p. 1.

Darity, William Jr. "Who Loses from Unemployment." *Journal of Economic Issues*, 33, no. 2 (June 1999): 491.

Davidson, P. (1978), *Money and the Real World*, London: Macmillan.

Dillard, Dudley. 1980. "A Monetary Theory of Production: Keynes and the Institutionalists". *Journal of Economic Issues*. 14: 255–273.

Foley, Duncan, 1989. "Money in Economic Activity", in John Eatwell, Murray Milgate, and Peter Newman (eds) *The New Palgrave: Money*, New York and London: W.W. Norton.

Forstater, Mathew. 1999. "Full Employment and Economic Flexibility" *Economic and Labour Relations Review*, Volume 11.

Forstater, Mathew and L. Randall Wray (eds) 2008. *Keynes for the Twenty-First Century: The Continuing Relevance of the General Theory*, Palgrave/Macmillan 2008.

Fullwiler, Scott, 2006. "Setting Interest Rates in the Modern Money Era", *Journal of Post Keynesian Economics*, 28(3) Spring: 495–525.

——. 2010 *Treasury Debt Operations – An Analysis Integrating Social Fabric Matrix and Social Accounting Matrix Methodologies,* September 2010 (edited April 2011), http://papers.ssrn.com/sol3/papers.cfm?abstract_id=1874795

Fullwiler, Scott T. 2003. "Timeliness and the Fed's Daily Tactics." *Journal of Economic Issues*, vol. 37, no. 4 (December): 851–880.

———. 2005. "Paying Interest on Reserve Balances: It's More Significant than You Think." *Journal of Economic Issues*, vol. 39, no. 2 (June).

———. 2008. "Modern Central Bank Operations: The General Principles."

———. 2009. "The Social Fabric Matrix Approach to Central Bank Operations: An Application to the Federal Reserve and the Recent Financial Crisis." In Natarajan, Tara, Wolfram Elsner, and Scott Fullwiler, (eds) *Institutional Analysis and Praxis: The Social Fabric Matrix Approach*: 123–169. New York, NY: Springer.

———. 2011. "Treasury Debt Operations: An Analysis Integrating Social Fabric Matrix and Social Accounting Matrix Methodologies." SSRN, located at: http://papers.ssrn.com/sol3/papers.cfm?abstract_id=1825303

Galbraith, James K. 2011. "Is the Federal Debt Unsustainable?" Levy Economics Institute Policy Note 2011/2.

Ginsburg, Helen. 1983. *Full Employment and Public Policy: The United States and Sweden*, Lexington, MA: Lexington Books.

Godley, Wynne. 1996. "Money, Finance and National Income Determination: An Integrated Approach", Levy Economics Institute, Working Paper 167, June, www.levy.org,

Godley, Wynne and Marc Lavoie. 2007. *Monetary Economics: An Integrated Approach to Credit, Money, Income, Production, and Wealth*. New York, NY: Palgrave Macmillan.

Goodhart, Charles A.E. 1989. *Money, Information and Uncertainty*. Cambridge, Mass.: MIT Press.

———. 1998. "Two Concepts of Money: Implications for the Analysis of Optimal Currency Areas." *European Journal of Political Economy*. 14: 407–432.

———. 2005. "Review of Credit and State Theories of Money: the contributions of A. Mitchell Innes," *History of Political Economy*, vol. 37, no. 4, winter, pp. 759–761.

———. 2008. "Money and Default", in Mathew Forstater and L. Randall Wray (eds) *Keynes for the Twenty-First Century: The Continuing Relevance of the General Theory*, 213–223 New York: Palgrave Macmillan.

Graeber, David. Interview. http://www.boston.com/bostonglobe/ideas/articles/2011/08/21/which_came_first_money_or_debt/

Graziani, A. .1990. "The Theory of the Monetary Circuit", *Economies et Societes*, series no. 7, June.

Harvey, P. 1989. *Securing the Right to Employment: Social Welfare Policy and the Unemployed in the United States*, Princeton, NJ: Princeton University Press.

———. 1999. "Liberal Strategies for Combating Joblessness in the Twentieth Century", *Journal of Economic Issues*, vol 33, no. 2, June: 497–504.

———. 2002. "Human Rights and Economic Policy Discourse: Taking Economic and Social Rights Seriously", *Columbia Human Rights Law Review*, vol 33, no. 2, Spring: 364–471.

Hayden, F. Gregory. 2006. *Policymaking for a Good Society: The Social Fabric Matrix Approach to Policy Analysis and Program Evaluation*. New York, NY: Springer.

——. 2009. "Normative Analysis of Instituted Processes." In Natarajan, Tara, Wolfram Elsner, and Scott Fullwiler, (eds) *Institutional Analysis and Praxis: The Social Fabric Matrix Approach*: 103–122. New York, NY: Springer.

Heilbroner, Robert. 1985. *The Nature and Logic of Capitalism*, New York and London: W.W. Norton and Company.

Hirway, Indira .2006. "Enhancing Livelihood Security through the National Employment Guarantee Act: Toward effective implementation of the Act", The Levy Economics Institute Working Paper No. 437, January, www.levy. org.

Ingham, Geoffrey. 2000. Babylonian Madness: On the Historical and Sociological Origins of Money. In John Smithin (ed.) *What Is Money*. London & New York: Routledge.

——. 2004a. "The Emergence of Capitalist Credit Money." In L.R. Wray (ed), *Credit and State Theories of Money: The Contributions of A. Mitchell Innes*, Cheltenham, 173–222, Edward Elgar.

——. 2004b. *The Nature of Money*, Cambridge: Polity Press Ltd.

—— (ed.). 2005. *Concepts of Money: Interdisciplinary Perspectives from Economics, Sociology, and Political Science*, Edward Elgar, Cheltenham.

Innes, A. M. 1913. "What is Money?" *Banking Law Journal*. May: 377–408.

——. 1914. "The Credit Theory of Money." *Banking Law Journal*, January, 151–68.

Innes, A. M. (1913, 1914) reprinted in L. R. Wray (ed.), *Credit and State Theories of Money*, Cheltenham, UK and Northampton, MA, USA: Edward Elgar (2004), pp. 14–49.

Kaldor, N. 1955–6. "Alternative theories of distribution" *Review of Economic Studies*, 23: 83–100.

Kalecki, Michal. 1971. "The determinants of profits," in M. Kalecki (ed.) *Selected Essays on the Dynamics of the Capitalist Economy*, 1933–1970, 78–92, Cambridge: Cambridge University Press.

Keynes, John Maynard. (1964) *The General Theory of Employment, Interest and Money*, Harcourt Brace Jovanovich, New York and London.

Keynes, J. M. (1971–1989), *The Collected Writings of John Maynard Keynes*, London: Macmillan and Cambridge University Press for the Royal Economic Society

Vol. XIII: *The General Theory and After. Part I Preparation*, 1973

Vol. XIV: *The General Theory and After. Part II Defense and Development*, 1973

Keynes, J. M.. 1914. "What is Money?", review article in *Economic Journal*, 24(95), September, 419–421.

——. 1930. *A Treatise on Money*. Volumes I and II (1976), New York: Harcourt, Brace & Co.

——. 1937. The *'Ex Ante'* Theory of the Rate of Interest, *Economic Journal*, December.

——. 1976. *A Treatise on Money*. Volumes I and II, New York: Harcourt, Brace & Co.

——. 1982. *The Collected Writings of John Maynard Keynes, Volume XXVIII*, Donald Moggridge (ed), London and Basingstoke: Macmillan.

King, J. E. 2001. "The Last Resort? Some Critical Reflections on ELR." *Journal of Economic and Social Policy* 5, no. 2: 72–76.

Klein, Peter G. and George Selgin. 2000. "Menger's Theory of Money: Some Experimental Evidence." In John Smithin (ed.) *What Is Money.* London & New York: Routledge.

Knapp, Georg Friedrich. (1924) 1973. *The State Theory of Money.* Clifton: Augustus M. Kelley.

Kregel, J.A. (1986), "Shylock and Hamlet: Are there Bulls and Bears in the Circuit?" *Economie et Société*, série MP 3, pp. 11–22.

Kregel, J. A. 1976. "Economic Methodology in the Face of Uncertainty: The Modeling Methods of Keynes and the Post-Keynesians," *Economic Journal*, vol. 86, no. 342: 209–225.

Kurke, Leslie. 1999. *Coins, Bodies, Games, and Gold*, Princeton University Press, Princeton, New Jersey, 1999; xxi, 385.

Lavoie, Marc. 1985. "Credit and Money: The Dynamic Circuit, Overdraft Economics, and Post Keynesian economics", in Jarsulic, Marc (ed.), *Money and Macro Policy*, 63, Boston, Dordrecht, Lancaster: Boston-Dordrecht-Lancaster.

Lerner, Abba P. 1943. "Functional Finance and the Federal Debt." *Social Research* vol. 10, 38–51.

——. 1947. "Money As a Creature of the State." *American Economic Review.* Vol. 37: 312–317.

Minsky, H.P. 1965. "The Role of Employment Policy," in M.S. Gordon (ed.), *Poverty in America*, San Francisco, CA: Chandler Publishing Company.

Minsky, Hyman P. 1986. *Stabilizing an Unstable Economy*, New Haven and London: Yale University Press.

——. 1993. "Schumpeter and Finance", in S. Biasco, A. Roncaglia and M. Salvati (eds), *Market and Institutions in Economic Development*, 103–115, New York: St. Martin's Press.

Minsky, H.P. 1975. *John Maynard Keynes*, Yale University Press.

Mitchell, William and Joan Muysken. 2008. *Full Employment Abandoned: Shifting Sands and Policy Failures*, Cheltenham, UK, Northampton, MA: Edward Elgar.

Mitchell, W.F. and Wray, L.R. 2005. "In Defense of Employer of Last Resort: A Response to Malcolm Sawyer," *Journal of Economic Issues*, vol. 39, no. 1: 235–245.

Moore, Basil J. 1988. *Horizontalists and Verticalists: The Macroeconomics of Credit Money*, Cambridge: Cambridge University Press.

Mosler, Warren. 2010. *The Seven Deadly Innocent Frauds of Economic Policy*, Valence Co., Inc.

Parguez, Alain. 2002. "A Monetary Theory of Public Finance". *International Journal of Political Economy*, 32(3), Fall.

Parguez, Alain and Mario Seccarrecia. 2000. "The Credit Theory of Money: The Monetary Circuit Approach". In John Smithin (ed.) *What is Money?*, 101–123, London and New York: Routledge.

Phillips, R.J. 1995. *The Chicago Plan and New Deal Banking Reform.* Armonk: M.E. Sharpe, Inc.

Rawls, J. 1971. *Theory of Justice*, Cambridge, MA: Harvard University Press.

Rezende, Felipe. 2009. "The Nature of Government Finance in Brazil." *International Journal of Political Economy*, 38, no. 1: 81–104.

Ritter, Lawrence S. 1963. "An Exposition of the Structure of the Flow-of-Funds Accounts." *The Journal of Finance*. vol. 18, no 2: 219–230.

Samuelson, Paul, *Economics*, New York: McGraw-Hill, Ninth Edition, 274–276 (1973).

Sardoni, C. and Wray, L.R. 2005. "Monetary Policy Strategies of the European Central Bank and the Federal Reserve Bank of the U.S.," Levy Economics Institute, Working Paper 431.

Sawyer, M. (2003), "Employer of last resort: could it deliver full employment and price stability?,: *Journal of Economic Issues*, 37(4): 881–908.

Schumpeter, J.A. 1934. *The Theory of Economic Development: An Inquiry into Profits, Capital, Credit, Interest and the Business Cycle*, Cambridge, MA: Harvard University Press.

Sen, A. 1999. *Development as Freedom*, New York, NY: Alfred A. Knopf.

Sraffa, Piero. 1960. *Production of Commodities by Means of Commodities*. Cambridge: Cambride University Press.

Taylor, N. 2008. *American-Made: The Enduring Legacy of the WPA: When FDR Put the Nation to Work*. Tantor Media

Tcherneva, Pavlina and L. Randall Wray. 2005. "Gender and the Job Guarantee: The impact of Argentina's Jefes program on female heads of poor households", Center for Full Employment and Price Stability Working Paper No. 50, December, www.cfeps.org.

Wray, L. Randall. 1998. *Understanding Modern Money: The Key to Full Employment and Price Stability*. Northampton, MA, Edward Elgar.

——. 1990. *Money and Credit in Capitalist Economies: The EndogenousMoney Approach*, Aldershot, UK and Brookfield, VT, USA: Edward Elgar.

——. 2003. "The Perfect Fiscal Storm," *Challenge*, vol. 46, no. 1: 55–78.

——. 2009. "The rise and fall of money manager capitalism: a Minskian approach", *Cambridge Journal of Economics*, vol 33, no 4: 807–828

——. (ed.) 2004. *Credit and State Theories of Money: The Contributions of A. Mitchell Innes*, Cheltenham, Edward Elgar.

Wray, L.R. and Forstater, M. 2004. "Full Employment and Economic Justice," in D. Champlin and J. Knoedler (eds), *The Institutionalist Tradition in Labor Economics*, Armonk: NY: M.E. Sharpe.

Index

accounting, 4–8, 21–7, 32–41, 54, 60, 96, 126, 130–3, 205, 210, 267
  nominal values, 1, 21, 127, 159–63, 244, 248, 263, 269
  real values, 2, 21–7, 62–5, 154, 244, 248
assets
  as another party's liabilities, 1–6, 8–11, 24–7, 34–5, 78, 81–3, 92–6, 146, 262
  financial, 1–11, 24–7, 34–5, 62–4, 101–2, 107–8, 129–30, 134, 143, 172–3, 184, 199–200, 208, 211, 218
  net financial, *see* net financial assets
  nonfinancial, 2, 25–6, 35
  also see wealth, nonfinancial (real)
Australia, 39–4, 46, 48, 50, 134, 143, 148, 224, 233, 276
automatic stabilizers, 16–17, 197, 207–8, 222–3

bank
  assets, 24–7, 63, 78–84, 89–91, 92–6, 99–104, 116, 120–3, 126, 201, 262, 270, 272, 279–80
  commercial, 83, 91, 269
  demand deposits, 44, 62–4, 78, 80, 85, 96–7, 113, 117–19, 205, 262, 279
  lending, 63, 79–80, 87–98, 115–17, 124–5, 144–5, 262, 270–2, 274
  liabilities, 1, 24–7, 59, 77–9, 84–7, 91–6, 99–104, 121–2, 262, 270, 272, 278–80
  reserves, xv, 53, 59, 64, 97–8, 108–18, 120–4, 142, 172, 194–200, 205, 211

  also see Federal Reserve System
  time deposits, 78, 85
borrowed reserves, 83, 90, 94–5, 103–4, 117, 172, 278
Brazil, 117, 147, 252–3
budget, 3–10, 68, 72–5, 133, 187–90, 194–7, 200–2, 208–15, 252–6
business cycle, 180, 194, 309, 227

Canada, 48, 79, 116–17, 276
capital, 12, 23, 91–4, 139, 211, 230
cash, *see* currency
central bank, xv, 78–83, 89–91, 97, 103–4, 112–19, 123–6, 128, 142, 172–3, 195, 256, 268
China, 131–2, 164–6, 213–15
Confederacy, 253–4
consumer price index, 57, 225, 241–6, 251–3
consumption spending, 11–17, 20, 28, 36–7, 59, 70, 209, 219, 224, 227–30, 260, 267, 273–4
convertibility, *see* currency
CPI, *see* consumer price index
credit, 12–14, 21, 60–5, 119, 142, 147, 194, 204, 257, 272
creditor, 85, 88–92, 158, 272
currency
  cash, 14, 63, 78–80, 91–3, 114, 195, 244–5, 275, 279
  convertibility, 45, 76–9, 86–7, 138, 141–5, 148–53, 167–9, 172, 185–6, 250–2, 263, 275
  defined, xv
  domestic, 39–42, 58–60, 77–8, 127–8, 141–3, 150
  government, 2–3, 39, 41, 44, 48–50, 54–5, 77, 83, 85–8, 110–34, 137, 172, 276–7, 279–80

currency – *continued*
  reasons for acceptance of, 44–58,
    276–7
  sovereign, *see under* sovereignty
  pyramiding, 85–8
current account, 12, 15, 18–19,
    29–30, 66, 71–2, 126, 129–34,
    138–45, 150, 165–6, 170,
    173, 176–8, 209–10, 212–15,
    219–20, 273

debt, *see under* private sector; public
    sector
debt-to-GDP ratio, 72–5, 127, 148,
    195
default, *see under* private sector
deficit hysteria, 15, 66, 72
deflation, 68, 140, 150, 163, 194,
    223, 244–5, 258, 271
deposits, *see under* banks
developing nations, 39–41, 54–6,
    134–5, 137, 165–6, 216–17,
    227–30
dissaving, 4, 14, 31–2

ECB, *see* European Central Bank
economic growth, 7–8, 18, 27, 70,
    87, 149–51, 181, 250, 259,
    263–4
ELR, *see* employer of last resort
employer of last resort, 217, 221–41,
    258–60, 282
  also see job guarantee
EMU, *see* European Monetary
    Union
endogenous money, *see under*
    money
endogenous versus exogenous, 97–8
Euro, 32, 39–41, 57–8, 61–2, 141–2,
    161–4, 169–84, 213–14,
    275–77
  crisis in, 173–81
European Central Bank, 89, 141–2,
    147, 170–5, 179–84
European Monetary Union, 39–40,
    164, 167–76, 180–84, 214
  see also Euro

European Union, 171, 183–4
exchange rates, 19, 36, 39, 45, 57,
    64, 76, 87, 97, 110–14, 119,
    127–33, 137–86, 188–9, 194,
    211–17, 225, 237, 249–52,
    258, 263, 275, 277, 282
exchange rate policies
  fixed regimes, 140, 148–53, 165,
    176, 211, 216, 251, 275
  floating regimes, 140, 148,
    150–2, 165, 211, 216, 226,
    251, 275
  "pegged," 57, 113, 137, 140,
    149–53, 165, 211, 230

Federal Reserve System
  coordination with U.S. Treasury,
    81–3, 91, 98–109, 115–17, 124,
    175, 204, 256
  discount window, 82, 85, 87, 90,
    116, 125
  federal funds rate, 79, 98, 115–17,
    122–5, 205
  reserve accounting, 126, 133
fiat money, *see under* money
finance, 9, 12–14, 22, 26, 28, 49, 87,
    92, 108, 134, 146, 155–6, 175,
    229, 257, 272, 274, 280
fiscal operations
  the case of a non-sovereign
    currency, 110–37
  the case of a sovereign currency,
    138–47
fiscal policy, 110, 113, 151, 170,
    179–84, 187, 210, 222, 236,
    250
flow of funds, 32, 37, 97
flows, 1–38, 58–69, 96–7, 272
  real versus nominal, 21–7, 62–5
foreign direct investment, 34, 137,
    145
foreign sector, 5–7, 10–12, 19–27,
    33–8, 41, 66, 119–20, 172–3
  debt, 6
  deficit, 6, 10, 12, 173
  surplus, 6, 10, 37
"free" market, 190–1

full employment, 19, 87, 97, 139–40, 151, 182, 189, 193–99, 208–11, 217–20, 221–60, 282
full employment policy, 221–60
   see also employer of last resort; job guarantee
Functional Finance, 193–203, 211–20, 221–7, 236–8, 241–2, 258–60, 282

GDP, *see* gross domestic product
Global Financial Crisis of 2007, 15, 68, 87–8, 98, 106, 171–81, 210, 227, 245
Godley, Wynne, 5, 7, 29, 39, 57
gold, 44–7, 49, 64–5, 81–3, 87, 141, 149, 151–4, 157–8, 159–62, 164, 186, 202, 238, 241, 244–5, 247, 249–51, 255–7, 259, 262–66, 259
gold standard, 47, 149–52, 164, 186, 238, 248–50, 257, 263–4, 275
Goldilocks economy, 7, 27–30, 178
government
   "big," 70, 191, 185, 238–9
   budget, 1, 15–19, 66, 70, 107, 109, 112, 114–31, 167, 171, 176, 180, 184, 197–8, 201, 208–10, 212–15, 223, 228–9, 236–8, 244, 253, 258
   budget constraint, 111, 198–217
   debt, 69, 72, 127, 141–2, 146, 166, 174–76, 203, 206
   deficit, 3, 8, 29–30, 66, 69–70, 100–4, 107–8, 120, 125–7, 138, 184, 195, 210, 212–15
   deficit as nondiscretionary, 15–19
   deficit spending, 33, 68–71, 101, 103, 106–8, 114–15, 121–3, 127–9, 172, 247
   "small," 193, 240
   state and local, 4, 30, 36, 171, 244
   surplus, 3, 6–7, 19, 29–30, 41, 67–8, 109, 115, 196–7, 209–10, 219, 236, 278

Greece, 54, 57–8, 66, 141–2, 146–7, 171–82, 214
   ancient Greece and money, 155–6, 159
gross domestic product, 8, 11–14, 18, 28–30, 36–7, 54–7, 67–9, 72–5, 127, 148, 165, 171, 174–80, 182–4, 195, 207, 209, 218, 226, 243, 253, 256, 267, 273

high powered money, 82, 197, 203, 257, 275, 277
   see also currency, government; reserve currency
horizontalism, 97, 124
households, 1–38, 40, 54, 56–8, 77, 86–7, 111–12, 130–1, 135, 145, 179, 190–1, 194–5, 198–201, 205, 210, 212, 229, 235, 260, 262, 274, 278–80
   see also private sector
Hungary, 167–8
hyperinflation, 154, 198–9, 204, 221, 238, 240–1, 246–58

imports, 18–19, 29, 33, 37, 40, 56, 71, 131, 134, 138, 140–4, 150, 185–6, 188, 212–13, 216–18, 225–30, 237–9, 256
income, 3–20, 30–3, 54–61, 114–15, 118, 120–3, 128, 132, 146, 150, 167–8, 189, 191, 193, 198, 208–9, 212–13, 216, 218–19, 233, 235, 246, 260
inflation, 27, 52, 55, 67–9, 70, 72, 79–80, 111–12, 125, 137, 151, 153–4, 163–4, 176, 180–1, 185, 189, 194–204, 207, 216–17, 221–6, 237–8, 240–6, 258, 261, 264, 271
interest rate target, 79–80, 98, 106, 111–13, 124–5, 183, 194, 241, 258, 264, 275
interest rates
   effects of government deficit on, 115–17, 123–4
   exogenous, 97, 179

inventories, 11–14, 20, 24, 30, 33, 36–7, 56–7, 111, 114, 180, 209, 217, 219, 229, 244, 267, 273–4
investment, 12–13, 37, 56, 111, 114, 209, 217–19, 224, 229, 273–4
IOUs, xv, 2–4, 22, 34–5, 49–50, 76–80, 83–9, 92–3, 109, 113–14, 136–8, 145, 152, 155, 161–2, 198, 206, 248–51, 262, 270, 274–80
issuer of currency, 30, 36, 39, 110–13, 138, 146, 167, 170–1, 184, 198, 204, 210, 258, 262, 282

job guarantee, 217, 221–41, 258–60, 282
Jefes program, 226, 230, 232, 235–6

Keynes, J.M., 23, 76, 121, 156, 232–3, 241, 244, 266–7, 271, 273, 277, 279

lender of last resort, 78–9, 84, 89–91, 171, 221–2, 275
    also see Federal Reserve System
Lerner, Abba, 193–9, 208, 211, 216, 221–2, 236, 241, 258–9
liabilities
    as another party's assets, 1, 3, 24–7, 78–9, 81–3, 95–6, 262
    clearing of financial, 84–6, 172
        see also payments system
    financial, 1–6, 8–9, 22, 24–7, 34–5, 61, 84–9, 134, 146, 172
    as government (public sector) debt, 3, 4, 85, 142
    as money, 40, 42, 51, 53, 77, 93, 262, 279–80
    pyramid of, 79, 83–8, 145, 262, 278–9
    settlement of, 89
liquidity, 124–5, 144, 245, 274–9

macroeconomic accounting, 1–37
macroeconomics, 19, 232, 281
medium of exchange, 42–4, 61–2, 153, 161–2, 280

Mesopotamia, 153–5
metalism, 153–63, 248
Minsky, Hyman, 146, 209, 235, 272, 279–80
Mitchell, Bill, 167, 217, 222–4, 233, 255
MMT, *see* modern money theory
modern money theory, 6–7, 39, 97, 138, 148–86, 193, 221, 238–41, 246–9, 253–4, 258–60
monetarist, 80, 246–8, 253, 256–7, 260
monetary economy, 23, 240, 244, 266–9, 271
monetary policy, 101, 105, 124, 137, 170, 182, 194–7, 241, 258, 264, 275
monetary sovereignty, 39
money
    commodity, 64, 152–63, 238, 248, 265
    creation of by banks, 80, 82, 92–6, 196–7, 207–8, 272
    as credit, 21, 61, 81, 86, 198, 206, 272
    as debt, 269–74
    defined, xv
    endogeneity of, 97–8, 112
    fiat, 44–7, 50–3, 109, 113–14, 211, 240, 244, 255–6, 265
    nature of, 44, 261–82
    origin of, 154–5
    supply of, 97, 164, 196, 201, 246–7, 260
money of account, 3, 21, 39–42, 44, 48, 50, 58–62, 76, 80, 83, 85, 136, 154–5, 241, 262, 264, 277
money "things," xv, 12, 44–5, 61, 82, 89, 92–3, 155–7, 159–62, 262–8, 268
Mosler, Warren, 166, 242

net financial assets, xv, 2
    accumulation of, 3, 5, 8, 11
    creation of, 63, 101
    two sector model; private sector net financial assets equal government liabilities, 3, 64, 108, 121, 211

nominalism, 153–63, 248–9

paradox of thrift, 15, 19–21
payments system, 60, 76, 85, 118
"PIIGs," 66, 141, 173–5, 178,
    179–81
policy space, 40–1, 138–9, 145, 151–2,
    164–9, 181–5, 194–5, 211,
    216–17, 237–8, 250–1, 258
Ponzi finance, 146–7
price stability, 19, 151, 193, 220,
    221–59
private sector, 2
    debt, 10, 28, 30, 64, 146, 179, 210
    deficit, 3, 7, 18, 28–30, 37, 67–70,
        109, 133, 176–80, 209–10
    surplus, 5, 12, 15, 29–30, 37, 68,
        130, 215
profits, 23, 37, 79–80, 198, 267,
    273–4, 280
public purpose, 100, 167, 190–4,
    282
public sector, 2
    debt, 3
        see also government debt
    default, 77, 114, 135–7, 141, 154,
        164–9, 171, 173, 175, 179,
        185–6, 239, 251
    deficit, 4
        see also government deficit
    surplus, 3–4
        see also government surplus

quantitative easing, 79, 97–8, 106,
    108, 119, 125, 200, 205, 247

recession, 179–80, 196–7, 208, 223,
    226
    Great Recession of 2007, 15–17,
        28–9
reserve currency, 133, 138, 166,
    211–12, 215
"rest of world," *see* foreign sector

saving, 3–6, 11, 15, 17–18, 31–8,
    114, 118–23, 132–3, 212–15,
    273–4
    net, 11–12, 120, 123

sectoral balances, 4–19, 27–9, 34–8,
    56–8, 129, 176–8, 184, 209,
    267, 273
    behavior of, 6–14, 70–1
    causation of, 7–13, 119–20,
        133–4
    deficits equal surpluses, 6, 8–10,
        29, 33–8, 176–7, 184
    three sector model, 3–7, 10, 15,
        18, 29, 56–7
    two sector model, 3, 33
settlement, interbank, 92–6
    see also payments system
sovereignty
    currency, 30, 36, 39, 42–5, 51, 53,
        138–41, 146, 148, 152, 167–9,
        174–5, 179–81, 185, 198,
        210–11, 216–17, 221, 237–8,
        258–9, 282
    defined, 39
    government, 9, 44, 50, 53, 57–8,
        70–2, 86, 88, 109–14, 133,
        135–6, 138–42, 146, 166, 168,
        175, 187, 203, 211, 219, 229,
        237–9, 251–2, 260, 264,
        275–6
spending, 3–20, 28–39
stock-flow consistency, *see*
    macroeconomic accounting
stocks, 1–38, 58–69, 96–7, 272
    real versus nominal, 21–7,
        62–5
sustainability conditions, 66–71
    of current account ratios, 71–2
    of government deficits, 66–71,
        184, 195, 210
    of government that borrows in
        foreign currency, 135–7

taxes, 17, 21, 33, 37, 41, 48–56,
    59–60, 72–4, 83, 98,
    115–26, 186, 196–7,
    208, 240, 247, 250,
    254–7, 276
taxes-drive-money, 23, 47–58, 77,
    100, 153, 220, 254, 277
transfer payments, 16–17, 37, 115,
    252

unemployment, 27, 150, 187, 193–200, 211, 216, 220–5, 232–3, 235, 236–7, 239, 250, 258, 259–60, 264, 266–8

unit of account, 21, 32, 40, 42, 59, 61, 83, 111, 155, 261, 268–72

U.S. Treasury, 41, 43, 63, 72, 81–3, 98–9, 109, 113–14, 131, 148, 175, 201–4
  debt operations, 105–9
  technical coordination with the Federal Reserve System, 81–3, 91, 98–109, 115–17, 129, 175, 204, 256

user of currency, 36, 170–3, 182, 210, 217

wages, 13–14, 18–19, 34, 40, 59–61, 140, 144, 165, 176, 180–1, 188–9, 198, 200, 218–19, 223–32, 240–6, 252–3, 260, 266–7, 273–4

Wealth
  financial
    inside financial wealth, 2, 10, 26, 89
    net financial wealth, 1–6, 8–12, 22–3, 26–7, 40, 54, 62, 64, 69
  nonfinancial (real), 2, 22–3, 35, 62, 64–5, 102, 244
  "outside," 2, 10, 27, 89

Weimar Republic, 58, 154, 198, 246–9, 251, 254–6

Zimbabwe, 58, 154, 198, 238, 246–7, 254–6